MW00895574

EURO-ARAB RELATIONS

A Study in
Collective Diplomacy

HAIFAA A. JAWAD

ITHACA PRESS
READING
1992

© Haifaa Jawad 1992

All rights reserved. No part of this book
may be reprinted or reproduced or utilized
in any form or by any electronic, mechanical or
other means, now known or hereafter invented,
including photocopying or recording, or in any
information storage or retrieval system
without permission in writing
from the publishers.

First published in 1992 by Ithaca Press,
8 Southern Court, South Street, Reading, UK

Typeset by BP Integraphics Ltd., Bath, Avon
Printed by Bath Press Ltd., Bath, Avon

British Library Cataloguing in Publication Data

A catalogue record for this book is available from the British Library

ISBN: 0 86372 129 X

CONTENTS

To my father, brother and sister, from whom
separation is not easy

ACKNOWLEDGMENTS

I would like to express my sincere thanks to my supervisor, Dr Tim Niblock, for his meticulous criticism and advice which were of great value. I consider myself to have gained considerably in academic terms from his constructive criticism. Thanks are also due to the departmental secretaries, Fay and Sue, for their co-operation and assistance.

Special thanks go to my friend, Reza, who was a morale booster through all my ups and downs during the years of research. Thanks are also due to my mother, brothers Emad and Jamal, and my sister Susan for their kind support and encouragement throughout my years of education. Finally, thanks must also go to my friend and colleague, Gerd Nonneman, for his support and initiative.

INTRODUCTION

Much attention has been paid to superpower rivalry and involvement in the Third World in general, and the Arab world in particular. But comparatively little has been said about the role of the regional powers in these areas, either in their own right, or in relation to the European Community, which has been attempting to augment its economic and political strength in the Third World. This attempt marked a shift in orientation on the part of the European Community: a bid to establish itself as a major actor on the international scene comparable to, if not quite equal to, the superpowers.

When the European Community was founded in 1957, the principal aim was to achieve economic and then political integration among its member states. For this reason, up to the 1970s, the Community's attention was directed inwards rather than outwards (e.g. by removing the trade barriers among the member states, building up its agricultural policy and achieving ever-improving standards of living for its members.

With the advent of the 1970s, the Community managed to achieve remarkable economic growth and hence enjoy an influence in world economic affairs. The general increase in importance of the European Community in the 1970s generated the desire on the part of many European states to pursue a coordinated, distinctly European foreign policy, through which the Community could influence events in world affairs. Therefore, since the 1970s, the European Community has started to stress its desire to shape events in the international system and strengthen its international role. The Middle East was one of the first regions to which the Community turned in the early 1970s, an area which, for historical and geographical reasons, is of vital interest to it. This coincided with the general growth of Middle East oil revenues and the concomitant increase of power which served to further highlight the strategic significance of the Middle East.

The first collective European approach towards the Middle East was the Mediterranean trade policy that was adopted in October 1972. The policy aimed at concluding comprehensive economic agreements with the southern and eastern Mediterranean countries. But the watershed for the Community's involvement in the Middle East came in the aftermath of the October War and the Brussels and Copenhagen Declarations of 1973, which marked the beginning of what was subsequently called the Euro-Arab dialogue between the EEC and the Arab world. It is to this dialogue that this study principally addresses itself: from its genesis, through its various stages of development, up to the deadlock between the two parties in 1979. Thereafter, the initiative launched by the Community towards the Arab Gulf states, and its efforts to reactivate the dialogue, will be the focus of analysis.

The work will attempt to trace and analyse the development of the Community's collective approaches to the Arab world, the impetus behind these approaches, their degrees of success and failure and, finally, their future.

The methodology for research and analysis is that of a historical analytical approach, which in the writer's view is appropriate to the material available on this subject.

The research is based mainly on official documents such as communiqués, statements, reports, official journals, and so on. The survey of materials proved to be a difficult task. Despite the huge number of official documents and reports (both in Arabic and English), the researcher found herself limited in several ways. Important issues often go uncovered in the official reports, and most of the documents and reports are dull and inaccurate. It might, however, be put forward that the researcher should find this a challenge, not a discouragement. It is hoped that the result will be useful.

I

ECONOMIC RELATIONS BETWEEN THE
EUROPEAN COMMUNITY AND THE LEAGUE
OF ARAB STATES

The countries of the League of Arab States—usually known as the Arab League—are collectively the most important trading partner of the European Community (EC), also referred to as the European Economic Community (EEC) or Common Market. The EEC and the Arab League have played a crucial role in coordinating, controlling and developing Euro-Arab relations. The two organizations have worked to bring together the two groups of countries and promote economic co-operation between them. Their efforts in this respect are undeniable. But before examining the economic relations between the two groups, we should take a close look at them. The EEC and the Arab League are both regional organizations, and have been the main bodies conducting the ongoing Euro-Arab dialogue.

FORMATION OF THE EUROPEAN COMMUNITY

The EEC was established in 1957 by the Treaty of Rome, which set up a permanent economic community, to be known as the European Economic Community. Initially it included France, West Germany, Italy, Belgium, the Netherlands and Luxembourg. Later the membership of the Community expanded. This expansion was first to the north, when it became a community of nine with the entry of the United Kingdom, Ireland and Denmark in 1973. Then it encompassed nations to the south, when it became a community of twelve with the admission of, first, Greece in January 1981, and then Spain and Portugal in January 1986.[1]

The chief objects of the European Community were:

(a) the abolition of all tariffs, quotas and other barriers to trade between the member states of the Community, within a transition period of 12 years;
(b) the free movement of capital and labour within the territories of the Community;[2]
(c) the establishment of a uniform schedule of tariffs to imports from countries outside the Community;
(d) the creation of a common agricultural policy;
(e) the creation of two investment funds, one to operate in Europe and the other in associated overseas territories, in order to direct capital from the developed to the less developed regions of the Community;
(f) the establishment of a social fund to 'help relieve negative externalities for workers resulting from the movement toward integration'.[3]

THE MAIN EEC INSTITUTIONS

The EEC has four major permanent institutions: the Council of Ministers, European Commission, European Parliament and Court of Justice.

Council of Ministers

This is the Community's main decision-making body, consisting of ministers from each of the member states. The ministers' function is to act independently in the interest of the Community as a whole. The presidency of the Council is held for six months by each country in turn. In general, the Council acts according to proposals from the European Commission.[4] In performing its work it is supported by a Committee of Permanent Representatives, which is in charge of coordinating the preparatory work of the Community's decisions. The Committee is assisted by working groups of senior officials from the member states, and supported by a General Secretariat and its staff.[5]

European Commission

The Commission is composed of 17 members who are supposed to be independent of their national governments and to act in the interest of the Community as a whole. The members are under direct supervision of the European Parliament, which has the right and the power to force them to resign collectively. The decisions of the Commission are made on a collegiate basis. The Commission's tasks are: to ensure that rules of the Community and the principles of the Common Market are respected, and to see that the decisions of the Community's institutions are fully implemented. The Commission has powers of its own in sectors such as coal and steel competition and nuclear energy, and is responsible for the administrative work of the Community.[6]

In negotiating with non-member countries, the Commission acts under the guidance of the Council of Ministers. The heads of state or government of the EEC nations meet twice a year to decide the general guidelines for European policy. The foreign affairs ministers of the Community also meet periodically in a separate framework of political co-operation, in order to reach common positions on broad international issues.[7]

European Parliament

The European Parliament is composed of members who represent the citizens of the European Community. The 518 members, who are directly elected to serve for five years, sit in the Parliament not in the form of national groups but as political party groups. At present the groups are: Communists, Socialists, the European Peoples Party, Liberal and Democratic Reformists, European Democrats, the European Renewal and Democratic Alliance, the Rainbow Group, and the European Right. Although the Parliament does not enjoy legislative powers like those of the national parliaments, it does have the power to dismiss the Commission by a two-thirds majority and to supervise the Commission and the Council. In addition, the Parliament has the responsibility for advising the Council of Ministers on the Commission's proposals. With the help of the Council of Ministers, the Parliament decides the Community budget. Finally it also has some political control over the Council and the Commission.[8]

Court of Justice

The European Court of Justice consists of 13 judges assisted by six advocates-general. Each judge and each advocate serves for a period of six years. The Court's task is to settle legal disputes involving Community law. All Community institutions, governments of the member states, companies and individual Community nationals have the right to ask the Court for judgments on issues concerning Community laws. All decisions and judgments of the Court are binding in every member country.[9]

FORMATION OF THE ARAB LEAGUE

The establishment of the League of Arab States came as a result of an agreement signed in Cairo on 22 March 1945 between seven Arab states: Egypt, Iraq, Lebanon, Saudi Arabia, Syria, Jordan and Yemen. The other Arab nations joined the League as they gained their independence. Today, the organization includes all of the 22 independent Arab states (although Egypt's membership was temporarily suspended as a result of its signing of the Camp David agreements). The Palestinians are represented by the Palestine Liberation Organization (PLO), which has enjoyed full membership of the Council of the League of Arab States since 1976. The structures of the Arab League are quite flexible and akin to that of the Organization for African Unity (OAU). The League respects the established government in each member state, and guarantees its sovereignty and independence.[10]

The main goals of the Arab League are:

(a) to secure and encourage solidarity among its members in the face of external threats;
(b) to guarantee peace between the member states of the League by arbitrating in any conflict that may arise between two or more member states and by prohibiting the use of force;
(c) to ensure and maintain social, legal, parliamentary, financial, economic and cultural co-operation between the member states.[11]

THE MAIN ARAB LEAGUE INSTITUTIONS

Like the European Community, the Arab League has various institutions that run most of its affairs.

Council of the Arab League

This Council is composed of representatives from all the member states. It holds general sessions twice a year and extraordinary sessions at the request of two members if circumstances require it. The tasks of the Council are: to ensure the implementation of the agreements passed by different member states, to decide the means by which the League is to cooperate with the United Nations and other international agencies, to mediate conflicts between member states or between members and non-member states, to coordinate the measures of defence in the face of attack or threat of aggression, to endorse the League budget, and finally to appoint the secretary-general of the League.[12]

Joint Defence Council

This Council was established in June 1950 for the purposes of reciprocal defence and economic co-operation. It is composed of the foreign affairs and defence ministers of all the member countries.

Economic and Social Council

This was set up to replace the earlier Economic Council. Its aims are to facilitate and ensure the economic and social development of the Arab world. In addition it coordinates the activities of the specialized agencies which belong to the Arab League. These are: the Arab Fund for Economic and Social Development, the Arab Fund for Assistance to Arab and African countries, the Arab Monetary Fund, the Arab Organization for Agricultural Development, the Industrial Development Centre for Arab States, the Arab Bank for Economic Development in Africa, the Arab Council for Civil Aviation, the Arab Postal Union, the Arab

Telecommunication Union, the Arab Labour Council and the Council for Arab Unity.[13]

Committees

The Arab League's committees fall into three categories. First, there are committees that can be set up by the principal organs of the League. In every general session the Council undertakes to set up committees for foreign affairs, economic affairs, social affairs, and so on. The duration of these committees is linked to the timing of the session. Secondly, the 'ad hoc committees' are in charge of specific tasks and then dissolved whenever their mandate expires. Thirdly, there are 'permanent committees' in charge of studying problems within their competence and then presenting their findings to the Council for endorsement. There are permanent committees for political, social, health, cultural and economic affairs, and for information, oil, finance and administration.

Secretariat General

The Secretariat General is headed by the secretary-general, who is usually appointed by the Council by a minimum two-thirds majority vote. The secretary-general can in turn appoint assistant secretaries with the approval of the Council. The secretary-general's task is to ensure the implementation of the decisions taken by the Council. His role is very important for he represents the Arab world at international level, and he usually holds the post for a period of five years.[14]

ECONOMIC RELATIONS BETWEEN THE EEC AND ARAB LEAGUE BEFORE THE EVENTS OF 1973–4

The level of Euro-Arab trade during the period 1968 to 1974 shows the substantial importance that the European Community and the Arab League constituted for each other. The European Community's exports to the Arab countries increased considerably after 1968 to reach $13.2 billion in 1974, accounting for 48 per cent of the total imports of the Arab League countries.

During the same period, the share of European exports to the Arab market increased steadily from 6.2 per cent in 1968 to 9.2 per cent in 1974.

However, the importance of the Arab League countries as export markets differed from one EEC country to another. Among the Community countries, Italy, France and West Germany were the biggest exporters to the Arab League. The share of exports to Arab markets as a proportion of total exports in 1974 was 10.2 per cent for Italy, 9.4 per cent for France and 5.3 per cent for West Germany.[15]

The Arab countries were also important suppliers to the European Community. Their share of the Community's total imports rose from 13.6 per cent in 1970 to 22.3 per cent in 1974, when the total reached $27.9 billion. Italy, France, the United Kingdom, the Netherlands and West Germany were among the European Community countries most dependent on imports from the Arab world. In 1974, the individual shares of these countries' imports from it in their total imports were: 23.6 per cent for Italy, 18.8 per cent for France, 15 per cent for the United Kingdom, 13.4 per cent for the Netherlands and 12 per cent for West Germany. Crude oil made up about 90.6 per cent of total Arab exports to the European Community. If other unprocessed raw materials such as phosphates and ores are added to the figure for oil, it rises to 93.8 per cent.[16]

Despite this level of interaction between the two sides, the European Community lacked a comprehensive strategy (at the Community level) towards the Arab world. This was in part because the Community was in the process of shaping its own agricultural and trading policies, with the internal integration between the member states as its main concern.[17]

For these reasons, the economic relations between the European Community and the Arab world before 1972 can be characterized as random, unsystematic and on a case-by-case basis. The only exceptions were the preferential trade agreements concluded in 1968–9 with the Maghreb countries of North Africa: Morocco, Tunisia and Algeria. Lebanon and Egypt were the only Mashraq countries that had preferential trade agreements with the EEC, signed in 1965 and 1972 respectively.[18]

It was not until 1972 that the European Community managed to develop a 'global approach' towards the countries of the southern Mediterranean basin. As we shall see later, within the framework of the 'global Mediterranean policy' the European

Community managed in 1976 to conclude bilateral co-operation agreements with three of the Maghreb countries: Algeria, Morocco and Tunisia; four Mashraq countries (Egypt, Lebanon, Syria and Jordan) followed suit in 1977. As for Sudan, Somalia, Mauritania and Djibouti, these were signatories of the Lome Convention in 1975.

With regard to the Arab countries of the Gulf region, the European Community was up to the end of the 1970s not interested in having an economic relationship with them—at the Community level. However, this strategy has since been changed. In 1980 and as part of the process launched by the European Community to strengthen and make new agreements with the countries of the Gulf and Arabian peninsula, a co-operation agreement was concluded for the first time with the Yemen Arab Republic (North Yemen). This was signed in 1984 and was the Community's first contractual tie with this country. It covered commercial, economic and development co-operation between both sides. Also, in March 1988, the European Community and the countries of the Gulf Co-operation Council (GCC) managed to conclude a co-operation agreement.

ECONOMIC RELATIONS BETWEEN THE EEC AND THE MAGHREB COUNTRIES

Before dealing with the economic relations between the EEC and the Maghreb countries in the 1960s, some explanation of the present status is necessary. Collectively, the member states of the European Community form the main trading partner of the Maghreb countries of North Africa. The EEC is the most important and largest market for their exports. But the degree of reliance on the EEC varies in nature and degree. Most exports from Algeria (98 per cent) are petroleum products and, although the European market is not negligible as far as other products are concerned, it is not absolutely vital for Algeria's economic and social stability.

The same is not true of the other two Maghreb countries. In the case of Morocco, more than a quarter of its exports are agricultural products (such as citrus fruits and vegetables), for which the European Community is the principal market. In Tunisia, the agricultural sector (especially olive oil production, which offers a living for about 200,000 farmers) is still of major economic and social importance, and the European Community imports more than half of Tunisia's olive oil exports.[19]

The European Community in turn provides an important outlet for the labour forces of the Maghreb countries. More than two million North African citizens are working in Europe, and the remittances they send home are of great importance to their countries of origin. The Community is also the chief supplier of the Maghreb countries—the main source of machines, transport equipment, manufactured goods and chemicals. In addition, the Community is the major source of financial and technical aid. So there is a degree of economic interchange between the EEC and the Maghreb countries.[20]

Although the economic dimension forms the centre of relations between the two sides, the political aspect of their relations should not be dismissed. The European Community, in an attempt not to emulate the patterns of influence practised by the two superpowers and as a result of lacking the diplomatic and military means to uphold its influence, has chosen to rely on trade means. It considers this an effective instrument to help the Community to play a balanced role, as well as promoting conditions for social, economic and political stability in the Mediterranean basin.[21]

THE ORIGINS OF EEC–MAGHREB ECONOMIC RELATIONS

When the Treaty of Rome was first signed in 1957, the founder members of the European Common Market hoped to raise their standards of living and establish close relations between the Community members. For this reason, in the course of the negotiations over the Treaty of Rome, attention focused mainly on economic co-operation among the six founder members, which was viewed as a means to overcome the effects of war in Europe. However, it was the French government which, wanting to keep intact its customs union with its own colonies and overseas territories, suggested (towards the end of the negotiations) that provisions be made for the 'overseas countries and territories' of the member states.[22] These were mainly the colonies and territories under French dominance, as well as some recently independent countries such as Morocco and Tunisia. France, during the negotiations, made it plain that its entry must not compromise any privileged economic relations or free trade arrangements it enjoyed with its partners overseas.[23]

The initial reactions of the other prospective members towards the French suggestion were negative. In fact the suggestion took the other members by surprise, and was met with strong opposition from some member states—especially West Germany. Other countries, such as Belgium and Italy, were prepared to accept the idea of associating overseas countries and territories with the newly emerging European Community. This approval was because, at that time, these two countries were colonial powers as well.[24]

After protracted discussions, the other member states of the European Community gave their support to the French suggestion. They outlined the principles of their economic co-operation with the overseas countries in a 'Declaration of Intent' in 1957. It stated that the European Community was willing to conclude agreements for economic association with the independent countries of the Franc Zone in so far as these countries were 'anxious to maintain and intensify the traditional trade flows between the member states of the European Economic Community and these independent countries and to contribute to the economic and social development of the latter'.[25]

Morocco and Tunisia

As for the Maghreb countries of North Africa, the declaration of intent concerned only Morocco and Tunisia (Algeria had not yet gained its independence). The special relations between the European Community and these two countries were thus provided for by the Treaty of Rome. A protocol annexed to the Treaty authorized France to maintain preferential trade arrangements with Morocco and Tunisia. It also made it possible for France to conclude a bilateral arrangement with Algeria, under which France could grant Algeria preferential treatment for certain of its exports.[26]

When the negotiations for the establishment of the European Community were first held, France still maintained her dominance over the Arab Maghreb countries. France and its colonies in North Africa formed a closed area in which they had special trade relations, a joint monetary system and arrangements over financial aid.

During the EEC negotiations, France insisted on maintaining the privileged economic system which it enjoyed with bound its North African colonies. The French government requested that the Arab Maghreb countries should be associated with the EEC through the establishment of a free trade area between the EEC and these two countries. After long discussions, the other Community member states accepted the French demand. As a result, Morocco and Tunisia were subject to the declaration of intent and the protocol annexed to the Treaty of Rome.[27]

The protocol gave a privileged economic position for Morocco and Tunisia in the French market. It maintained their preferential treatment, so that nearly 50 per cent of their exports entered free of customs duties. Then when Morocco and Tunisia gained their independence, most of the advantages provided by the privileged system remained intact and the two countries continued to benefit from it.

As time went by, the European Community started to stress its dissatisfaction in maintaining this privileged status after the transitional period, arguing that continuing the protocol would create an anomalous situation. It considered that keeping it would be an obstacle to the functioning of the Common Market. Therefore, the Community insisted that the protocol should be eliminated and substituted by new agreements at Community level.[28]

The response of the Maghreb countries was negative. They argued that they regarded the protocol as permanent and that it should remain in effect until new agreements were reached. They also contended that if the new agreements did not cover all products, the protocol should remain in use for the products which were not included in the agreements. This did not satisfy the European Community, and to this end the Community expressed its desire to conclude new contractual agreements with both countries.[29] The outcome was that the legal basis of the 'special relations' between the European Community and the Maghreb countries remained confused and unformulated throughout the whole of the 1960s.[30]

Despite the urgent need to replace the protocol with contractual arrangements, the opening of the negotiations between the two sides had to wait for some time. This was due to many reasons on both sides. The Maghreb countries were not interested, at the time, in establishing a close relationship with the Community. First, this was for psychological reasons: the

European Community was viewed by most Third World countries as a colonial grouping. Secondly, there were economic reasons: because the European Community was busy with its internal integration, the Maghreb countries feared that the Community was not in a position to grant them important concessions. Thirdly, there were political reasons: Morocco and Tunisia were concerned about the political situation in Algeria. The two Maghreb countries therefore found it difficult to start negotiations while the Algerian conflict was not settled.

With respect to the European Community, the success of France in convincing the rest of the Community to have association agreements with the African countries (the Yaounde Convention) was viewed by the other Community members as a major concession favouring the sales of French exports in Africa. The other EEC members therefore showed no interest in launching negotiations with the Maghreb countries, especially in view of the fact that France already had privileged relationship with these two countries. Some of the Community members, moreover, gave more emphasis to the expansion of the Community towards the north to include the United Kingdom and the Nordic countries than to expansion towards the south.[31]

As mentioned earlier, the two Maghreb countries (Morocco and Tunisia) were subject to a declaration of intent regarding their association agreements. They were also subject to a protocol annexed to the Treaty of Rome that allowed them to keep their preferential treatment in the French market. In 1962, both countries concluded agreements with the European Community that contain great economic similarity. Thus we shall deal with these two countries together as one political unit.

The Maghreb countries presented their official demand for the conclusion of contractual agreements with the Community in October 1963. Morocco and Tunisia asked the EEC to open negotiations with a view to reaching association agreements. They expressed their desire that the agreements would cover not only trade arrangements, but also other aspects of their economic relations such as financial and technical co-operation and the issue of North African labour in Europe.[32]

Exploratory talks took place between the two sides in October 1964. During the negotiations, the Maghreb countries demanded, first, the establishment of a free trade area that would take account of the differences in the economic structures between the Community and the Maghreb countries; secondly, the application of the same treatment that was applied among the Six on their agricultural products; thirdly, the initiation of financial and technical co-operation; and fourthly, the maintenance of the privileged access they enjoyed to the French market.

After long discussions, the European Commission presented a report to the Council of Ministers on the outcome of the negotiations between the two sides. The Council therefore issued its first negotiating mandate on 15 June 1965. This mandate was rejected by the Maghreb countries because it did not contain any provisions for financial or technical co-operation nor any provisions concerning the conditions of migrant workers in Europe. It covered only a limited part of the commercial exchange, leaving out some important products of the Maghreb countries such as olive oil, wine, fruit and vegetables. In fact the Community member states were not then interested in establishing immediate relations with the Maghreb countries. This was because:

(a) the European Community, at the time, was engaged in Kennedy-round GATT negotiations;
(b) some of the Community member states, especially the Netherlands, were opposed to the idea of the enlargement towards the south, where the political tensions in some Arab states threatened;
(c) the Italian government had reservations, which it expressed in a memorandum issued on 4 May 1964, over granting any concessions (especially in the agricultural sector) to the Maghreb countries. The agricultural products of Italy were similar to those of the Maghreb countries and were in strong competition with them.[33]

The stagnation of the negotiations continued until 23 June 1967, when the Council of the European Community instructed the Commission to take the initiative and start a new round of negotiations. This time the negotiations culminated in the signing of a trade agreement on 28 March 1969 with Tunisia, and one on 31 March 1969 with Morocco. Each agreement was for a period of five years. The agreements were less comprehensive than had initially been envisaged. Both countries had hoped that they would be more generous and more broad in their scope. But the agreements were restricted to trade arrangements, leaving aside other things such as financial and technical co-operation and the migrant labour question.[34] The reasons for this were:

(a) the European Community was still in the process of shaping its common agricultural policy (CAP);
(b) there was a conflict of interests between the Community members and the Maghreb countries over some sensitive products such as wine, olive oil and citrus fruit;
(c) some member states did not agree to include financial, technical and labour co-operation in the agreements. They stated that it was too early to launch such co-operation.

Nevertheless, the agreements were regarded by both sides as a first step towards wider co-operation, which was accomplished seven years later.[35]

Under the 1969 agreements, the Community offered (in the agricultural sector) a preference of about 80 per cent of the common external tariff for citrus fruit exported to the Community from the two countries. All other products, especially olive oil, were excluded from the concessions. This was, as mentioned before, because of the strong competition between the interests of some of the EEC members and the Maghreb countries.[36]

In the industrial field, the Community granted free access for almost all industrial products except cork articles (which faced a tariff quota) and refined petroleum products (which faced a special safeguard clause). In return, the Maghreb countries agreed to remove the tariffs and quantitative restrictions (QRs) on EEC imports, except where this could cause serious disruption. Finally, an association council consisting of members of the European Commission and representatives of the Moroccan and Tunisian governments was established. The council's main task was to administer the workings of each agreement.[37]

Algeria

Algeria's situation was rather different. Until independence, it was considered to be part of the EEC and treated as a European territory belonging to France, as was clear during the setting up of the European Common Market. At the time, in regulating relations with their overseas territories within the framework of the Treaty of Rome, the six member states indicated that those countries would gain their independence some day. In the case of Algeria, France did not show any intention of granting the country its independence. Consequently, special exception was made for Algeria under Article 227 of the Treaty of Rome. This article explained the treatment of the relations between Algeria and the European Community, especially Paragraph 2 which concerned the geographic application of the Treaty of Rome.[38] The paragraph stated: 'With regard to Algeria and the French overseas departments, the general and particular provisions of this Treaty relating to the free movements of goods, agriculture save for Article 40 (4), the liberalization of services, the rules on competition, the protective measures provided for in Articles 108, 109 and 226, the institutions, shall apply as soon as this Treaty enters into force.'[39]

The text of Article 227 thus indicated that the provisions of the Treaty of Rome would apply to Algeria as an integral part of France.

Independence and de facto continuation

In 1962, Algeria gained its independence. It immediately approached the Community seeking a 'special relationship' in which Algeria was ready to grant tariff preferences on a unilateral basis to the products of the Common Market. Algeria asked the Community to keep the *status quo* concerning trade preferences, which was embodied in the provisions of Article 227. The Community response was positive: there was a general agreement among the member states to continue applying the regulations originally agreed under the Treaty of Rome. Algeria had thus managed to gain a *de facto* continuation of its preferential trade arrangements with the European Community.[40]

Attempts at a contractual relationship with the EEC

In 1963, the Algerian government, in an attempt to shape its future relations with the EEC, expressed its desire to start negotiations with the aim of concluding an overall agreement. The Community response was negative. The Council of Ministers did not authorize the Commission to start negotiations, and it was not until late 1972 that the Community decided to launch discussions with Algeria on the basis of an offer covering only trade arrangements.[41]

The reasons behind the delay were mostly political. At least four among the six member states of the European Community at the time were reluctant to have an agreement with Algeria. The Belgian government, for example, harboured ill-feelings towards Algeria because of its support for the rebels in the Congo as well as its readiness to extradite Moise Tshome to the Congo. The West Germans did not admire the militancy of the Algerian regime. They considered the Algerian government even more militant than Nasser's in Egypt, which had severed its diplomatic relations with West Germany because of the latter's recognition of Israel. The Netherlands was also cool towards the political hard line of the Algerian government. In 1967, when the Algerian government refused to accept the United Nations cease-fire in the 1967 Arab–Israeli war, the Dutch declined even to have the Algerian application (for concluding an agreement with the Community) debated in the Council. Italy, for economic considerations, was reluctant to allow the Community open its market to Algerian exports which stood in direct competition with Italian products.

Moreover, the status of the relations between France and the five other members had an important impact on the progress of the talks. France was viewed by the Community members as the *demandeur* on behalf of Algeria, and when the relations between France and the other five were disrupted, Algeria became the victim.[42]

Opening of negotiations

The *de facto* status granted to Algeria after its independence did not last long. This created an unsatisfactory situation, because over time the precise application of the Treaty of Rome (by the Community members) was gradually decreased. Consequently a diversity of systems—according to products and member states—prevailed between Algeria and the European Community.[43]

The years 1967–8 witnessed an era during which each member state of the EEC was free to employ the preferential system in a way that could suit its own interests. For example, France continued to give Algerian products duty-free entry to its market (except for wine, in which special agreement was concluded between the two sides). Italy and West Germany, on the other hand, denounced Article 277 and regarded Algeria as a Third Party. The Benelux countries applied a partial customs tariff, favourable in particular to Algerian citrus fruit.[44]

As time went by, the member states began to feel that it was impossible to continue with such a random relationship. Consequently, they expressed their desire to clear up the obscure status of their relations with Algeria. This wish was coupled to the fact that negotiations were due to start with Morocco and Tunisia for the renewal of their association agreements. The combination of these factors made it imperative for the Community members to approach the problem of relations with the Maghreb countries in a comprehensive way.[45]

Thus it was in 1972 that the Community took the initiative and decided to start the negotiations with Algeria. The same year witnessed the creation of the 'Mediterranean policy', whereby the then nine members of the European Community examined their future relations with the Mediterranean countries and then laid down the main points for the agreements which would have to be concluded or renewed with the countries concerned. This policy emphasized the question of financial and technical co-operation. Within the framework of this policy, a Community-level agreement was concluded with Algeria for the first time in 1976.[46]

LEBANON

Lebanon was the first Arab country to have contractual relations with the European Community. It approached the EEC as early as 1962, asking for an agreement on tariff concessions. However, the approach proved to be fruitless because at that time the Community was not willing to grant Lebanon any such concessions.

The second approach made by Lebanon came through a memorandum submitted by its government in December 1963 and February 1964. In this memorandum, the Lebanese government asked for an economic co-operation agreement. This time the Community's response was positive. At its session of 13–15 April 1964, the Council of Ministers instructed the Commission to start negotiations with Lebanon aimed at concluding an economic agreement. The negotiations were successful and agreement was reached almost eleven months later.[47] It was a non-preferential trade agreement, signed on 21 May 1965, and came into force on 1 July 1968. The agreement has special importance because it was not exclusively concerned with trade—it also involved technical co-operation.[48]

The technical assistance provisions in the agreement exceeded the competence of the Treaty of Rome, and as a result the agreement had to be signed by the Community members individually as well as by the Council of Ministers.[49]

The main provisions of the agreement were:

(a) On trade , the EEC and its member states on the one hand and the Lebanon on the other agreed to grant each other 'most favoured nation treatment'. This was in the broad sense of the term, including non-tariff obstacles to trade. Subsequently, a joint committee composed of Community representatives (from the Commission and the member states) and Lebanese representatives was set up to supervise the implementation of the trade side of the agreement.

(b) With regard to technical assistance, a joint working group on technical co-operation was formed. It was composed of representatives of the member states, the Commission and Lebanon. The working group was charged with coordinating technical assistance activities by the six members with the Lebanese Republic. This would be done by sending experts for teaching or setting up research institutions in Lebanon; supplying technical training for Lebanese nationals in the EEC; providing technical equipment; and preparing surveys on Lebanese resources.

In addition, a protocol on oranges and a declaration concerning credit insurance for Community exporters to Lebanon were annexed to the agreement. The agreement was to be renewed every three years.[50]

The 1972 agreement between the EEC and Lebanon

The 1965 agreement did not, however, live up to the expectations of the Lebanese government. Trade relations between the two sides developed in a manner which favoured only the EEC, and no substantial progress was achieved in the field of technical assistance. Consequently, on 1 October 1970 the Lebanese government requested a new agreement with more substance than the first one. The negotiations started in 1970 and lasted almost two years. They culminated in the signing of a preferential agreement in December 1972, on the basis of Article 113 of the Treaty of Rome. This included matter of more economic substance than the first agreement.[51]

The new agreement was for a period of five years. It did not replace the first non-preferential one, because both sides had agreed in a declaration laid out in the annex to the new agreement that the 1965 agreement would continue to operate in areas that were not covered by the new one.[52]

It dealt mainly with trade preferences and did not cover financial and technical co-operation. The concessions being given by the Community were a 30 to 50 per cent tariff reduction for Lebanese exports to the EEC, and an immediate tariff reduction of 45 per cent for industrial products (except textiles and petroleum products). In the agricultural sector, concessions were given for certain products such as citrus fruits, onions, garlic, bananas, mango and avocados. In return, Lebanon reduced its customs duties on EEC exports, ranging from 6 to 30 per cent, according to an agreed timetable.[53]

Finally, a joint committee composed of representatives from both sides undertook the responsibility of implementing the agreement and then presenting recommendations. It was to meet once a year on the initiative of its chairman, and whenever necessary at the request of one of the contracting parties. It would form a working party to help it to perform its duties.[54]

Over time, because of insufficient trade concessions and the lack of financial and technical co-operation, the Lebanese government became dissatisfied with the agreement. In 1974, it asked the Community to launch another round of negotiations, aimed at concluding a new agreement—this time to be based on the EEC's global approach towards the Mediterranean countries. The Lebanese government hoped that such an arrangement would include not only trade arrangements but also other aspects of economic relations, such as financial and technical co-operation. The Community accepted the request, and in December 1975 the Council of Ministers issued its first negotiating mandate for Lebanon, as well as for other Mashraq countries. The negotiations with Lebanon culminated in the signing of a comprehensive agreement in 1977, based on Article 238 of the

Treaty of Rome and within the framework of the Community's Mediterranean policy.[55]

EGYPT

Egypt's preferential agreement with the EEC was signed in December 1972, and came into force in 1973. Its aim was to establish a free trade area. Accordingly, Egypt cut tariffs by up to 50 per cent on one-third of its imports from the EEC, subject to a safeguard clause and quantity restriction on some EEC products. In return, 90 per cent of Egyptian industrial exports were guaranteed preferential access to the EEC market (the major exceptions were cotton yarn and fabric, aluminium, cars and petroleum products), and over half of its agricultural exports received tariff cuts (although these were limited in the case of rice by a tariff quota, and in the case of citrus fruits by a requirement that prices had to exceed the CAP minimum). However, as time went by, it became clear that a free trade area was not feasible. This was due to the low capacity of the Egyptian products to compete in the Common Market and the growing trade deficit between Egypt and the EEC. Therefore, in 1976, the relations between both sides were re-formulated within the framework of the European Mediterranean policy.[56]

CONCLUSION

Clearly the first generation of agreements fell short of satisfying the aspirations of the Arab countries that signed them. The agreements did little to contribute to the economic and social development of the countries concerned, because they dealt solely with trade. It was in view of this situation, and of the desire of the EEC to establish a broad cohesive co-operation policy which could live up to the expectations of the Mediterranean countries, that the Community worked out a global approach in 1972.

THE COMMUNITY'S MEDITERRANEAN POLICY, 1972

The Mediterranean region forms an area that is characterized by special historical links and a level economic interdependence in some decisive areas. These factors combine to make the region of crucial importance for the European Community. The EEC countries that occupy the northern part of the Mediterranean basin have historically been bound to the countries on the southern and eastern coasts by different kinds of economic, political, social and cultural ties. These ties go back to ancient times.[57]

EVOLUTION OF THE MEDITERRANEAN POLICY

The first expression of global co-operation came in May 1964, in the so-called Italian memorandum. In this memorandum the Italian government suggested to the European Council the following: first, the establishment of a free trade area for industrial goods between the European Community and the Mediterranean countries; secondly, financial aid to be afforded by the rich members of the Community to the less developed countries in the area; thirdly, restricted concessions to be offered for the Mediterranean countries in the agricultural sector. These agricultural concessions could be granted only on condition that the interests of the Community's southern region were suitably accommodated through the necessary trade incentives, structural aids and the establishment of an EEC regional policy. The proposals in the Italian memorandum were not accepted by the European Council of Ministers, but the memorandum did later play a significant role in the formation of Community policy.

In 1966, the European Commission proposed an EEC global approach towards the Maghreb countries. This initiative also failed to gain acceptance. In the absence of any agreement between the Community member states to launch a coherent Mediterranean policy, and after its failure to gain the approval of the European Council for its global co-operation approach to the Maghreb countries in 1966, the Commission resolved to go ahead and use the only instrument the Treaty of Rome had given it: the establishment of trade co-operation agreements with the Mediterranean countries.[58]

The European Commission consequently became involved in a network of preferential and non-preferential trade agreements, as well as of agreements of association. They were as follows: association agreement with Greece and Turkey in June 1962 and 12 September 1963 respectively, with Morocco and Tunisia in March 1969, with Malta on 5 December 1970, and with

Cyprus on 19 December 1972. Preferential trade agreements
with Spain on 27 June 1970, with Egypt in September 1972 and
with Portugal in July 1972. Israel signed a non-preferential trade
agreement as early as 1963 followed by a preferential trade
agreement in June 1970. Lebanon also signed a non-preferential
agreement with the Community in 1965, followed by a preferential agreement in 1972. Finally a non-preferential agreement
was signed with Yugoslavia in March 1970.[59]

*Community members' attitude towards attempts at a Mediterranean
policy*

Up to the early 1970s, the attitude of the Community member
states towards the attempts to establish a coherent Community
Mediterranean policy varied and differed from one member
state to another. This was due to the divergent positions of the
Community governments, as well as those of different economic
lobbies and interest groups within each member state. Among
the members most closely concerned with the situation in the
Mediterranean region were the so-called Mediterranean coastline Community members. They included Italy in the first place,
then France.

Italy

Geographically, Italy was well placed to have close relations
with other Mediterranean countries, and from the beginning its
ambition to establish a Mediterranean policy was clear. But
Italy's position was difficult. On the one hand, Community
Mediterranean policy could enormously benefit Italy because it
would allow it to move from the periphery of the Community to
the centre of a larger integrated area. Furthermore, a Mediterranean policy was more important for Italy's security than to
that of its northern partners. On the other hand, the economic
vulnerability of Italy (especially the structural weakness of its
'Mezzogiorno') could not permit it to undertake alone the structural adjustments called for by the increased competition it faces
through the lowering of tariffs in the Mediterranean area. This
explains why Italy hesitated between brave initiatives (such as
the Moro Memorandum of 1964) and an unwillingness to risk
new policies in this sphere.

Italy was ultimately prepared to compromise on condition that it would gain some compensation for the sectors most likely to be affected by the Mediterranean policy. In 1975, during the negotiations with the Maghreb countries, Italy declined to accept the additional concessions that were suggested by the Commission for the Maghreb countries, unless compensation was provided by the Community for its southern farmers. Equally, Italy favoured granting better terms to migrant labour from the Maghreb, but on condition that Community preference for migrant workers from within the Community (mostly Italy) was clearly established.[60]

France

The interests of France in the Mediterranean region were mostly, for political and economic reasons, in the direction of the Iberian Peninsula and the Maghreb countries. Its main concern (especially after Charles de Gaulle came to power) was how to build a role for itself in the Mediterranean region—a role that would be independent of the two superpowers. Expressions such as 'Europe extended to Africa' meant that France aimed at building up its strength and influence, and affirming European and its own national leadership in the region. This ambition to have a world role in the Mediterranean area was to become a key factor in the French policy towards this area.

However, for many years France lacked the concept of a global Community relationship with the Mediterranean countries. This was for many reasons. First, the French government, at the time, was constantly under pressure from its farmers in relation to any concessions on agricultural imports. The agricultural unions were opposed to any attempt by the French government to try to establish a coherent Community Mediterranean policy. They argued that such a policy would sharpen competition with countries which produced similar agricultural goods and lead to a real threat to their own interests.

Secondly, the political crisis that followed the Bizerta incident in Tunisia and the nationalization of petroleum firms in Algeria prevented France from playing a mediating role between the Community and the Maghreb countries.

Thirdly, the French government at the time generally favoured bilateral relations and gave priorities to national actions at the expense of Community actions. This bilateral approach was in contrast to the positions of the other Community member states. Later the situation changed. France started to realize that its ambition in the Mediterranean region would not be accomplished alone, due to its limited political and economic influence. It realized also that its own interests could work together with wider Community interests in the area, and that the Community could form a means for the fulfilment of French aspirations in the Mediterranean.[61]

By 1970s, the French government began to emphasize the importance of the area and the importance of having a global policy in it. The Mediterranean, said the French minister of agriculture commenting on the Libyan arms deal of 1970, was 'one of the few areas in which independent and concerted action by Europe would have positive significance'. President Pompidou talked of the need 'to improve Europe's equilibrium by making Mediterranean and Latin influences more clearly apparent'.[62]

The French government in due course became the champion of a Mediterranean policy. It even succeeded in convincing its partners to stress the importance of this policy in the final communiqué at the Paris summit meeting of October 1972.[63]

Other Community member states

West Germany, the Netherlands and, later, Great Britain and Denmark, all showed a lack of enthusiasm for the idea of establishing a coherent Mediterranean policy. More than once, these countries expressed their reservations about any initiative in the Mediterranean. They reminded their partners in the Community that any further progress in co-operation with the countries bordering the Mediterranean was linked to new Community initiative in development co-operation world-wide. The objections of these countries stemmed from the fact that they were trying to avoid antagonizing the United States, which was opposed to the Community developing Mediterranean policy. They feared that such a policy would only increase the tension which already existed with the United States and endanger the Atlantic Alliance.

Despite such initial reservations, these four countries did by the early 1970s modify their positions and began to lean towards favouring the policy. West Germany, for example, after the failure of the so-called 'Hallstein doctrine', stressed that a Community Mediterranean policy was well suited to improving relations with the Arab countries, on a new basis. In 1972, West Germany, the Netherlands, Britain and Denmark approved the idea of an overall Mediterranean policy at the Paris summit meeting.

Belgium, Ireland and Luxembourg all followed a positive attitude towards the idea of setting up a co-operation policy with the Mediterranean countries. Contrary to their European partners, they supported and endorsed the Commission initiative in the Mediterranean region.[64]

THE PARIS SUMMIT MEETING AND THE ACCEPTANCE OF THE MEDITERRANEAN POLICY

Up to the beginning of the 1970s, there was no European agreement to a collective, coherent Mediterranean policy. But from 1970 onwards, the European Community began to show more interest in the Mediterranean region and more emphasis was placed on the need for a coherent Community policy in the area. This policy was part of a more outgoing international one. After the 1972 Paris summit conference, the Community initiated a new programme which aimed at increasing and upholding its international role: Europe should establish a 'European identity' in world affairs, and should 'seek increasingly to shape events' in the international system. 'Europe must be able to make its voice heard in world affairs, and to make an original contribution commensurate with its human, intellectual and material resources.'[65]

This original contribution was seen to be based on the notion of Europe as a 'civilian power'. Consequently, the Community had to employ fully its economic potential through establishing partnerships with third countries or with groups of countries. It was conceived that the Community could become a leading force in an evolutionary change of the international system, based on democratic and human values.[66]

It was within this context that more emphasis was placed on the Mediterranean region. Since then the Community has continuously proclaimed its vital and permanent interests in the region. The highest-ranking officials of the EEC 'have attributed essential importance ... to the fulfilment of (the Community) commitments to the countries of the Mediterranean Basin.'[67]

> The Mediterranean is an area of considerable importance to which the Community, for historical and geographical reasons, is in a unique position and has responsibilities it cannot shirk ... To secure peace in Europe as well as to stabilize trade flows, the Community has to contribute to the solution of conflicts in northern Africa, the eastern Mediterranean and the Middle East. Europe must play its rightful role on the international scene and particularly in the Mediterranean. To assert its presence and strengthen its identity, the Community must equip itself with the instruments of diplomacy and joint action which it still lacks at the level of policy and security.[68]

At the same time and parallel to these developments at the political level, the Commission was in the process of assessing its economic relations with the Mediterranean countries. Given the broad policy which the Commission had followed during the 1960s and up to 1972, the need was felt for a coherent framework. Being aware of this, the Commission took the initiative in 1971 and presented a memorandum on this subject to the European Council of Ministers.

In the memorandum the Commission evaluated its economic record with the southern Mediterranean countries. It stated that the 'considerable overlap of political and economic interests, and the influence that Europe could have in this region made it possible to see the development of the Mediterranean basin as a natural extension of the European integration'.[69] The memorandum went on to explain that the agreements which were concluded with the countries of this region were insufficient to safeguard European interests.[70]

This time the European Council of Ministers responded positively by instructing the Commission to take stock of the overall pattern of the economic relations between the European Community and its Mediterranean partners. Three months later, the Commission submitted its suggestion for a global Mediterranean policy based on trade, economic, technical and social co-operation. On 19 October 1972, the Paris summit of European heads of state and government gave its support to the Mediterranean approach.[71]

The summit resolutions declared that the Community attached vital importance to the implementation of its commitments to the countries of the Mediterranean basin with which agreements had been or would be concluded and that these agreements were to be the subject of an overall and balanced approach.[72] The geographical range was specified: it would cover the countries of the Mediterranean coastline (Spain, Yugoslavia, Albania, Cyprus, Malta, Syria, Lebanon, Israel, Egypt, Libya, Tunisia, Morocco, and Algeria) as well as Jordan and Portugal. Greece and Turkey were the signatories of association agreements intended to lead to a full membership at a later stage.[73]

MOTIVES UNDERLYING THE GLOBAL MEDITERRANEAN POLICY

The chief factors affecting the formulation of the EEC's global Mediterranean policy were political, strategic and commercial considerations.

Political considerations

Political considerations were the main motive behind the Community's desire to conduct the new type of agreements with its Mediterranean partners on the other side of the sea.

In the post-Suez era, one can discern the declined of European (mainly British and French) influence in the Middle East. Meanwhile, the United States moved in to fill the vacuum created by the departure of the colonial powers. It also undertook the responsibility to safeguard and protect Western interests in the area. In addition, the Suez crisis offered an opportunity for the Soviet Union and gave it a foothold in the region, especially in the crucial eastern Mediterranean. Initially, this infant involvement did not cause any significant worries. But slowly Western fears of Soviet influence began to mount, because of the arrival of a strong and permanent Soviet fleet in the Mediterranean region[74]. The precise date that most authorities give as marking the beginning of a permanent Soviet naval presence there is June 1964, although full-force levels were not reached until 1967.[75]

The emergence of the Soviet presence in the Mediterranean basin, where Europe's southern flank was directly exposed to the Soviet influence, was regarded as a serious threat to Western interests in the area. It alarmed the European allies and threw into question the American defence credibility. As a result, Europe's security position underwent change. The international polarization of the area round the Arab–Israeli conflict (the United States was committed to Israel's defence whereas the Soviet Union lent its support to the Arab countries) helped to increase the state of tension and instability in the area as a whole. Conflict such as the Arab–Israeli dispute, the Greek–Turkish quarrel over Cyprus, and so on, all created political destabilization and facilitated the penetration of the superpowers into the region. These conflicts also threatened the security of the area and opened up the possibility of a direct clash between the two superpowers in a volatile region where Europe found itself most vulnerable.[76]

For these reasons Europe was eager to reduce the influence of the superpowers in the area and to establish equitable and beneficial relationships with its Mediterranean partners on the other side of the shore. The desire to clear the region of superpower rivalry found a positive response from most of the the Mediterranean countries, which expressed their desire to see less superpower dominance. They looked to the EEC as a counterweight likely to offset the domination of one or other of the superpowers, or both taken together. Thus they had a common interest to free the region from superpower competition.[77]

Strategic considerations

The strategic considerations related mainly to the security of the European Community's oil supply. The countries of the EEC, as other developed countries, depend heavily on oil for their economic development. Most of the Community's oil comes from the Middle East through the pipelines, port terminals and shipping routes of the Mediterranean.[78] This fact made the Mediterranean of special significance to Europe as a route through which its oil supplies pass, and made it vital for Europe to keep this route away from any threats whether from countries within the area itself or from hostile outside powers.[79] The oil crisis of 1973, and its economic and political repercussions, increased the importance of the Mediterranean region. It also upheld the idea of establishing close relations with the Arab Mediterranean countries in order to secure the supply of oil and other raw materials.[80]

Progress made in the building of Europe

By the beginning of 1970, after having achieved customs union and set up the agricultural common market, the Community had the means to carry out a more ambitious co-operation policy. With the entry of the United Kingdom, Ireland and Denmark scheduled for 1 January 1973, the EEC would become the biggest trading power of the Western world. The Mediterranean countries were becoming aware of the growing importance of their European partner.[81]

Commercial considerations

Commercial motives were also behind the desire of the Community and its Mediterranean partners to take another look at their co-operation. For example, the United Kingdom's accession to the Community meant not only that it had to gradually align its customs tariffs with that of the Common Customs Tariff (CCT) but also take into consideration the trade agreements the 'Six' had concluded previously. Consequently, there was on the one hand the prospect of changing trade patterns in the Euro-Mediterranean area, and on the other the evident need to renegotiate or 'adapt' certain agreements. Moreover, several of these agreements were about to expire at this time.[82]

Establishment of the generalized system in 1971

The idea of a generalized system of preferences (GSP) was launched by the developing countries as a group during the first United Nations Conference on Trade and Development in 1964. At the time, the developing countries asked the industrial countries to provide them with preferential treatment for their exports so that they could boost their industry. The demand did not receive a favourable response from the developed countries, which were unwilling to accept the idea. They were reluctant to encourage imports of manufactured goods from Third World countries that could compete unfairly with their own products.

However, in the early 1970s all industrialized nations recognized the need for a system of tariff preferences, under which Third World exports of manufactured products would be exempt from import duties. The EEC took the initiative and introduced its own preference system in 1971, for a period of ten years. This expired in 1981 and was extended for a further ten years. The EEC example was followed by other industrialized countries which launched their own schemes: the American scheme, and the Japanese scheme.[83]

In general, the object of the GSP is to encourage the industrialization of the developing countries. This would be accomplished by making it easy for them to export their semi- manufactured and manufactured products to the industrialized countries. Under the GSP, exports from developing countries enter the markets of the industrial countries either duty-free or at lower rates of duty. It also provides Third World exporters with a price advantage over exporters from industrialized nations.

Currently, about 20 OECD countries (including the EEC countries) offer preferential treatment for the developing countries under the GSP. The product and country coverage, as well as the margin of preference, differ from one country to another. The EEC's scheme covers all semi-manufactured and manufactured products, including textiles and clothing and a large number of processed agricultural products. All industrial products and more than 20 per cent of agricultural products enter the EEC market duty-free. Morover, there are tariff reductions of between 20 and 60 per cent for other agricultural products.[84] Countries benefiting from the Community's GSP need not grant reciprocal tariff concessions. The preferences are given to all developing countries without discrimination and are not negotiated. It constitutes an attempt by the Community to meet the needs of developing countries.[85]

The Community GSP scheme currently covers 128 independent countries and 22 dependent territories. It has, however, been the most advanced economies within the developing countries that have gained most from the scheme. Consequently, and in order to encourage others to make more use of the scheme, the Community has since 1982 replaced the old global ceiling and quotas by individual limits for each country. In addition, the less developed countries (among the developing countries) enjoy other benefits such as duty-free entry for all agricultural products imported under the GSP, and duty-free entry and no quantitative limits for industrial and textiles products.[86]

However, as time went by, the development of this system threatened to damage the Mediterranean countries' trade positions *vis-à-vis* the European Community. This accelerated the demand for the re-negotiation of the existing agreements.[87]

External pressure

The outside pressure on the European Community to try to put its external commercial policy into harmony was enormous. On the one hand, the Tokyo round of multilateral trade negotiations was in prospect. On the other, there was the constant opposition by the United States to the reverse preferences offered to the Community by the Mediterranean countries.[88]

THE CONCLUSION OF THE CO-OPERATION AGREEMENTS

In November 1972, the European Council of Ministers approved the Mediterranean policy. In June 1973, the Council issued its first directives to the European Commission instructing it to start negotiations on behalf of the Community with the Mediterranean countries.[89]

The negotiations with the Arab Mediterranean countries took place in two parts. Negotiations with the Maghreb countries started in July and October 1973, carried on in the autumn of 1974 and in April 1975 and reached their final stage in January 1976.[90] As for the Mashreq countries, in 1973 and 1974 these states demanded the opening of negotiations with a view to concluding co-operation agreements. These negotiations did not start, however, until January 1976 and entered their final stage in 1977.[91]

The negotiations proved to be tough and arduous, and were beset with difficulties. First, there were disagreements between the member states of the European Community itself over the agricultural aspect of the Mediterranean policy. The consumer countries, such as Britain, welcomed the possibility of gaining cheap food from the Mediterranean countries. The producer countries, such as France and Italy, considered this a threat to their own agricultural interests and they strove to safeguard these.[92] This was because of the direct competition between these countries and the Arab Maghreb countries in relation to certain types of products. It was difficult for the negotiators from both sides to find satisfactory conditions for the access of

agricultural goods to the EEC Common Market.[93] Secondly, due
to the lack of general guidelines, much time was wasted debat-
ing trivial matters such as the question of whether an EEC
customs duty reduction of 55 per cent would apply only to
tinned fruit salads weighing over one kilogram, or also to those
weighing under a kilo.[94]

Thirdly, the political and economic disparities among the
southern Mediterranean partners, as well as their different
interests, all hindered the application of this policy and caused
delay in completing the negotiations.[95] Among the main obstacles causing difficulty were the political complications that
followed from the Arab boycott against Israel. This latter problem was settled by reaching a compromise including a non-
discrimination clause in the agreements, while at the same time
allowing the Arab countries a qualification of this clause in a
separate letter.[96]

Negotiations were finally brought to a successful end with the
signing in 1976 of co-operation agreements with the Maghreb
countries of North Africa: Tunisia, Morocco and Algeria. The
agreements with Tunisia and Morocco were to replace the early
agreements of 1969. The agreement with Algeria was the first
one to be made at the Community level. As for the four Mashreq
countries, the agreements with Egypt, Syria and Jordan were
signed in January 1977, while the signing of the agreement with
Lebanon was delayed until May 1977. The latter delay was due
to the country's political problems. In the cases of Syria and
Jordan, this was the first time they had contractual relations with
the Community. Lebanon and Egypt had early agreements with
the EEC.

Thus the EEC currently has contractual relations with 12 Arab
countries: the Maghreb countries (Tunisia, Morocco and
Algeria), the Mashreq countries (Egypt, Syria, Jordan and Lebanon) and Sudan, Somalia, Mauritania and Djibouti. The Community also has a co-operation agreement with the Yemen Arab
Republic signed in 1984 and with the GCC countries signed in
1988.

Structures of the co-operation agreements

The co-operation agreements signed between the European
Community and the seven Arab countries in 1976–7 were identi-

cal in outline. They were based on the same model, which reflects the Community's concern to have a coherent overall Mediterranean approach. The agreements established co-operation between the European Community and its Mediterranean partners in different aspects of their relations. They had financial protocols which provided loans and grants to fund economic development in the countries concerned. All the agreements were of unlimited periods, except for the protocols fixing the amount of the financial aid which were of limited periods—usually five years.[97]

The co-operation agreements between the EEC and the seven Arab countries covered different fields.

Trade preferences

The agreements provided free access to the European Common Market for all industrial goods (except refined petroleum products and certain textiles). The EEC, in order to protect its textile industry, was following a strict textile import policy. The repercussions of this policy in relation to the Arab Mediterranean countries were enormous because it tended to hinder their ability to increase their export production. The countries most affected by these measures were the non-oil exporting countries and the poorest ones in the group, such as Tunisia, Morocco and Egypt.

In the agricultural sector the situation is not that favourable either. Tariff concessions have been confined to special conditions, such as only for certain kinds of fruit and vegetables during certain times of the year.[98] The purpose behind this is to provide the Community with the products of these countries in the off-season. For example, Moroccan vegetables enjoy a 60 per cent reduction if they are available between 1 November and 30 April. Also canned citrus fruits enjoy a concession of 80 per cent on the normal duty if the total weight of the can and contents is 1 kilogram or less.[99]

Financial and technical co-operation

The agreements aimed at establishing technical co-operation as well as providing European financial assistance for the economic development of the seven Arab countries. The amount of the aid under the first protocols, covering 1978–82, was 669 million ecu distributed between the countries in question. Further financial protocols were concluded covering the period 1982 to 1986, with a total increase in funds of 52 per cent. In distributing the funds between the recipient countries, the less developed and the poorest countries such as Egypt, Morocco and Lebanon took priority over the rest of the group.[100] In 1987, the Community concluded a third financial protocol with six Arab countries (the protocol with Syria was not renewed due to the British veto).[101]

The agreements also contained arrangements for joint operations between the Community and other donors. This, it was hoped, would stimulate potential suppliers of funds to become more interested in investing in countries that had signed the agreements, if they could be sure to reap the benefits of guaranteed access to the Community market for products they might manufacture in the Arab countries. In addition, a broad range of economic co-operation between the two sides was envisaged:

(a) sales promotion and marketing;
(b) encouragement of private investment;
(c) industrial co-operation;
(d) co-operation in scientific, technological and environmental fields.[102]

Social matters

The agreements with the Maghreb countries contained a special section concerning Maghreb nationals working in the Community. Because a considerable number of Maghreb nationals are working in Europe, the co-operation agreements included provisions related to the living conditions of these workers, such as provisions for social equality and welfare of various types. In return the Maghreb countries promised not to discriminate against EEC citizens working in their respective countries.[103]

Joint institutions

Each agreement is managed by a Co-operation Council composed of representatives from both sides, who meet annually to assess the work. Extra meetings can be organized at the request of either side. The council is presided over alternatively by a member from each side. It possesses the power to take decisions in order to reach objectives in the agreements. Council decisions are taken by mutual consent and are binding on both sides. The Council can make recommendations to safeguard the implementation of the agreements. It can also take a decision to set up Specialist Committees to help it carry out its duties. The Specialist Committees can in turn organize contacts between the members of both sides in order to speed up the exchange of views. The European Commission is represented permanently by a delegation in each of the seven Arab countries concerned, as is the case with the Arab countries which signed the Lome Convention. The delegations offer information and administer the projects laid down in the agreements.[104]

THE UNITED STATES AND THE EUROPEAN MEDITERRANEAN POLICY

The position of the United States concerning the Mediterranean policy of the European Community stems from its attitude to the EEC common agricultural policy as well as the Community preferential trade relations with the developing countries in general. For a long time, the EEC common agricultural policy and its associated system of prices and barriers to trade had been the main cause of disagreement and conflict in USA-EEC agricultural trade relations. But first, an explanation of the American attitude towards the European common agricultural policy (CAP) is needed.[105]

From the inception of the EEC, the United States emphatically encouraged and endorsed the establishment of the European Common Market. The American government considered the Community as an ally and partner, and a huge long-term consumer market for the American agricultural and industrial products. This has proved to be wrong because the American government underestimated the desire felt by the Community to create its own internal and international commercial policy where the latter would be dependent upon the former.[106]

Initially, the United States gained substantially from the creation of the Common Market. Continually from 1958 to 1971, the United States enjoyed a large surplus in its trade balance with the Community, and even in 1972 when the trade balance changed to be in favour of the Community, the United States trade deficit of roughly $500 million was far smaller than that with Canada ($2 billion) or Japan ($4 billion).[107]

Over time, and especially after the European Community succeeded in building up its own customs union and its common agricultural policy (CAP), the situation changed. Conflict arose between the two sides over their interests in many areas. Agriculture was the most affected sector. After the application of the different import levies by the Community under the common agricultural policy, United States agricultural exports to Europe became severely restricted. This did not please the American government, which viewed it as a major obstacle to their export policy. Consequently, the American administration reacted strongly against it and criticized the Community for imposing such restrictive rules. The disagreements over their interests reached its peak when the American government called into question the basic idea of support for European union.

Furthermore, in order to increase pressure on its European partners to grant some economic concessions, the United States tried to link trade and defence matters, hinting that the United States should receive better treatment to compensate for maintaining its troops in Europe.[108] In the view of Secretary of State Kissinger, trade relations with the European Community could not be separated from other aspects of policy towards Western Europe, such as defence, other politico-strategic considerations, and monetary co-operation.[109]

The other issue in which disagreement between both sides became acute was the preferential trade relations with the developing countries, including those in the Mediterranean basin. From the outset, the United States was opposed to any EEC preferential relations with developing countries. Up until the early 1970s, its position was to stress the importance of complying with the GATT rules in this matter. The United States, at the time, argued that the trade arrangements of the Community in Africa would never reach the free trade area stage, as promised. Hence any preferential agreement with the less developed countries based on reciprocity, such as free trade areas, should be dismissed.

When the Community launched its ambitious plan for an overall Mediterranean policy, the American attitude was negative. But in the face of the Community's determination to go ahead with its Mediterranean plan, the United States had to withdraw its objection to the Community preferences and finally reluctantly accept it. In 1972, when the European Community adopted officially the Mediterranean policy, the American government responded to the European Community's favouring some countries more than others as 'accepted by the United States insofar as the favoured countries were helped thereby'.[110]

However, despite this acceptance, tension between the two sides over the Community Mediterranean preferential trade arrangements began to build up. The fact is that after 1975, the Community started to reduce tariff rates for the produce of the several African and Arab Mediterranean countries. This did not find favour with Washington. The American government considered this policy a clear violation of the rules of the General Agreement on Tariffs and Trade (GATT) and fought, through GATT negotiations in 1977 and 1978, to change some of the Community's import policies. Because the Mediterranean countries are mainly agricultural countries, the new links between them and the Community were viewed by Washington as a major challenge to American agricultural interests. In 1978, a numbers of American citrus fruit producers were forced to divert their exports from the Community markets and look for new ones, such as in the Arab Gulf. Moreover, the Community's share of American fruit exports slumped from about 2 per cent in 1975 to 1.5 per cent in 1979. Parallel to that, its share of American vegetable exports fell from 2.73 per cent in 1976 to only 1.39 per cent in 1979.

These facts angered Washington and generated a strong complaint from the United States. The American government's complaint focused on the pricing policies of the Community which, on the one hand, extended some quota preferences to Mediterranean and African produce, to the exclusion of American farm exporters and, on the other, subsidized EEC farm exports to Third World countries.[111]

The United States complained that the Community subsidies were creating unjust competition for American food exports. The Community argued that the European food exports were sold at the world price, and that the cost per head of subsiding farmers was less in the Community than in the United States. Moreover, the Community stated that GATT rules did not forbid subsidies, the rules only prohibited misuse of them—such as taking an unjust share of the market. The Community also stressed that its agricultural trade deficit with the United States (which totalled 5,000 million ecu in 1980) did not justify American complaints against the Community.[112]

Furthermore, from 1970 to 1980 the Community's share of world agricultural trade had declined from 16.6 per cent to 14 per cent, while the American share had increased from 38.9 per cent to 44.8 per cent. So in the light of these facts, combined with the lack of tangible evidence that the American difficulties were generated by the Community subsidy policy, the Community saw no ground for the American complaint.

All in all, the Community showed on many occasions some sort of flexibility over its trade problems with the United States, and stressed its readiness to enter into a dialogue on issues of conflict. But having emphasised this, the Community confirmed that there would be no question of abdicating either the main principles of the CAP or the preferential agreements with the Mediterranean countries whose political importance had been stressed by the United States itself.[113]

Effects of the Community's enlargement on the Mediterranean countries

The repercussions of the Community's enlargement, which included Greece after 1981, and Spain and Portugal after 1986, had less effect on international economic relations than the first one in 1973. Although the admission of the three southern European countries into the Community was politically and economically desirable, enlargement nevertheless required profound changes and some essential adjustments by the Community. These involved both its internal policies and its behaviour towards some of its trading partners with whom the Community had contractual relations, such as the countries of the southern and eastern Mediterranean region. Our main concern here will be with the effects of enlargement on the countries of the southern Mediterranean area. This region, according to Community usage, covers the seven countries of the Arab Maghreb (Algeria, Tunisia and Morocco) and Mashreq (Egypt, Jordan, Syria and Lebanon), in addition to Israel.

These were not the only countries that were at risk of being affected by the enlargement; other Mediterranean countries such as Turkey, Cyprus and Malta were also involved. But their position was rather different. Turkey, for example, is a potential candidate for full Community membership, while Cyprus is looking for a customs union arrangement.[114]

There was consensus among the Mediterranean countries (European and non-European) that enlargement would have a positive impact. First, enlargement would enhance the political and economic weight of the Community in the world, and would strengthen its status as the world's foremost trading power.[115] This would in turn allow the Community to play a decisive role in stabilizing and then increasing the security of the whole region.

Secondly, the new members had traditionally strong ties with the Arab world. This revived the hopes of some of the Mediterranean partners (non-EEC members) that the Community might become more active in finding solutions to the problems of interstate divisions in the region.

Thirdly, some of the Community's Mediterranean partners had substantial economic relations with the new members, especially Spain. These economic ties had been enhanced over the years. This trend, according to the Community, would be encouraged 'by the incorporation of these links into the preferential agreements of the Community'.[116]

However, enlargement of the Community was viewed with anxiety by the southern and eastern Mediterranean countries. They all agreed that the enlargement would accentuate the problems and exacerbate the crisis already existing in their relations with the Community. Apprehension was mainly aroused by the threat the enlargement might pose not only to the traditional agricultural exports of these countries, but also to their manufactured goods produced for the EEC market, often with political and financial encouragement from the Community.[117] The southern Mediterranean countries feared that the enlargement might take place at the expense of their interests, leading finally to the erosion of their share in the Community market which they considered of great importance to their exports.[118] They also feared that the EEC's enlargement might change the trade balance created between the Community and its partners in the south of the Mediterranean. This was due to the prospective reduction in the EEC's imports of certain products and the growth of protectionism against countries with similar economies to those of the new entrant. Therefore, this would pose serious problems for the southern Mediterranean countries that were not major oil-producing countries and whose exports to the Community included a large share of agricultural and manufactured goods (such as Morocco, Tunisia and Egypt).[119]

MOROCCO, TUNISIA AND EGYPT

Among the Arab countries, Morocco, Tunisia and Egypt were the most concerned about the impact of the Community enlargement on their economies.

The agricultural sector

In the agricultural sector, Morocco and Tunisia would have been the worst affected, and the hardest hit products would have been olive oil, fruit, vegetables and wine. The effect of enlargement on Algeria and the Mashreq countries would have been less because the volume of their agricultural exports to the Community was very small. The new members' production, moreover, would be increased as a result of the privileged access to the Common Market.[120] Spanish membership in particular would increase the Community production of vegetables by 25 per cent, of fresh fruit by 48 per cent, and of olive oil by 59 per cent. Thus, the rate of self-sufficiency of the Community would reach 100 per cent or even more in Mediterranean products such as wine, fruit, vegetables and olive oil.[121]

Morocco and Tunisia were among the southern Mediterranean states with a broad range of agricultural exports. Their production had been developed and directed towards the EEC market, and they were likely to face difficulty in finding substitute outlets for their exports.[122] Agricultural exports from Morocco are mainly citrus fruit, tomatoes, potatoes, olive oil, fruit juices and wine. These products are very important to Moroccan farmers. In the case of Tunisia, olive oil forms its main agricultural export to the Community. It constitutes 43 per cent (in value) of the country's total agricultural exports and provides income for 20 per cent of the population.[123] According to EEC Commission estimates, the Community of twelve was going to have a surplus of olive oil of roughly 200,000 tonnes. That was equal to about four times of what Tunisia, its biggest single supplier, exported annually to the Nine in recent years. Morocco and Tunisia therefore, had little room for manoeuvre. It was difficult for them to find alternative markets for their traditional products, or even to convert them to new ones. Although the two countries had recently expanded their agricultural sales to neighbouring states, this was far from replacing any potential losses in the EEC market.[124]

The industrial sector

Although the share of agricultural products in the overall exports of southern Mediterranean states had in the main been failing in recent years, they had expanded their exports to the Community of manufactured industrial goods. This was particularly true in the textile and clothing sectors, where the southern Mediterranean states had successfully managed to develop their production capacities. This was often done with European help in the form of financial aid, joint ventures with EEC firms or processing deals with Community companies which sent them half-finished articles to be processed through using cheaper labour in the southern Mediterranean countries. Footwear was another area where southern Mediterranean countries had also increased their own productivities.[125]

Consequently, in the industrial sector Morocco, Tunisia and Egypt would have been the most affected countries, and the hardest hit products would have been textiles, clothing and footwear. Textile and clothing industries are crucial for these countries and the Community constitutes the main consumer for their exports in this field. During the years 1978–80, the Community represented 80 to 90 per cent of total textile exports for Morocco and Tunisia.[126] As for the footwear industry, the southern Mediterranean countries had only a very modest share of the Community market. But it was likely that major footwear producers like Spain and Portugal would have prevented these exports from flourishing in the future.[127]

The erosion of the real value of the bilateral agreements between the southern Mediterranean countries and the Community

The enlargement of the European Community could not alone be held responsible for bringing on the crisis in relations between the EEC and its southern Mediterranean partners. The crisis was already existing but latent. With or without the enlargement, the Mediterranean policy of the Community was no longer satisfying the aspirations of the Community's southern partners. The entry of Spain and Portugal had come only to exacerbate the situation and aggravate the Community partners's worries about their future cooperative relations with the enlarged Community. So, the fear of the enlargement was only a cover for an already growing disenchantment among the Community's partners. This discontent concerned the real value of their bilateral agreements with the EEC. The Mediterranean partners complained that over the years, the advantages they hoped to gain from these bilateral agreements with the EEC were gradually reduced. They also stressed that the agreements had not yet been able to create a true global Community policy in the region. This was especially clear in commercial matters, where the extent of the opening of Community market to exports from the Mediterranean countries remained, especially for some sensitive products, below the 'prospects held out by the co-operation agreements'.[128]

The Community's attitude towards tackling the effects of its enlargement on the southern Mediterranean countries

As mentioned earlier, the entry of the three southern European countries, especially Spain and Portugal, had accentuated the concern of the non-Community Mediterranean countries at the implications of the enlargement for their co-operation agreements with the Community. To ease the anxieties of the southern Mediterranean countries, the Commission, from the outset, responded positively. As early as 20 June 1979, the European Commission adopted a report on the possible effects of the enlargement of the Community on non-member countries. The Commission, at the time, stressed that it was not in a position to evaluate the outcome of the Community enlargement. Nonetheless, it promised to keep a close watch on the negotiations so that 'as soon as the enlargement negotiations are sufficiently far advanced, it will be in a position to put forward concrete proposals designed to maintain the key principle of the Community policy towards non-member countries'.[129]

Following up the undertaking of the 1979, the European Commission sent the Council in June 1982 a report on the implementation of a Mediterranean policy for the enlarged Community. In this report the Commission stated that the problems affecting the 1972 Mediterranean policy, stemming mainly from the deterioration in the international economic situation and internal difficulties within the Community, were likely to be aggravated by its enlargement. The Commission therefore suggested what the enlarged Community should do to avoid exacerbating the economic and hence social and political problems of the southern Mediterranean countries which, quite apart from their strategic interest, were very important trading partners for the Community. The measures suggested by the Commission covered the following:

(a) the development of traditional trade flows;
(b) a vigorous commercial co-operation campaign in the interests of avoiding crises, and technical, technological and financial co-operation to ensure better Community participation in the development of the countries concerned;
(c) the promotion of intra-Mediterranean co-operation.

The Commission proposed, moreover, that exploratory talks with southern Mediterranean countries should be conducted in order to determine the implications of the accession of the new members to the Community.[130] On 25 January 1983, the Council of Ministers took a decision authorizing the Commission to start exploratory talks with the southern Mediterranean countries 'with a view to examining the problems which enlargement might pose for them and looking ahead to their future relationship with the enlargement Community'.[131] The Council decision pointed out that the exploratory talks were to be conducted simultaneously with the enlargement negotiations, so that the Council would be able to 'have an overall picture of the problems encountered and the measures which might be considered for solving them with a view to determining any political guidelines and decisions on amending the co-operation or association agreements which might appear necessary'.[132]

In March 1984, the European Commission reported to the Council on the outcome of the exploratory talks with the southern Mediterranean countries. The Commission recommended 'maintaining and strengthening the preferential links between the (southern) Mediterranean countries and the Community of twelve as regards their traditional trade and the development of co-operation in all spheres of mutual interest'.[133]

THE EUROPEAN COUNCIL STATEMENT, MARCH 1985

When the accession negotiations with Spain and Portugal reached their final stage, the European Council of Ministers adopted a statement on 30 March 1985. In it the Council stressed the importance of the co-operation and association relations between the Community and the southern Mediterranean countries, and expressed the desire to strengthen these relations further with the enlargement of the Community. The Council confirmed the global concept of the Community's Mediterranean policy, which aimed to contribute to the economic development of the southern Mediterranean countries and to promote the harmonious and balanced progress of relations and trade with those countries.

Within this context, the Community would look for mutually satisfactory solutions to the worries repeatedly expressed by the southern Mediterranean countries concerning the possible effects of the Community enlargement on their traditional exports. The Community therefore determined to keep these traditional patterns and to launch initiatives aimed at providing effective support for these countries' efforts to reduce their agricultural and food deficit and to move progressively towards self-sufficiency in food and diversification of their production. The Community moreover, would speed up its efforts to pursuing financial and technical co-operation with the southern Mediterranean countries.

The aim was to make an appropriate contribution to the southern Mediterranean countries' economic and social development. In addition, the Council stated that the Mediterranean policy of the enlarged Community 'would have to be of an ongoing nature and both as regard trade in industrial and agricultural products and in terms of economic development, make for significant and stable results in the medium term'.[134]

Finally, the Council asked the Commission to submit (according to the above guidelines) negotiating directives for the adaptation of the co-operation and association agreements with the southern Mediterranean countries.[135]

Following the Council's statement, on 18 July 1985 the Commission suggested to the Council that the trade provisions of the co-operation or association agreements linking the Community with the southern Mediterranean countries be adapted to ensure that the traditional export trade of these countries be maintained after the enlargement. This suggestion was followed by elaborate proposals put to the Council by the Commission on 26 September 1985.[136]

THE COMMISSION GUIDELINES FOR ECONOMIC CO-OPERATION BETWEEN THE COMMUNITY AND THE SOUTHERN MEDITERRANEAN COUNTRIES, SEPTEMBER 1985

On 26 September 1985 the Commission sent the Council suggestions for the future of economic co-operation between the Community and the southern Mediterranean countries after the enlargement of the Community. In its guidelines, the Commission reaffirmed the importance of the southern Mediterranean countries to the Community, which together made up the Community's third largest export market and provided its largest trading surplus. The Commission argued that enhanced co-operation could increase the region's political stability, stressing that the current financial protocols which would expire in 1986, focused mainly on short-term operations of a conventional nature. The Commission therefore suggested that the Community should narrow the focus, concentrating its relations on just a few target areas with the aim of establishing a longer-term approach. Future co-operation between the Community and the southern Mediterranean countries, the Commission proposed, should follow three main guidelines:[137]

(1) The first need was to reduce the present excessive dependence of the southern Mediterranean countries. The Commission pointed out that in the period 1981–3, Egypt's cereal crop covered only 53 per cent of domestic demand. Algeria was even worse, producing a mere 31 per cent of its requirements. The Commission, therefore, suggested that the

Community should support the southern Mediterranean
countries' efforts to improve domestic food production. This
would be achieved through launching multi-annual supply
commitments which had proved effective with Operation
Flood in India. Training and trade promotion schemes
should be also introduced to help these countries diversify
their agricultural exports.

(2) The second policy objective was to use industrial, scientific
and technical co-operation action as a means of achieving
greater degree of complementarity between the economies
of the Community and the non-Community Mediterranean
countries. This required liberal and stable trade provisions,
including a gradual lifting of the restrictions on trade in
textile products. There would also be incentives for joint
investment projects. Special budget provision of 5 to 10
million ecu for five years was envisaged, to help Community
firms take part in joint ventures with the southern Mediterranean countries.

(3) The third element consisted of support for regional and
multilateral co-operation. The Commission wanted the
southern Mediterranean countries to achieve greater
economic integration and looked forward to the conclusion
of a comprehensive agreement linking the two Mediterranean regions once political conditions permit. For the time
being, the Commission would continue to give priority to
regional operations and to support private or semi-state
bodies with a multinational trade and economic co-operation centre.[138]

The Commission's proposals were discussed several times at the
Council meetings and on 26 November 1985, after intensive
work, the Council agreed to the negotiating directives under
which the Commission was to open negotiations with the non-
Community Mediterranean countries 'with a view to adapting
the co-operation and association agreements following the
accession of Spain and Portugal to the Community'.[139] The
directives offered, with regard to trade, favourable tariff
measures for all agricultural products covered by the agreements and traditionally exported to the Community. The directives also provided special measures for certain countries
covering a number of sensitive products such as citrus fruit,
tomatoes, olive oil and wine. The procedures by which the new

member states were to progressively apply the trade provisions of the agreements were also set out in the directives.[140]

The Council also approved the Commission's guidelines for implementing co-operation, especially with regard to the new financial protocols which would be negotiated with the Mediterranean countries to replace the protocols due to expire in November 1986. The guidelines (as mentioned earlier) were concerned with the reduction of food dependence, efforts to achieve greater economic complementarity and support for regional and multilateral co-operation. On the basis of these directives, the Commission opened negotiations with the non-Community Mediterranean countries in December 1985.[141]

START OF THE NEGOTIATIONS WITH THE NON-COMMUNITY MEDITERRANEAN STATES, DECEMBER 1985

In accordance with the negotiating directives approved by the Council on 26 November 1985, the Commission started in December 1985 a first round of negotiations with the non-Community Mediterranean countries. The aim was to conclude, with regard to economic matters, agreements of adaptation to the co-operation and association agreements following the enlargement of the Community. In March 1986, the Commission reported to the Council on the outcomes of the negotiations.

In the report the Commission proposed to the Council that a number of amendments must be made to the original negotiating directives in order to bring the negotiations to a satisfactory conclusion. The amendments, which covered the trade aspects, were approved by the Council on 21 October 1986 and offered 'a relaxation of the quantitative framework of certain concessions, adjustments to certain timetables, and the inclusion of a number of new products in the list of those covered by the agreements'.[142] Moreover, a review clause was also included to enable the Community and the southern Mediterranean countries to examine, after 1 January 1995, the outcomes of their co-operation so as to 'assess the situation and the future prospects for their relations in the light of the goals laid down in the agreement in question'.[143]

Following the amendments of 21 October 1986, the Commission managed in 1987 to conclude agreements of adaptation on economic matters with Egypt, Lebanon, Jordan, Algeria and

Tunisia. The adaptation agreements with Morocco and Syria were concluded in 1988. The aim of these agreements was to ensure that the southern Mediterranean countries could continue their traditional exports of agricultural produce to the Community. The agreements also contained technical provisions required for their implementation by Spain and Portugal.[144] As for the financial protocols, in 1987 the Commission succeeded in renewing the financial protocols with Algeria, Tunisia, Egypt, Lebanon and Jordan.[145] The financial protocol with Morocco was concluded in 1988, while the financial protocol with Syria has not been completed because of the British objection following the Hindawi affair in 1987.[146]

NOTES

1. *European Unification: The Origins and the Growth of the European Community*, Office for Official Publications of the European Communities, Luxembourg, 1986, pp. 11–16.
2. W. O. Henderson, *The Genesis of the Common Market*, Frank Cass & Co. Ltd., London, 1962, p. 160.
3. Samy Afify Hatem, *The Possibilities of Economic Co-operation and Integration Between the European Community and the Arab League* (published doctoral thesis), Munchen: Florentz, Germany, 1981, p. 13.
4. *Europe At a Glance: A Brief Guide to the European Community and Britain's Share in its Activities*, Publications of London Office, Commission of the European Communities, London, 1982, p. 1.
5. *The Institutions of the European Community*, Office for Official Publications of the European Communities, Luxembourg, 1982, p. 3.
6. *The Institutions of the European Community*, Office for Official Publications of the European Communities, Luxembourg, 1986, pp. 3–4.
7. *The European Community and the Arab World*, Commission of the European Communities, Directorate-General for Information, Brussels, 1982, p. 10.
8. *The Institutions of the European Community*, pp. 6–7.
9. See *The Court of Justice of the European Communities*, Office for Official Publications of the European Communities, Luxembourg, 1986.
10. *The European Community and the Arab World*, Commission of the European Communities, pp. 5–6.
11. *Ibid*, p. 6.
12. Robert W. MacDonald, *The League of Arab States: A study in the Dynamics of Regional Organization*, Princeton University Press, Princeton, 1965.
13. *The European Community and the Arab World*, Commission of the European Communities, pp. 6–7.
14. *Ibid*, p. 7.

15. Samy Afify Hatem, *The Possibilities of Economic Co-operation and Integration Between the European Community and the Arab League*, p. 88.
16. *Ibid*, pp. 88–9.
17. Colette Cova, *The Arab Policy of the EEC*, Bureau d'Information Européen, S.P.R., Brussels, 1983, p. 2.
18. *Ibid*, p. 2.
19. *Europe-South Dialogue*, Commission of the European Communities, Directorate-General for Information, Brussels, 1984, p. 5.
20. *Ibid*, pp. 5–6
21. Avi Shlaim, 'The Maghreb Countries and the EEC', *The Maghreb Review*, August–September, No. 2, 1976, p. 10.
22. Malcolm Subhan, *The EEC's Trade Relations with the Developing Countries*, Commission of the European Communities, Directorate-General for Information, Brussels, 1985, p. 30.
23. *Europe-South Dialogue*, Commission of the European Communities, p. 4.
24. Michael Dauderstadt, Holger Mirek, Sylvia Nett-Kleyboldt, Werner V.d.ohe Brita Steinbach, *The Outlook for Community Policy on Co-operation with the Developing Countries in the Light of Changing North-South Relations and the Future Development of the Community*, Commission of the European Communities, Directorate-General for Information, Brussels, 1982, p. 6.
25. *Co-operation Agreements Between the EEC and the Maghreb Countries*, Commission of the European Communities, Directorate-General for Information, Brussels, 1982, p. 1.
26. *Europe-Third World Rural Development*, Commission of the European Communities, Directorate-General for Information, Brussels, 1979, p. 10.
27. Samy Afify Hatem, *The Possibilities of Economic Co-operation and Integration Between the European Community and the Arab League*, pp. 90–1.
28. Hassan Abdel Hak Gadel Hak, *The Mediterranean Policy of the European Economic Community with Special Reference to Egypt* (published doctoral thesis), Institute of Arab Research and Studies, League of Arab States, Cairo, 1978, p. 251.
29. *Ibid*, p. 252.
30. Richard Pomfret, *Mediterranean Policy of the European Community: A Study of Discrimination in Trade*, Macmillan for the Trade Policy Research Centre, London, 1986, pp. 18–19.
31. Hassan Abdel Hak Gadel Hak, *The Mediterranean Policy of the European Economic Community with Special Reference to Egypt*, p. 253.
32. *Co-operation Agreements Between the EEC and the Maghreb Countries*, Commission of the European Communities, p. 1.
33. Hassan Abdel Hak Gadel Hak, *The Mediterranean Policy of the European Economic Community with Special Reference to Egypt*, pp. 254–5.
34. Philip Mishalani, Annette Robert, Christopher Stevens, Ann Weston, 'The Pyramid of Privilege', in Christopher Stevens (ed.), *EEC and the Third World: A Survey 1*, Hodder and Stoughton in Association with the Overseas Development Institute and the Institute of Development Studies, London, 1981, p. 62.

35. *EEC-Morocco Co-operation Agreement*, Commission of the European Communities, Spokesman's Group and Directorate-General for Information, Brussels, 1980, pp. 2–3.
36. Hassan Abdel Hak Gadel Hak, *The Mediterranean Policy of the European Economic Community with Special Reference to Egypt*, pp. 255–6.
37. Philip Mishalani, Annette Robert, Christopher Stevens, Ann Weston, 'The Pyramid of Privilege', in Christopher Stevens (ed.), *EEC and the Third World: A Survey 1*, p. 62.
38. Hassan Abdel Hak Gadel Hak, *The Mediterranean Policy of the European Economic Community with Special Reference to Egypt*, pp. 267–8.
39. Abderrahman Rogana, 'The Maghreb Economic Co-operation in Retrospect', *The Maghreb Review*, May–August, 1978, p. 14.
40. Peter Coffey, *The External Economic Relations of the EEC*, Macmillan Press, London and Basingstoke, 1976, p. 15.
41. *Co-operation Agreements Between the EEC and the Maghreb Countries*, Commission of the European Communities, p. 2.
42. Gordon L. Weil, *A Foreign Policy for Europe? The External Relations of the European Community*, College of Europe, Bruges, Belgium, 1970, p. 179.
43. Peter Coffey, *The External Economic Relations of the EEC*, p. 15.
44. Hassan Abdel Hak Gadel Hak, *The Mediterranean Policy of the European Economic Community with Special Reference to Egypt*, p. 270.
45. Jean Siotis, 'The European Economic Community and its Emerging Mediterranean Policy', in Frans A. M. Alting Von Geusau (ed.), *The External Relations of the European Community*, Saxon House, England, 1974, p. 76.
46. *Co-operation Agreements Between the EEC and the Maghreb Countries*, Commission of the European Communities, p. 2.
47. Stanley Henig, *External Relations of the European Community: Associations and Trade Agreements*, Chatham House, London, 1971, p. 45.
48. *Memorandum on a Community Policy on Development Co-operation*, Commission of the European Communities, Brussels, 1972, p. 148.
49. Gordon L. Weil, *A Foreign Policy for Europe? The External Relations of the European Community*, p. 191.
50. *Eighth General Report on the Activities of the Community (1 April 1964–31 March 1965)*, Publishing Services of the European Communities, Brussels, 1965, pp. 299–300.
51. Hassan Abdel Hak Gadel Hak, *The Mediterranean Policy of the European Economic Community with Special Reference to Egypt*, p. 287.
52. *Twentieth Review of the Council's Work (1 January–31 December 1972)*, Office for Official Publications of the European Communities, Luxembourg, 1972, p. 161.
53. Hassan Abdel Hak Gadel Hak, *The Mediterranean Policy of the European Economic Community with Special Reference to Egypt*, p. 288.
54. *Twentieth Review of the Council's Work*, p. 170.
55. Hassan Abdel Hak Gadel Hak, *The Mediterranean Policy of the European Economic Community with Special Reference to Egypt*, pp. 289–90.

56. Philip Mishalani, Annette Robert, Christopher Stevens, Ann Weston, 'The Pyramid of Privilege', in Christopher Stevens (ed.), *EEC and the Third World: A Survey 1*, pp. 67–8.
57. Avi Shlaim and G. N. Yannopoulos, *The EEC and the Mediterranean Countries*, Cambridge University Press, p. 1.
58. Corrado Pirzio-Biroli, 'Foreign Policy Formation within the European Community with Special Regard to the Developing Countries', in Leon Hurewitz (ed.), *Contemporary Perspectives on European Integration*, Aldwych Press, London, 1980, p. 237.
59. *The European Community External Trade (1958–1974)*, Office for Official Publications of the European Communities, Luxembourg, 1976, p. 18.
60. Corrado Pirzio-Biroli, 'Foreign Policy Formation within the European Community with special regard to the Developing Countries', in Leon Hurewitz (ed.), *Contemporary Perspectives on European Integration*, pp. 238–89.
61. Hassan Abdel Hak Gadel Hak, *The Mediterranean Policy of the European Economic Community with Special Reference to Egypt*, pp. 153–4.
62. Dorothy Pickles, *The Government and Politics of France*, Methuen & Co. Ltd., London, 1973, p. 326.
63. Hassan Abdel Hak Gadel Hak, *The Mediterranean Policy of the European Economic Community with Special Reference to Egypt*, p. 154.
64. Corrado Pirzio-Biroli, 'Foreign Policy Formation within the European Community with Special Regard to the Developing Countries', in Leon Hurewitz (ed.), *Contemporary Perspectives on European Integration*, p. 239.
65. Cited in Elfriede Regelsberger and Wolfgang Wessels, 'European Concepts for the Mediterranean Region', in Giacomo Luciani (ed.), *The Mediterranean Region*, Croom Helm, London, 1984, pp. 239–41.
66. *Ibid*, pp. 241–2.
67. *Ibid*, pp. 239–40.
68. *Ibid*, p. 240.
69. *Europe-South Dialogue*, Commission of the European Communities, p. 10.
70. *Ibid*, p. 10.
71. Corrado Pirzio-Birloi, 'Foreign Policy Formation within the European Community with Special Regard to the Developing Countries', in Leon Hurewitz (ed.), *Contemporary Perspectives on European Integration*, p. 238.
72. *The Mediterranean Policy: Thirty Years of Community Law*, Office for Official Publications of the European Communities, Luxembourg, 1983, p. 391.
73. *The European Community and the Developing Countries*, Office for Official Publications of the European Communities, Luxembourg, 1975, p. 8.
74. Wolfgang Hager, 'The Community and the Mediterranean', in Max Kohnstamm and Wolfgang Hager (eds.), *A Nation Writ Large? Foreign Policy Problems before the European Community*, Macmillan, London, 1973, p. 179.
75. Jesse W. Lewis, Jr., *The Strategic Balance in the Mediterranean*, American Enterprise Institute for Public Policy Research , Washington DC, 1976, p. 58.

76. Wolfganfg Hager, 'The Community and the Mediterranean', in Max Kohnstamm and Wolfgang Hager (eds.), *A Nation Writ Large? Foreign Policy Problems Before the European Community*, pp. 197–8.
77. Jean Siotis, 'The European Economic Community and its Emerging Mediterranean Policy', in Frans A. M. Alting Von Geusau (ed.), *The External Relations of the European Community*, p. 71.
78. Wolfgang Hager, 'The Community and the Mediterranean', in Max Kohnstamm and Wolfgang Hager (eds.), *A Nation Writ Large? Foreign Policy Problems Before the European Community*, pp.200–1.
79. Stanley Henig, 'Mediterranean Policy in the Context of the External relations of the European Community: 1958–1973', in Avi Shlaim and G. N. Yannopoulos (eds.), *The EEC and the Mediterranean Countries*, p.310.
80. Robert Taylor, 'Implications of EEC Enlargement for Arab Exports', in *Euro-Arab Co-operation*, Colloquium held in Brussels 20–22 April 1983, Arab-British Chamber of Commerce Publication, London, 1893, p. 90.
81. Colette Cova, *The Arab Policy of the EEC*, p. 6.
82. *Ibid*, pp. 6–7.
83. *The EEC's Trade Relations with the Developing Countries*, Commission of the European Communities, Directorate-General for Information, Brussels, 1985, pp. 4 and 32.
84. *Ibid*, p. 34.
85. *The European Community's External Trade (1958–1974)*, p. 19.
86. *Europe—South Dialogue*, Commission of the European Communities, p. 12.
87. Colette Cova, *The Arab Policy of the EEC*, p. 7.
88. Richard Pomfret, *Mediterranean Policy of the European Community: A Study of Discrimination in Trade*, p. 21.
89. Corrado Pirzio-Biroli, 'Foreign Policy Formation within the European Community with Special Regard to the Developing Countries', in Leon Hurewitz (ed.), *Contemporary Perspectives on European Integration*, p. 238.
90. *Co-operation Agreements between the EEC and the Maghreb Countries*, Commission of the European Communities, p. 2.
91. Colette Cova, *The Arab Policy of the EEC*, p. 10.
92. Richard Vaughan *Twentieth-Century Europe: Paths to Unity*, Croom Helm, London, 1979, p. 242.
93. *Fact Sheets on the European Parliament and the Activities of the European Community*, European Parliament, Directorate-General for Research, Office for Official Publications of the European Communities, Luxembourg, 1987.
94. Richard Vaughan, *Twentieth-Century Europe: Paths to Unity*, pp. 242–3.
95. *The European Parliament and the World at Large*, Office for Official Publications of the European Communities, Luxembourg, 1981, p. 14.
96. H. Maull, *Europe and the World Energy*, Butterworths, London, 1980, p. 295.
97. *Europe—South Dialogue*, Commission of the European Communities, p. 7.
98. *The European Community and the Arab World*, Commission of the European Communities, pp. 23–4.

99. Saleh A. Al-Mani and Salah Al-Shaikly, *The Euro-Arab Dialogue*, Frances Pinter, London, 1983, p. 83.
100. *Euro-South Dialogue*, Commission of the European Communities, p. 8.
101. *Telex Mediterranean*, 9 November 1987.
102. *The European Community and the Arab World*, Commission of the European Communities, p. 25.
103. *Ibid*, p. 25.
104. See Commission of the European Communities, Spokesman's Group and Directorate-General for Information: *EEC-Syria Co-operation Agreement 1978, EEC-Egypt Co-operation Agreement 1978, EEC-Jordan Co-operation Agreement 1978*. See also, Commission of the European Communities, Directorate-General for Information: *EEC-Lebanon Co-operation Agreement 1980*. Also, *The Co-operation Agreements between the EEC and the Maghreb Countries 1982*.
105. Saleh A. Al-Mani and Salah Al-Shaikly, *The Euro-Arab Dialogue*, p. 128.
106. Peter Coffey, *The External Economic Relations of the EEC*, p. 19.
107. Robert J. Lieber, 'Expanded Europe and the Atlantic Relationship', in Frans A.M. Alting Von Geusau (ed.), *The External Relations of the European Community*, p. 56.
108. *Ibid*, pp. 54–56.
109. Alfred Tovias, *Tariff Preferences in Mediterranean Diplomacy*, Trade Policy Research Centre, London, 1977, p. 76.
110. *Ibid*, pp. 76–8.
111. Saleh A. Al-Mani and Salah Al-Shaikly, *The Euro-Arab Dialogue*, pp. 128–9.
112. *The Europe-United States-Japan: Trade Controversy*, Office for Official Publications of the European Communities, Luxembourg, 1983, p. 4.
113. *Ibid*, p. 4.
114. Robert Taylor, *Implications for the Southern Mediterranean Countries of the Second Enlargement of the European Community*, Commission of the European Communities, Directorate-General for Information, Brussels, 1980, pp. 2–3.
115. *The Enlargement of the European Community*, Commission of the European Communities, Directorate-General for Information, Brussels, 1983, p. 3.
116. *Report to the Council on the Exploratory Talks with the Mediterranean Countries and the Applicant Countries, Commission Proposal Concerning the Implementation of a Mediterranean Policy for the Enlarged Community*, Commission of the European Communities, Com (84) 107 Final, Brussels, 1984, p. 5.
117. Robert Taylor, *Implications for the Southern Mediterranean Countries of the Second Enlargement of the European Community*, Commission of the European Communities, p. 3.
118. *The Second Enlargement of the European Community*, Office for Official Publications of the European Communities, Luxembourg, 1979, pp. 22–3.
119. Robert Taylor, 'Implications of the EEC Enlargement for the Arab Exports', in *Euro-Arab Co-operation*, p. 90.
120. Colette Cova, *The Arab Policy of the EEC*, p. 138.

121. *Problems of Enlargement: Taking Stock and Proposals,* Commission of the European Communities, Directorate-General for Information, Brussels, 1983, p. 1. (See especially Annex Analysis by Sector.)

122. Robert Taylor, *Implications for the Southern Mediterranean Countries of the Second Enlargement of the European Community,* p. 10.

123. *Telex Mediterranean,* 30 July 1985.

124. Robert Taylor, *The Implications for the Southern Mediterranean Countries of the Second Enlargement of the European Community,* pp. 10–11.

125. *Ibid,* p. 12.

126. Didier Buysse, *The Effects of Enlargement on Other Mediterranean Countries,* Europe News Agency, Brussels, 1984, p. 25.

127. Robert Taylor, *Implications for the Southern Mediterranean Countries of the Second Enlargement of the European Community,* p. 13.

128. Didier Buysse, *The Effects of Enlargement on the Other Mediterranean Countries,* pp. 4–5.

129. *Bulletin of the European Communities,* 7/8, 1979.

130. *Sixteenth General Report on the Activities of the European Communities in the 1982,* Office for Official Publications of the European Communities, Luxembourg, 1983, pp. 250–3.

131. *Seventeenth General Report on the Activities of the European Communities in 1983,* Office for Official Publications of the European Communities, Luxembourg, 1984, p. 270.

132. *Thirty First Review of the Council's Work (1 January–31 December 1983),* Office for Official Publications of the European Communities, Luxembourg, 1984, p. 141.

133. *Eighteenth General Report on the Activities of the European Communities in 1984,* Office for Official Publications of the European Communities, Luxembourg, 1985, p. 263.

134. *Thirty Third Review of the Council's Work (1 January–31 December 1985),* Office for Official Publications of the European Communities, Luxembourg, 1986, pp. 140–1.

135. *Ibid,* p.141.

136. *Bulletin of the European Communities,* 7/8, 1985, p. 87.

136. *Bulletin of the European Communities,* 9, 1985, p. 18.

138. *Ibid,* p. 18.

139. *Nineteenth General Report on the Activities of the European Communities in 1985,* Office for Official Publications of the European Communities, Luxembourg, 1986, p. 300.

140. *Bulletin of the European Communities,* 11, 1985, p. 87.

141. *Ibid,* p. 87.

142. *Thirty Fourth Review of the Council's Work (1 January–31 December 1986),* Office for Official Publications of the European Communities, Luxembourg, 1987, p. 124.

143. *Ibid,* p. 124.

144. *Twenty First General Report on the Activities of the European Communities in 1986*, Office for Official Publications of the European Communities, Luxembourg, 1987, p. 302.
145. *Twenty Second General Report on the Activities of the European Communities in 1987*, Office for Official Publications of the European Communities, Luxembourg, 1988, p. 366.
146. *Bulletin of the European Communities*, 2, 1988, pp. 67–8.

II

THE ORIGINS OF THE EURO-ARAB

DIALOGUE

The starting point of the Euro-Arab dialogue can be found in the events of autumn 1973 and spring of 1974. After the outbreak of the October War of 1973, the Arab oil-producing countries, in an attempt to boost the Egyptian–Syrian front in the war with Israel, announced their decision to impose an embargo on oil supplies to the United States and the Netherlands. These events were followed by a major and unprecedented increase in the price of crude oil.

The developments on the Middle East stage hit the European Community hard, and for the first time the Community felt that its interests and indeed its whole economic survival was at stake. The result was a joint statement on the situation in the Middle East, issued on 6 November 1973. The statement was considered to be the most important development so far in the Community's attitude towards the Arab–Israel conflict. It was viewed by the Arab side as a satisfactory response and a positive attitude towards understanding Arab demands in the struggle with Israel. The statement signalled a new era in Arab–European relations and was later to pave the way for the birth of the Euro-Arab dialogue.

Despite this, it is essential to stress that the declaration was not exactly a volte-face or a sudden break with the past. It was, rather, the culmination of a series of changes which had been occurring within the EEC on a national level as well as on a Community level. These changes were accelerated by the war. So, before dealing with the October War and the Community response to it, we need to trace the development of the Community's position prior to the war, and its attempts to formulate a common understanding among the Community member states with regard to the Middle East situation.[1]

THE ATTITUDE OF THE EUROPEAN COMMUNITY BEFORE
THE OCTOBER WAR OF 1973

At the end of World War II, some European countries (especially
France and Britain) had to face independence movements in
their colonies in the Middle East. This marked the diminishing
of European power in the area, and restricted greatly its ability to
exert any pressure over events in the region. The Suez adven-
ture in 1956 was the last significant attempt to do so, and it ended
with considerable damage for European influence and prestige.
As a result of the Suez crisis, European ties with the Arab world
suffered damage and were further weakened. This situation
continued until the mid-1960s.[2]

When the Six-Day War erupted in June 1967, the European
approach to it was an asymmetrical one. The six countries of the
European Community, because of their lack of a common strategy in the field of foreign policy, reacted differently; they
adopted different positions according to their national interests.
France condemned the aggressor and leaned towards favouring
the Arab position at the United Nations. West Germany strongly
supported Israel and emphasized the special relationship linking the German and Jewish states. The Italians were divided into
two sections. Fanfani, the foreign minister, adopted a rather
pro-Arab position, while on the other side most of the Christian
Democrats, the Socialists and President Saragat sided with Israel
and assured it of their friendship. Belgium tried to take recourse
in the United Nations institutions. The Dutch response to the
conflict was the most striking, and completely in contrast with
that of France. The Dutch government fully and strongly supported Israel in its conflict with the Arabs.

However, despite the Community's divergent attitudes
towards the conflict, and the lack of a joint position at Community level, from that time most of the European countries
began the gradual process of reassessing and then adjusting
their Middle East policies in the direction of more and greater
balance between the two conflicting parties. On the international stage, the June War managed to bring into greater
international prominence the existence of the Palestinian problem. The PLO (which had been established in 1964) was
to become, especially after 1968, an important factor. From
1969 onwards, the European Community started the process of

preparing for a joint policy on the Arab–Israel conflict in which the Palestinian dimension was to have an important place.[3]

EUROPEAN POLITICAL CO-OPERATION

The converging positions of the European countries on the Middle East problem coincided with the initiation and the establishment of 'European political co-operation'. The latter was decided upon by the European heads of state and government at the Hague Conference in December 1969 and set up in the framework of the Davignon Committee, the process of European political co-operation. This instrument of policy making 'is a purely inter- governmental body. It is, therefore, distinct from the Community activity that proceeds from the Juridical engagement subscribed by the member states in the framework of the Treaty of Rome'.[4]

Following the Hague summit conference, the Davignon Committee (later to be called the Political Committee) laid the foundation of the Davignon Report, which concerned Community political co-operation. The Committee introduced its report to the foreign ministers in July 1970. It suggested meetings of the foreign ministers to be held every six months, as well as provisions for summit conferences; and a committee of political directors of foreign ministers to assume the responsibility of preparing for the foreign ministers' sessions.

The Directorate was to meet at least four times a year and was to form a number of working groups. The chairmanship and venue were to rotate in accordance with the presidency of the Council of Ministers, which changes every six months. When matters within the competency of the Community were to be debated, the European Commission was to be invited to be represented.

The Davignon Report was approved and accepted by the foreign ministers in October 1970, as a first step towards enabling Europe to speak with one voice.[5] Setting up the process of political co-operation was of great help in overcoming the different perceptions among different European countries. This was accomplished through the sharing of information and expertise; and through the willingness of European countries to compromise on a given position held with sufficient strength by one or more member states. The 'mechanism proved also to be very important for the information of the smaller European countries that have no part in the important bilateral meetings'.[6]

The first topic that European political co-operation dealt with was the Middle East question. It was one of the two initial political priorities; the other was the conference on security and co-operation in Europe. The choice clearly indicated the importance the Community attached to this strategic region.[7]

The movement in the Community's attitude towards the Middle East problem raised Israel's fears. According to the Israeli government, this was a serious development: it indicated that the policies of the Community members which, as noted above, had been very different at the time of the Six-Day War, now tended to become reconciled. From the Israeli point of view the 'reflexive element of the EPC (European political co-operation) was perceived as having a negative potential on the supportive policies of its friends among the Six. Reflexivity was considered as being one-directional: coordination away from Israel'.[8]

The first European political co-operation meeting took place in Munich on 19 November 1970. The aim of the meeting was mainly to prepare a common position on the Middle East conflict. The meeting was chaired by Walter Scheel, the German foreign minister. During the meeting, exchange of views on the Middle East problem took place. The discussions proved to be difficult, and positions on the Middle East question seemed irreconcilable. The meeting ended with no agreement on the idea of a joint policy to be pursued on the Middle East situation.[9]

THE SCHUMANN PAPER OF MAY 1971

Despite the drastic outcome of the first political meeting, the Community efforts to formulate a joint position on the Middle East question did not come to a standstill. In early 1971, the French government stepped up diplomatic manoeuvres in an attempt to persuade its European partners of the advisability of having a common position on the Arab–Israeli conflict. The French efforts bore fruit. In February 1971, the political committee discussed the possibility of publishing a joint paper on the Middle East question. The discussions showed that there was considerable disagreement among the Community member states over several issues. These issues were: the question of the

Arab refugees; the demilitarized zones to be established between the conflicting parties; the composition of the troops to be stationed in the area; and the question of the city of Jerusalem.

Despite the sharp disagreement which appeared during the political committee debate, a reconciliation among the Six was achieved between February and May 1971. As a result, a joint move would be made by them, and indeed in early May it was clear that the announcement of a joint Community paper was on the way. Israel laboured to hinder the Community's progress in this matter, but its efforts were in vain.[10]

At a meeting in Paris on 13 May 1971, the foreign ministers of the European Community approved a report of their Political Committee, establishing a common position on the Arab–Israeli conflict within the framework of the newly established system of European political co-operation. The report was known as the Schumann Paper, after the French foreign minister, Maurice Schumann, who played a major role in producing it.[11] After the meeting, M Schumann made the following statement: 'Political co-operation has made a good start. Far from splitting, we have, on the contrary, considerably narrowed the gap between our points of view.'[12]

The Schumann Paper was regarded by the French government as a diplomatic triumph for its efforts to have a common position on the Middle East conflict. On 1 June 1971, M Schumann commented on what he felt was the political significance of the paper. Support was claimed by him for the French interpretation of Security Council resolution 242. 'I will keep to the main point' of the resolution, approval for which the ministers of foreign affairs had reaffirmed on 22 November 1967, and he underlined the necessity of applying it in all its parts. He also stated that the interest of the Community members was not to present the Community as a new mediator in the dispute, but to uphold the international community whose will was expressed in the United Nations by the intervention of the General Assembly and 'of the Security Council whose four permanent members have always recognized the existence of an interest superior to national interests or finally by the secretary-general, U Thant, to whom I renew the assurance of our sympathy'.[13]

The paper was never published, but its contents were later leaked to the press. It contained the following suggestions: the establishment of demilitarized zones between Israel and the Arab states; the stationing of United Nations troops to separate the conflicting parties; an Israeli withdrawal from all occupied territories with minor border modifications; the internationalization of the city of Jerusalem; solution of the refugee problem by either repatriation in stages or compensation under the supervision of an international commission;[14] and the regulation of shipping in the Gulf of Aqaba and the Suez Canal.[15]

Two characteristics of the Schumann Paper need to be stressed. First, the paper was in accordance with the United Nations Resolution 242; and secondly, it addressed the problem of the 'Arab refugees' and not the Palestinians—a point that was later to become the crux of EEC declarations on the Middle East question. Although the paper did not add anything new to United Nations Resolution 242, it did constitute an important step in laying down the Community attitude towards the Arab–Israeli conflict. It represented the first Community joint stand on the Middle East dispute. It was perhaps of more importance internally than externally. The paper managed impressively to harmonize the development of the positions of each Community member state at the beginning of 1970, and brought them together for the first time.[16]

The paper was received with approval in the Arab capitals, whereas it provoked a hostile reaction from Israel which denied the Community's right to interfere and involve itself in the Middle East dispute.[17]

The highly coordinated policy adopted during the Paris meeting proved to be futile. As mentioned earlier, the Schumann Paper was never officially published. This was because of the reservations of at least three member states: West Germany, Italy and the Netherlands. Moreover, the West German foreign minister, Walter Scheel, soon afterwards played down the significance of the convergence of positions among the Community member states shown in the Paris meeting.[18] During a visit to Israel in July 1971, Herr Scheel stressed that the so-called document of the Six was only a working paper which was far from being approved. On the subject of what interpretation to attach to the Security Council Resolution 242, Herr Scheel asserted that 'There are differences between the French and West German positions with respect to the Near East . . . the attitude of Bonn supports the interpretation given by Washington and London to the Security Council resolution of November 1967.'[19]

The basic difference between the French and English translations of the Security Council Resolution was that the English

version spoke of withdrawal 'from occupied territories',
whereas the French version referred to withdrawal 'from *the*
occupied territories' (italic added). 'There is no necessity that
Israel commit itself to a total retreat of its troops as a precondi-
tion to the opening of peace negotiations,' said Herr Scheel.[20]
The Schumann Paper, he went on, was a 'basis for further
discussions'. These remarks, at the time, roused considerable
anger from the French government whose efforts to have a
Community coordinated position on the Middle East dispute
were strong and clear.

The policy of muddling through continued to characterize the
Community's behaviour in relation to the Middle East situation.
No other joint paper at the Community level followed the Schumann Paper, but the attitude of each member of the EEC continued to develop towards positive reassessment of Arab
demands. These developments indicated that the Community
was, by the end of 1973, on the threshold of launching a major
political move. That was what happened in the aftermath of the
October War of 1973.[21]

THE EUROPEAN COMMISSION MEMORANDUM OF
OCTOBER 1972 AND THE ATTEMPT TO OPEN A DIALOGUE
WITH THE ARAB WORLD

The first initiative to open a dialogue with the Arab oil-producing countries came from the European Commission. In October
1972, it presented the Council of Ministers with a memorandum,
suggesting (among other things) opening such a dialogue. The
Commission's proposal stated that 'economic and social co-
operation between the two groups ... in all areas of common
interests ... could facilitate the industrial and economic development of the oil-exporting regions and the establishment of
a desirable stability in the relations between equal partners'.[22]
The Commission recommended the following: setting up a
mechanism for dialogue with the oil-producing states; dispatch-
ing (at the same time) groups of industrialists from the Community to the oil-producing countries, and vice versa, to
examine possible economic co-operation between the two sides;
and negotiating co-operation agreements which could observe
the following principles:

(1) An undertaking by the Community to favour the economic

and social development of the exporting countries by making available technical and perhaps financial assistance, as well as to open its markets for the industrial and agricultural products of these countries.

(2) An undertaking by the exporting countries and the Community to observe certain rules and guarantees for commercial transactions and industrial investments.[23]

The Commission's attempt to have a dialogue with Middle East oil countries did not go ahead, however, because it failed to raise any positive response from the Community member states. It even met with fierce resistance from some members, notably the Netherlands and West Germany. The Council of Ministers, moreover, did not take it seriously. The proposal was rejected on the basis that the Community did not have any firm and unified foreign policy.[24]

It is worth mentioning here that an attempt to open a dialogue between the Community and the Arab world also came from the Arab side just before the 1973 war started—from Libya. On 2 September 1973, two days after Libya nationalized 51 per cent of the oil companies in its territory, Libyan premier Abdul Salam Jalud declared: 'Libya is ready to cooperate with Europe for mutual advantage in forging a new and mutual partnership based on Arab oil and European technology and experience.'[25] He expressed his hope that the European Community would increase its investment in the Arab countries. Despite this open invitation, a proper response at Community level was at the time out of the question.[26]

THE OCTOBER WAR AND THE ARAB OIL EMBARGO

The October War

On 6 October 1973, war broke out in the Middle East between Egypt and Syria on the one hand and Israel on the other. The war quickly spread and took the shape of a major confrontation between the two superpowers. The United States, from the beginning of the war, sided with Israel, stepped up its aid, and initiated an airlift of weapons to equip her. The Soviet Union gave support to the Arab side. The first call for a cease-fire between the two belligerents came from the United States in the first days of the war. The United States urged both sides to return to the 1967 cease-fire lines (which meant the pre-6 October positions). The Arabs, who at the time were in a good position militarily, especially after their initial success in crossing the Suez Canal, showed little early interest in the call.

By the end of the second week of the war, the situation began to change drastically. After a meeting between Kosygin and Sadat in Cairo on 17 and 18 October, the Soviets called for a cease-fire. The United States publicly agreed but privately did not press hard on Israel to accept. The military situation had shifted in favour of Israel as a result of Israel's success on the west bank of the Canal. On 22 October, the two superpowers officially agreed on the terms of a cease-fire to be implemented between the parties concerned. By the time the cease-fire was put into practice, Israel had succeeded in launching a major offensive on the Egyptian front.

The offensive enabled Israel to cross the canal, move southwards (after the cease-fire) and then cut off the forces of the Third Army Corps on the eastern side of the Canal. These developments put the Egyptians in serious trouble.[27] Consequently, the Egyptian leader Sadat asked the superpowers to intervene and save the situation. He urged them to send their troops to monitor the implementation of the cease-fire and ensure that Israel would respect it. He stressed that the two powers had to take swift action, both because they were a permanent members of the Security Council and because they had originally engineered the truce resolution of 22 October.

The United States immediately rejected the Egyptian call for Soviet–American troops to police the truce, and warned the Soviet Union against sending troops to the area. 'We hope that other outside powers will not send troops to the Middle East,' said the White House spokesman Gerald Warran.[28] The United States officials also stressed that the United Nations Truce Supervision Organization should assume the responsibility of monitoring the cease-fire, and not the superpowers.[29]

The Soviet government, on the contrary, responded favourably to the Egyptian proposal and characterized it as 'fully justified'. It also called for sanctions against Israel in order to bring it to respect the truce. In the light of continuous Israeli violation of the cease-fire and the threat which was posed on the Egyptian front by its advance, the Soviet government on 24 October sent a direct message to President Nixon. The message stated that if the cease-fire of 22 October was not respected by Israel, and if the United States declined to cooperate in a joint force, the Soviet government would be faced with the necessity of considering urgent and appropriate action unilaterally. This letter was viewed by Washington as threatening direct Soviet involvement in the Middle East. The result was the decision by the United States to put its military forces on alert, thus creating the possibility of a direct Soviet-American confrontation. On 25 October, the two powers agreed officially on a Security Council resolution involving the creation of peace-keeping forces which excluded the participation of the big powers.[30]

THE ARAB OIL EMBARGO AND THE INCREASE IN THE PRICE OF CRUDE OIL

In the wake of the October War, two separate yet interconnected developments took place: first, the decisions adopted by the Arab oil-producing countries to impose a general production cut-back and a selective embargo on exports to specific countries; secondly, the decisions taken unilaterally by members of OPEC to increase the price of crude oil. The Arab boycott, whether cut-back or embargo, implied the idea of utilizing the oil as a political weapon in the struggle with Israel.[31]

Kuwait was the first country to call for a meeting of the Organization of Arab Petroleum Exporting Countries (OAPEC). The purpose was to draw up a common Arab policy on how Arab oil could best be used in the battle. Immediately before this meeting took place, the six Gulf states, at a meeting in Kuwait on 16 October, decided unilaterally to raise the posted price of crude oil by 70 per cent. The increase in the posted price was roughly 2 dollars per barrel (from about 3 dollars to 5 dollars), with an effective increase in payment by the oil companies to the host country of about 1.25 dollars per barrel (from roughly 1.75 to 3 dollars).[32]

The October Kuwait meeting

The Kuwait meeting took place on 17 October. The oil ministers who attended represented the following countries: Kuwait, Iraq, Libya, Algeria, Saudi Arabia, Egypt, Syria, Abu Dhabi,

Bahrain and Qatar. During the meeting the ministers adopted decisions to cut monthly their oil production by a minimum of 5 per cent from the September level, with effect from October, 'until such time as total evacuation of Israeli forces from all Arab territory occupied during the June 1967 war is completed and the legitimate rights of the Palestinian people are restored'.[33] Or, the resolution went on, until the production of each member state reached the situation in which its economy could not allow further reduction without serious damage to its national or Arab obligations.

During the meeting it was decided that the reduction would not affect any friendly country which had helped the Arab countries materially and effectively, and would continue to receive its full share of Arab oil supplies at the rate prevailing before the cuts were introduced. Similar exceptional treatment was offered for any country which could take special measures against Israel to compel it to end its territorial occupation of the Arab lands. In addition, there was a recommendation that accompanied the decisions. In it the Arab oil ministers specified the United States as an unfriendly country. Accordingly it was to be subjected to 'the most severe cut in proportion to the amounts of crude oil and products it imports from every exporting country'. The recommendation added that 'this progressive reduction would lead to a total halt in Arab supplies to the United States'.[34]

It is worth stressing that the measures concerning the United States were dealt with as a recommendation and not as a binding decision, because of pressure exerted by Saudi Arabia. Saudi Arabia wanted to try to give the United States government time to reconsider the hostile position it had adopted during the war. This explains why the Kingdom did not declare immediately an embargo on shipments to the United States. However, all Saudi efforts went in vain. On 19 October President Nixon declared that he had demanded from Congress the allocation of a sum of 2.2 billion dollars in the existing financial year for military aid to Israel. This announcement provoked Saudi anger, and on 20 October the Saudi government declared that 'in view of the increase of American military aid to Israel, the Kingdom of Saudi Arabia has decided to halt all oil exports to the United States of America for taking such a position'.[35]

Consumer countries were therefore divided into three categories:

(a) hostile countries, on which a ban on exports was imposed;
(b) friendly or most favoured nations which were to gain as against the September level of exports;
(c) neutral countries, among which the remaining production was to be apportioned.

Within the European Community, France and Britain were declared to be friendly, while the Netherlands (because of its pro-Israel position) was singled out with the United States as a hostile country.

So within few days the signatory countries reduced their production by either 5 or 10 per cent and imposed a total embargo on oil shipments to the United States and the Netherlands.[36] The embargo against the United States involved directly some 6 per cent of United States consumption, much coming from Saudi Arabia. The embargo against the Netherlands had serious implications not only for that country but also for others. This was because much of the crude oil refined in the port of Rotterdam was then re-exported. Countries that relied heavily on the Rotterdam refineries therefore suffered as well.[37]

The second Kuwait meeting 4–5 November 1973

This meeting was preceded by another, also in Kuwait, between President Sadat of Egypt, President Asad of Syria and Sheikh Sabah Al-Salem Al-Sabah, Emir of Kuwait. On his way back to Egypt, President Sadat visited Riyadh. There he conferred with King Faisal of Saudi Arabia and gained his support for the decisions that were taken by the three heads of state during their meeting in Kuwait. These decisions were to be the basis of the official ones taken at the second ministerial meeting held in Kuwait on 4 and 5 November 1973.[38]

During this meeting, the ministers decided to speed up the reduction in Arab oil production, imposing an immediate cut of 25 per cent below the September level. They decided that a further reduction of 5 per cent from the November level would be applied in December, but stipulated that this reduction should not harm the share which any friendly state was receiving from any Arab exporting country during the first nine months of 1973. Finally, the conference instructed the oil minister of Algeria, Belaid Abdesselam, and the oil minister of Saudi Arabia, Sheikh Ahmed Zaki Yamani, to visit Western capitals and clarify the measures taken by the two meetings of the Arab oil ministers.[39]

Within this context, it must be stressed that Iraq was the only country among the Arab states to oppose the cut-back decisions. Iraq officially explained its position by stressing that the cut-back would harm friendly countries, because it would not differentiate between friends and enemies. It would, rather, penalize both of them alike. Therefore, Iraq advocated the nationalization of the foreign oil companies. The Iraqi government cited its experience of nationalizing the American and Dutch shares in the Basrah Petroleum Company on 7 October as an example and urged other Arab countries to follow suit. The Iraqi government did join the rest of the Arab countries in imposing a total ban on the United States and the Netherlands, but it publicly dissociated itself from the cut-back decisions adopted by the Arab oil ministers at their meetings on 17 October and 4 and 5 November 1973.[40]

REACTION OF THE EUROPEAN COMMUNITY TO DEVELOPMENTS IN THE MIDDLE EAST

When the Arab–Israeli war of October 1973 broke out, with the Arabs employing their oil as a political weapon, Europe felt that its economic security and its very existence were directly threatened. This resulted in a serious crisis within the European Community, as well as within the Western alliance. There were disagreements within the alliance, based on the degree of new states' vulnerability and dependency. This gave rise to different assessments of, and then responses to, the Middle East crisis.[41]

Despite the fact that the economic structures (standard of living, level of industrial development, level of technology, rate of economic growth, and quality of life and culture) of Europe and the United States were all based on and hence relied on oil energy, the degree of this reliance was different. Although the United States was the biggest oil consumer in the world, its need for Middle East oil was small. With a cut of roughly 10 per cent in its domestic consumption, the United States could easily decrease the pressure on her economy in time of emergency and free itself from depending on Middle East oil. In other words, the United States was relatively autonomous *vis-à-vis* Middle Eastern oil.

The European Community, on the other hand, depended on oil coming from the Middle East for almost 60 per cent of its total energy requirement. This heavy dependency had become an established fact, and the countries of the European Community had accommodated themselves accordingly,[42] and hence their concern and their high sensitivity towards securing access to oil and ensuring the stability of the region. When the fighting started, it was obvious that Europe would react differently from its ally the United States. Europe concentrated on the elimination of the Arab–Israeli conflict through suggesting an overall comprehensive solution, whereas the United States' main concern was with the East–West aspect of the conflict and a possible Soviet attempt to gain from the crisis. Washington had failed to understand the vulnerability of the European Community.[43]

Europe's reaction to the situation in the Middle East went through two stages: the individual reactions, and then the joint Community reaction.

INDIVIDUAL REACTIONS OF THE COMMUNITY MEMBER STATES TO THE CRISIS

The initial reactions of the Community member states to the war and its development were confused, chaotic and uncoordinated. The disarray within the Community was reflected in the positions taken by each of the Community member states. These positions ranged from that of the French government, which adopted a relatively pro-Arab stance, to the Netherlands' clear anti-Arab attitude.[44] When the war erupted in the Middle East, the French foreign minister, Michel Jobert, immediately stated that the French government was always in favour of a 'peaceful and negotiated' solution for the Arab–Israel conflict. Then he asked, employing a famous phrase: 'Does trying to go back home necessarily constitute an unexpected aggression?'[45]

The French prime minister, Pierre Messmer, stated on 9 October that the attitude of the French government in relation to an ultimate cease-fire would be dictated by the wish that the cease fire would pave the way for real negotiations in a framework to be defined in accordance with Security Council resolution 242. The definitive settlement of the conflict, he added, should be accepted by everyone, and included the necessary security guarantees.[46] Also on 9 October, M Jobert stated that since the

European countries were directly interested in the region, by virtue of historic, geographic and economic links, it was imperative for them to play an essential role in the Middle East crisis.[47]

The French government sharply criticized the United States and the Soviet Union for their ambiguous role in the Middle East war. It accused both superpowers of trying to dominate the world and requested that France and other permanent members of the Security Council should be allowed to take part in the peace-keeping process.[48] President Pompidou, in his statement of 31 October, expressed his regret at Europe's absence from the Middle East bargaining, and his concern that the United States and the Soviet Union had been left to arrange a cease-fire. 'This way of doing things is dangerous,'[49] he told his cabinet. Experience had shown, he said, that a private understanding between the two great powers 'can just as easily lead to confrontation as to detente'.[50] He also urged the European countries to adopt a positive common stand on the Middle East dispute, because they had direct interests in the area.[51] France, alongside Britain and to a less extent West Germany, refused to cooperate with the United States either in its arms supply to Israel or in the diplomatic manoeuvres that followed the war.[52]

As for Britain, within a few days of the war starting, it had officially declared its decision to embargo all arms exports to the countries of the battlefield. During the war consultations between British and French officials often took place.[53] The British government stressed, shortly after the war broke out, that the immediate need in the Middle East was to achieve a just and lasting settlement of the conflict. It affirmed that reconciliation could not be accomplished on the basis of the retention by Israel of large areas of Arab lands. This would only pave the way for continuous hostility and then intensive fighting.[54] The British prime minister, Edward Heath, declined to give his support for an American proposal for an early cease-fire at the Security Council, which later provoked Kissinger's rage.[55] Britain refused to permit the United States to use its bases in Cyprus to supply Israel with weapons during the fighting. With France, Britain refused to back the United States in its objection to the Egyptian proposal for a joint Soviet–American troop presence to monitor the application of the cease-fire in Sinai.[56]

The West German government's initial reaction was one of regret at the renewal of the fighting and of hope for an immediate peaceful solution for the conflict. The German government stated that Germany was 'firmly' in favour of United Nations Security Council Resolution 242. The Chancellor of the Republic stressed, shortly after the war started, that West Germany had a significant interest in the establishment of a lasting peace in the Middle East. Parallel to that, the Chancellor also stated that if peace was to have a real chance of success, the right of existence of each state in the region should be respected.[57]

But Germany was at odds with France and Britain in relation to the United States airlift of weapons to Israel. Germany did not refuse outright the use of the American bases on its territory for this purpose. So when the war broke out, initially West Germany allowed the United States to re-supply Israel from the Ramstein and Schweinfurt air bases on its territory. The government maintained silence until the news leaked to the press. Agency France Press quoted military sources as saying that huge quantities of United States war material were taken from the American base at Schweinfurt to be dispatched to Israel. Israeli ships were observed transferring arms and ammunition from the port of Bremerhaven. These incidents put the government in an embarrassing situation because it clearly compromised the neutrality of West Germany, which it had declared at the beginning of the war.

In the light of these developments, the German foreign ministry issued a statement on 25 October, asking the United States to halt all arms deliveries to Israel from its territory. It also informed the United States chargé d'affaires in Germany, Frank Cash, that any arms deliveries by the United States through West German territory to one of the conflicting parties would not be allowed. Germany's strict neutrality prohibited any arms deliveries.[58]

In addition, the German foreign minister 'warned Israel that even though their two countries had special relations, since 1965 the Federal Republic had developed special relations with the Arab countries, who in the past had been angered by its supply of capital and arms deliveries to Israel'.[59] Therefore, and in order to secure its good relations with the Arabs, especially economic relations, it was imperative for West Germany to maintain and observe carefully its neutral posture on the Middle East conflict.

As for the smaller countries, both the Netherlands and Denmark officially sided with Israel and adopted an anti-Arab policy. The prime minister of the Netherlands, Den Uyi, and his foreign minister Van Der Stoel 'pronounced themselves in line with Israel's policy'. In a meeting with Arab representatives in the Hague shortly after the war started, the Dutch foreign minister attacked the Arabs and accused them of starting the war. The Dutch government permitted the United States to use its territory for arms supplies to Israel and it set up a centre for volunteers to go and defend Israel. In the daily press, publicity notices appeared, signed by three ex-prime ministers (Biesheuvel, De Jong and Drees), accusing both Egypt and Syria of being the aggressors. The Netherlands vigorously manifested its anti-Arab policy when government members, shortly after the war started, participated in a demonstration of solidarity with Israel. The Danish prime minister, Anker Joergensen, expressed his 'deep' sympathy towards Israel and declared that 98 per cent of the Danish public regarded the Arabs as the aggressors.[60] Both Denmark and the Netherlands refused to allow France and Britain to speak on behalf of the Community in the Security Council at the United Nations.[61]

Italy followed an attitude of unconcerned neutrality, despite the fact that a major sector of opinion (on the Left) showed sympathy and solidarity with the Arab case.[62] Italy later joined the three key countries within the Community (France, Britain and West Germany) and advocated an urgent Community contribution to the search for a peaceful solution to the Middle East conflict. 'Europe must actively contribute to this aim,' said the Italian prime minister. He went on: 'In my view time is ripe for a step in this direction.'[63]

To protect its interests during the war, the Belgian government held in abeyance the delivery of arms and ammunition to the Middle East. The government denied the rumour that a centre for volunteers for Israel had been set up in Belgium. It emphasized that such a centre would not be permitted.[64]

THE JOINT REACTION OF THE EUROPEAN COMMUNITY

During the 1973 Middle East crisis, the three key countries within the Common Market (France, Britain and Germany) chose a policy of neutrality, or to be precise neutrality with a pro-Arab tilt. Two countries, Britain and West Germany, had considerably shifted their positions towards the line that France had been pursuing in the Middle East. It seems that all the 'big three', moreover, had reached one conclusion: that it was imperative for the Community to overcome its internal differences and adopt a joint position on the Middle East problem.[65]

The first joint response of the Community came a few days after the outbreak of hostilities. The Council of Ministers, in a statement issued on 13 October, called for a cease-fire. The nine governments of the Community expressed their concern over the renewal of hostilities in the Middle East and asked both sides to stop the fighting, so that negotiations could be started on the basis of Security Council resolution 242.[66] On 17 October, during its Wednesday sitting, the European Parliament adopted a resolution in which it deplored the renewal of the fighting in the area, which constituted a grave threat to world peace, and approved the initial efforts made by the Community to end the fighting. It stressed the Community's responsibility in the world in general and in the Mediterranean in particular, and called for an emergency meeting of the Council of Ministers. The aim was to utilize the Community's good offices with a view to achieving a cease-fire followed by direct or indirect negotiations, such as might guarantee a lasting peace. The Parliament then forwarded the resolution to the Council of Ministers, the Commission and the governments of the member states so that they could take note of it.[67]

The 6 November declaration

The decisive common response, which was considered to be a watershed in the Community attitude towards the Middle East crisis, came on 6 November 1973, after major efforts to coordinate policies among the members. The declaration started with the emphasis by the Community that the views set out in the statement were only a first contribution on their part to seek a comprehensive solution to the crisis. The main points of the statement were as follows:

(1) The Community member states strongly urged that the forces of the conflicting parties in the Middle East conflict should return immediately to the positions they occupied on 22 October, in compliance with resolutions 339 and 340 of the Security Council. They stressed their belief that a return to these positions would pave the way for a solution to other pressing problems, such as that of prisoners of war and of the Egyptian Third Army.

(2) They had the firm wish that following the adoption by the
Security Council of resolution 338 of 22 October, negotiations would start for the re-establishment in the Middle
East of a just and lasting peace via the application of Security
Council resolution 242 in all its parts. The Community declared its willingness to do what it could to contribute to that
peace, and emphasized that those negotiations must take
their course in the framework of the United Nations. They
recalled that the charter of the United Nations had entrusted
to the Security Council the principal responsibility for international peace and security. The Council and the secretary-
general had a special role to play in the making and keeping
of peace through the application of resolution 242.[68]

(3) They believed that a peace agreement must be based on the
following points:
   (a) the inadmissibility of the acquisition of territory by force;
   (b) the need for Israel to end the territorial occupation which
       it has maintained since the conflict of 1967;
   (c) respect for the sovereignty, territorial integrity and inde-
       pendence of every state in the area and their right to live
       in peace within secure and recognized boundaries;
   (d) recognition that in the establishment of a just and lasting
       peace account must be taken of the legitimate rights of
       the Palestinians.

(4) They stated that, according to resolution 242, the peace
settlement should be the subject of international guarantees.
They emphasized that such guarantees should be enforced
through sending peace-keeping forces to the demilitarized
areas envisaged in article 2 of resolution 242. Such guarantees were of great importance in settling the overall situation
in the Middle East, in accordance with resolution 242. They
reserved the right to make proposals in this connection.

(5) The Community on this occasion recalled the different ties
which linked them to the states of the south and east of the
Mediterranean. They stated that they had intended to negotiate co-operation agreements with those countries within
the framework of the Community Mediterranean policy.[69]

Although the 6 November declaration reiterated parts of an
already established theme, its importance was as follows: first,
the text of the statement removed the ambiguity from Resolution 242, by demanding the withdrawal of the Israeli forces

from 'all the occupied territories'; and secondly, the statement recognized the necessity of taking into account the 'legitimate rights of the Palestinian people'.[70] This meant that the Community no longer treated the Palestinian question as a 'refugee problem'. The Community, after the 6 November declaration, started to emphasize recognition of the legitimate rights of the Palestinian people. This emphasis on Palestinian collective rights was later to become the theme of European policy.[71] Finally, the text underlined clearly the role of the Security Council and the necessity of international guarantees in the peace settlement.[72]

THE REACTIONS OF THE PARTIES CONCERNED

Israel

The Israeli government's reaction to the EEC declaration was very bitter and highly negative. The government believed that the statement was of no help in reducing tension in the Middle East and saw the European Community, apart from the Netherlands, 'as having submitted to the Arab blackmail' over oil supplies. The declaration was viewed by the Israeli government as an alignment by the Common Market with the Arab and Soviet interpretation of Security Council resolution 242, calling on Israel to withdraw from the lands occupied in 1967. The Soviet–Arab interpretation from the beginning was that the call for withdrawal meant withdrawal from all the territories. Israel did not accept this interpretation and stated that the word 'all' was specifically omitted.[73]

The Israeli officials were very critical of the statement. The Israeli ambassador to the EEC expressed his 'dismay and surprise' at the declaration adopted by the Nine.[74] The prime minister, Mrs Meir, sent a message to the European Community expressing her alarm at the position taken by the Community on the Middle East conflict. Mr Allon, the envoy to Belgium and the EEC, stated that the declaration by the Community had supported and advocated the Franco–Soviet theme, which represented and advanced the Arab position in an attempt to gain guaranteed oil supplies. He stated that the statement was viewed in Jerusalem as a 'repudiation' of resolution 242 which had been engineered and advocated by the British government.

Mr Allon accused Britain of having relinquished resolution 242.[75]

In a public statement issued on 9 November, Abba Eban, the Israeli foreign minister, stated that the Community declaration meant 'oil for Europe and not peace in the Middle East'. The text, he went on, showed 'feudal considerations' because it did not allow enough room for the sovereignty of the countries concerned. The declaration was released at an inappropriate time. The essential aim of the Community statement, he said, was to make an attempt and induce the governments of the Arab countries not to reduce their oil exports. It put forward an arrangement for the territorial question void of any international legal ground and therefore did not tie Israel in any way whatsoever. In addition, the statement failed to take into account the views of the countries that were most concerned. Eban rejected the suggestions made by the Community concerning the way in which negotiations for peace should be conducted, how the peace process should be guaranteed, and what should be done for the Palestinian people. He concluded that the European Community had acted as if Israel and the Arab countries were not independent states and 'were still living in the ancient bonds of servitude'. He added: 'The least the world could do, if it wants to contribute to a sovereign and negotiated peace is precisely to refrain from making such declaration in the future.'[76]

In the view of Israeli officials, the European Community could, by all means, help the countries of the Middle East to meet each other so as to conduct direct negotiations. But by no means should the Community impose the terms of the peace agreement. The Israelis could possibly accept the idea of Europe conducting a purely technical role, as played by France during the Paris negotiations between the United States and Vietnam. This role took the shape of, for example: providing the meeting place; initiating good circumstances for the negotiations; solving material problems; and providing good offices, and so on.[77]

Comments from the Community member states

For the European Community, the November declaration represented a major move forward in foreign policy co-operation and a significant effort to reaffirm European influence in the Middle East. The British foreign secretary, Sir Alec Douglas Home, stated that the declaration constituted another important step towards a common foreign policy[78] and 'a third success for the process of political consultation of the Nine'. He underlined that the statement addressed itself to one basic and essential thing. That was to achieve a just and lasting agreement in the Middle East conflict.[79] The Middle East, he said, was a region of particular concern to many people in Britain.

Britain had been closely tied with its political development in this century as well as before. This enhanced the sympathy which Britain in particular felt for nations that were eagerly looking forward to establishing new societies, while nourishing what was precious and essential to them in their past.[80] 'We had it in mind, too, to prove to the Arabs that they had friends and that the Russians were not the only people on whom they could rely for justice.'[81] 'The momentum of peace-making must be sustained ... what has happened has been that almost every country in the world, including the United States, is concluding that withdrawal and peace are synonymous.' Europe did not want to push itself on the Middle East negotiations, 'but before the end of this dispute, which has lasted for so many years, we will find that Europe is able to play a constructive part in arriving at a settlement'.[82]

The reaction of the French government was one of triumph. It viewed the statement as something of a victory for French diplomacy. The French foreign minister, Michel Jober, said that the United States should not oppose the statement because it proved that Europe was also looking for a solution, following its initial absence from the Middle East crisis.[83] France believed that Europe would gain a decisive influence in the Middle East once a peace agreement had been reached. According to M Jobert, sooner or later the Soviet Union and the United States would be 'fed up with confronting each other', and both the Israelis and the Arabs would ask the Community for help.[84]

The West German government supported the statement and emphasized that the call for Israel to withdraw its forces from the occupied territories must be linked with the right of every state in the region to live in peace within secure and recognized boundaries.[85] In a speech at the European Parliament, Chancellor Willy Brandt stated that the tragedy in the Middle East—an area so close to Europe geographically, culturally and historically—was a challenge to Europe. What went on in that agonized neighbouring region affected Europe directly, therefore

Europe must contribute towards solving the problem. He went on to stress that Europe's success in setting out its position in a joint paper would lend weight to the Community's role. This would ultimately be in the interests of the countries directly involved in the conflict.[86]

Considering the smaller states, it is important to stress that the statement was supported even by the countries who adopted an anti-Arab position during the October War, such as the Netherlands and Denmark. The Dutch foreign minister, Max Van der Stoel, stated shortly after the release of the statement that he was fully satisfied with the declaration.[87] The Dutch foreign office commented that Dutch policy was completely in harmony with the stance adopted by the countries of the Nine in their declaration of 6 November 1973.[88] In an official statement the Danish prime minister expressed his support for the declaration adopted by the Community and said that he fully backed it.[89]

The Arab reaction

The European statement was greeted favourably by the Arab countries. Government spokesmen and newspapers throughout the Arab world acclaimed the European Community's new stance in the Middle East conflict. The declaration was seen by the Arab governments as a major step forward regarding Europe's outlook on the Middle East conflict and predicted that the declaration would usher in a new era of Arab–European friendship. One Beirut newspaper which, capturing the mood of many, demanded that the Arabs should reciprocate in kind by providing Europe with cheap oil and increasing trade relations with it.[90] The newspaper stated: 'Europe which remains steadfast against the policy of American partiality towards Israel, deserves more than an Arab salutation. It deserves lower petroleum prices, and more dealings by the Arabs so that Europe's independence from the USA may increase.'[91]

The positive Arab response to the EEC statement also manifested itself in the decisions adopted by the Arab oil ministers during their meeting on 18 November in Vienna. The conferees decided to exempt the Community members (apart from the Netherlands) from the 5 per cent cut in exports scheduled for December. The communiqué issued in Vienna stated that 'in appreciation of the political stance taken by the Common Market countries in their communiqué regarding the Middle East crisis, it has been decided not to implement the 5 per cent reduction for the month of December as it applies to Europe only'.[92]

The Algerian summit conference of 26–28 November 1973

During their summit meeting in Algeria, the Arab heads of state responded positively to the European gesture. On the initiative of President Sadat of Egypt and President Asad of Syria, an Arab summit meeting took place in Algeria on 26 November. The conference was attended by President Boumedienne of Algeria, who acted as chairman of the conference, President Sadat, President Asad, King Faisal of Saudi Arabia, King Hassan II of Morocco, President Bourguiba of Tunisia, President Frangieh of Lebanon, the Emir of Kuwait, the Sultan of Oman, the rulers of Bahrain and Qatar, the president of the United Arab Emirates, President Al-Iriani of the Yemen Arab Republic (North Yemen), President Rubayyi Ali of the People's Democratic Republic of Yemen, President Nimeiry of Sudan, President Mokhtar Ould Daddah of Mauritania, Yassir Arafat, chairman of the PLO, and Bahjat Talhouni representing King Hussein of Jordan.[93] Iraq and Libya refused to attend the conference.

In a statement issued on 19 November, the official Iraqi news agency stated that Egypt and Syria were trying to employ the summit to gain approval for the 'unilateral decisions' they had taken during the Arab–Israel war. The spokesman of the foreign ministry stressed that, in the view of the Iraqi government, the summit meeting would 'not achieve the ambitions of the Arab masses and their aims of liberation and continuation of the struggle'.[94]

In Libya there was no official statement, but in an interview shortly after the cease-fire with the French newspaper *Le Monde*, the Libyan leader stated that he would not participate in the Algerian summit conference, emphasizing at the same time that the conference was formed to ratify a 'capitulation' by Egypt and Syria.[95]

During the meeting, the conferees took stock of the situation in the Middle East and ended with the adoption of the following:

(a) a political declaration;
(b) a declaration on Africa;
(c) three declarations on the attitude of the Arab States *vis-à-vis*

Western Europe, the Socialist countries, and the non-aligned states;

(d) a resolution on Arab oil policy.

In regard to Western Europe, the statement started by saying that the Arab kings and heads of state had 'noted with attention and interest the first signs of a better understanding of the Arab cause among the states of Western Europe'. The document went on to remind the Community that Europe was 'linked to the Arab countries across the Mediterranean by affinities of civilization and by vital interests which can only develop within the framework of confident and mutually beneficial co-operation'.[96] It stressed that by taking a just and equitable attitude, by making every efforts to secure the withdrawal of the Israeli armed forces from the occupied areas including Jerusalem, and by helping to restore the legitimate right of the Palestinian people, Europe would reinforce both its will for independence and its role in world affairs.[97]

The Copenhagen summit meeting of 14–15 December 1973

The summit meeting at Copenhagen was held on the initiative of President Pompidou. He had suggested that, in the light of the developments in the Middle East, the heads of the Community member states should gather before the end of the year 1973, to discuss the Middle East question.[98] During the meeting, France and Britain strongly advocated the idea of establishing a special relationship with the Arab world. This would include both diplomatic efforts to gain oil supplies and intensified trading relationships to provide Europe with recycled funds.[99]

In the course of the meeting, four Arab foreign ministers made an unexpected visit to the conference. The ministers were authorized by the Arab summit conference, which had taken place in Algeria, 'to put the conference's conclusions on the Middle East War and the future of the Mediterranean area to the European leaders' meeting at Copenhagen'.[100]

The outcome of the deliberations was a communiqué in which the Community confirmed the stance it had adopted on 6 November. The heads of the Community member states stressed also that the requirement of sovereignty and the requirement of security could only be achieved through the conclusion of a peace settlement, which included among other items international guarantees and the setting up of demilitarized zones.[101] Finally the Community heads of state 'confirmed the importance of entering into negotiations with oil-producing countries on comprehensive arrangements comprising co-operation on a wide scale for the economic and industrial development of these countries, industrial investments, and stable energy supplies to the member countries at reasonable prices'.[102] One can reasonably assert that the Euro-Arab dialogue began here.

NOTES

1. Hans Maull, 'The Strategy of Avoidance: Europe's Middle East Policies After the October War', in J.C. Hurewitz (ed.), *Oil, the Arab–Israel Dispute, and the Industrial World: Horizons of Crisis*, Westview Press, Boulder, Colorado, 1976, p. 118.
2. *Ibid*, p. 110.
3. Ilan Greilsammer and Joseph Wiler, 'European Political Co-operation and the Palestinian–Israeli Conflict: An Israeli Perspective', in D. Allen and A. Pijpers (eds.), *European Foreign Policy-Making and the Arab–Israeli Conflict*, Martinus Nijhoff Publishers, the Hague, 1984, pp. 131–2.
4. Dominique Moisi, 'Europe and the Middle East', in Steven L. Spiegel (ed.), *The Middle East and the Western Alliance*, George Allen and Unwin, London, 1982, p. 42.
5. G.L. Goodwin, 'A European Community Foreign Policy?', *Journal of Common Market Studies*, Vol. 12, 1973–4, p. 21.
6. Dominique Moisi, 'Europe and the Middle East', in Steven L. Spiegel (ed.), *The Middle East and the Western Alliance*, p. 25.
7. *Ibid*, p. 25.
8. Ilan Greilsammer and Joseph Wiler, 'European Political Co-operation and the Palestinian–Israeli Conflict: An Israeli Perspective', in D. Allen and A. Pijpers (eds.), *European Foreign Policy-Making and the Arab–Israeli Conflict*, p. 132.
9. *Bulletin of the European Communities*, 1, 1971, p. 15.
10. Ilan Greilsammer and Joseph Wiler, 'European Political Co-operation and the Palestinian–Israeli Conflict: An Israeli Perspective', in D. Allen and A. Pijpers (eds.), *European Foreign Policy-Making and the Arab–Israeli Conflict*, pp. 132–3.
11. Stephen J. Artner, 'The Middle East: A Chance for Europe?', in *International Affairs*, Vol. 56, No. 3, Summer, 1980, p. 430.
12. *Bulletin of the European Communities*, 6, 1971, p. 32.
13. Quoted by Edward A. Kolodziej, *French International Policy Under De Gaulle and Pompidou*, Cornell University Press, Ithaca, New York, 1974, pp. 510–1.
14. Hans Maull, 'The Strategy of Avoidance: Europe's Middle East Policies

After the October War', in J. C. Hurewitz (ed.), *Oil, the Arab–Israeli Dispute, and the Industrial World: Horizons of Crisis*, p. 118.

15. Stephen J. Artner, 'The Middle East: A Chance for Europe?', *International Affairs*, p. 431.
16. Ilan Greilsammer and Joseph Wiler, 'European Political Co-operation and the Palestinian–Israeli Conflict: An Israeli Perspective', in D. Allen and A. Pijpers (eds.), *European Foreign Policy-Making and the Arab–Israeli Conflict*, p. 133.
17. Stephen J. Artner, 'The Middle East: A Chance for Europe?', *International Affairs*, p. 431.
18. Panayiotis Ifestos, *European Political Co-operation: Towards A Framework of Supranational Diplomacy*, Gower Publishing, England, 1987, p. 421.
19. Quoted by Edward A. Kolodziej, *French International Policy Under De Gaulle and Pompidou*, p. 511.
20. *Ibid*, p. 511.
21. Ilan Greilsammer and Joseph Wiler, 'European Political Co-operation and the Palestinian–Israeli Conflict: An Israeli Perspective', in D. Allen and A. Pijpers (eds.), *European Foreign Policy-Making and the Arab–Israeli Conflict*, p. 133.
22. Quoted by Wolfgang Hager, 'Western Europe: The Politics of Muddling Through', in J. C. Hurewitz (ed.), *Oil, the Arab–Israel Dispute, and the Industrial World*, p. 38.
23. *Ibid*, pp. 38–9.
24. *Ibid*, p. 39.
25. Quoted by Benjamin Shwadran, *Middle East Oil Crisis Since 1973*, Westview Press, Boulder, Colorado, and London, 1986, pp. 98–9.
26. *Ibid*, p. 99.
27. Barry Rubin, 'US Policy, January–October 1973', *Journal of Palestine Studies*, Vol. III, No. 2, Winter 1974, pp. 108–9.
28. *The New York Times*, 25 October 1973.
29. *Ibid*.
30. Galia Golan, *Yom Kippur and After*, Cambridge University Press, London, 1977, pp. 121–2.
31. George Lenczowski, *Middle East Oil in a Revolutionary Age*, American Enterprise Institute for Public Policy Research, Washington D.C., 1976, p. 12.
32. *Keesing's Contemporary Archive*, 26 November–2 December 1973, pp. 26, 224–5.
33. Quoted by Fuad Itayim, 'Arab Oil: The Political Dimension', *Journal of Palestine Studies*, p. 90.
34. *Ibid*, pp. 90–1.
35. *Ibid*, p. 91.
36. George Lenczowski, *Middle East Oil in a Revolutionary Age*, pp. 14–15.
37. *Keesing's Contemporary Archives*, p. 26, 224.
38. *The New York Times*, 3 November 1973.

39. *Keesing's Contemporary Archives*, 1973, p. 26,224.
40. George Lenczowski, *Middle East Oil in a Revolutionary Age*, p. 15.
41. Hans Maull, 'The Strategy of Avoidance: Europe's Middle East Policies After the October War', in J.C. Hurewitz (ed.), *Oil, the Arab–Israel Dispute and the Industrial World*, p. 115.
42. Benjamin Shwadran, *Middle East Oil Crisis since 1973*, p. 90.
43. Hans Maull, 'The Strategy of Avoidance: Europe's Middle East Policies After the October War', in J.C. Hurewitz (ed.), *Oil, the Arab–Israel Dispute and the Industrial World*, p. 117.
44. *Ibid*, p. 117.
45. Quoted by Ibrahim Sus, 'Western Europe and the October War', *Journal of Palestine Studies*, p. 66.
46. For more Details on the French Reaction During the War see Daniel Colord, 'La politique méditerranéenne et proche-orientale de G. Pompidou', *Politique Etrangère*, 43, No. 3, 1978, pp. 283–306.
47. *Daily Star*, 1 November 1973.
48. *International Herald Tribune*, 15 November 1973.
49. *International Herald Tribune*, 1 November 1973.
50. Quoted by James O. Goldsborough, 'France, the European Crisis and the Alliance', *Foreign Affairs*, Vol. 52, No. 3, 1974, p. 549.
51. *International Herald Tribune*, 1 November 1973.
52. Janice Gross Stein, 'The Politics of Alliance Policy: Europe, Canada, Japan, and the United States Face the Arab–Israel Conflict', in Janice Gross Stein and David B. Dewitt (eds.), *The Middle East at the Crossroads*, Mosaic Press, Canada, 1983, p. 151.
53. *The Times*, 17 October 1973.
54. *Daily Telegraph*, 1 November 1973.
55. See *The Washington Post*, 1 November 1973.
56. Joan Garratt, 'Euro-American Energy Diplomacy in the Middle East, 1970–1980: The Pervasive Crisis', in Steven L. Spiegel (ed.), *The Middle East and the Western Alliance*, p. 84.
57. Ibrahim Sus, 'Eastern Europe and the October War', *Journal of the Palestine Studies*, p. 72.
58. Edmund Ghareeb, 'The US Arms Supply to Israel During the War', *Journal of Palestine Studies*, pp. 117–18.
59. Ibrahim Sus, 'Western Europe and the October War', *Journal of Palestine Studies*, p. 72.
60. *Ibid*, pp. 70–2.
61. Janice Gross Stein, 'The Politics of Alliance Policy: Europe, Canada, Japan, and the United States Face the Arab–Israel Conflict', in Janice Gross Stein and David B. Dewitt (eds.), *The Middle East at the Crossroads*, p. 151.
62. Ibrahim Sus, 'Western Europe and the October War', *Journal of Palestine Studies*, p. 71.
63. *Daily Star*, 11 November 1973.
64. Ibrahim Sus, 'Western Europe and the October War', *Journal of Palestine Studies*, p. 71.
65. Hans Maull, 'The Strategy of Avoidance: Europe's Middle East Policies

After the October War', in J.C. Hurewitz (ed.), *Oil, the Arab–Israel Dispute and the Industrial World*, pp. 123–4.
66. *Bulletin of the European Communities*, 10, 1973, pp. 105–6.
67. European Parliament, Information, Parliament in session, Luxembourg: European Parliament, 1973, pp. 23–4.
68. *Bulletin of the European Communities*, p. 106.
69. *Ibid*, p. 106.
70. Claude Imperiali and Pierre Agate, 'France', in D. Allen and A. Pijpers (eds.), *European Foreign Policy-Making and the Arab–Israeli Conflict*, p. 4.
71. Janice Gross Stein, 'The Politics of the Alliance Policy: Europe, Canada, Japan and the United States Face the Arab–Israeli Conflict', in Janice Gross Stein and D. Dewitt (eds.), *The Middle East at the Crossroads*, p. 151.
72. Claude Imperiali and Pierre Agate, 'France', in D. Allen and A. Pijpers (eds.), *European Foreign Policy-Making and the Arab–Israeli Conflict*, p. 4.
73. *Daily Telegraph*, 7 November 1973.
74. *The Guardian*, 7 November 1973.
75. *The Times*, 8 November 1973.
76. Ilan Greilsammer and Joseph Weiler, 'European Political Co-operation and the Palestinian–Israeli Conflict: An Israeli Perspective', p. 135. See also *The Jerusalem Post*, 11 November 1973.
77. *Ibid*, p. 136.
78. *Financial Times*, 7 November 1973.
79. *The Times*, 7 November 1973.
80. *Financial Times*, 13 November 1973.
81. *The Times*, 17 November 1973.
82. *The Times*, 27 November 1973.
83. *The Times*, 7 November 1973.
84. *The Guardian*, 7 November 1973.
85. *The Times*, 7 November 1973.
86. *Bulletin of the European Communities*, 11, 1973, p. 5.
87. *The Times*, 7 November 1973.
88. *Daily Star*, 6 November 1973.
89. *Financial Times*, 7 November 1973.
90. *The Times*, 8 November 1973.
91. Quoted by George Lenczowski, *Middle East Oil in a Revolutionary Age*, p. 17.
92. Quoted by *ibid*, p. 18.
93. *Keesing's Contemporary Archives*, 17–23 December 1973, p. 26, 245.
94. *Ibid*, p. 26, 246.
95. *Ibid*.
96. *Ibid*, p. 26, 245.
97. *Ibid*.
98. *Bulletin of the European Communities*, 12, 1973, p. 6.
99. Robert J. Lieber, *Oil and the Middle East War: Europe in the Energy Crisis*, Centre for International Affairs, Harvard University, 1976, p. 18.
100. *The Times*, 15 December 1973.
101. *Bulletin of the European Communities*, p. 10.
102. *Ibid*, p. 11.

III

THE PREPARATORY STAGE OF
THE DIALOGUE (1974–1975)

ARAB–EUROPEAN PREPARATIONS FOR THE DIALOGUE

After the Copenhagen Declaration of 15 December 1973, the contacts between the two sides—the Arab and the European—were continued. In January 1974, the French government presented a concrete plan for the initiation of a dialogue, and laboured to convince its Community partners of the importance of having a unified approach towards the Arab world. In the following weeks the Community member states produced a consensus formula. It stressed the view that the initiative should not hinder international efforts in the oil and raw material sectors nor interfere with the diplomatic efforts for a peace settlement in the Middle East. Thus it was clear from the beginning that the Arab–Israel conflict would be absent from the agenda of the dialogue.[1]

On 4 March 1974, the nine foreign ministers, meeting in the context of European political co-operation in Brussels, announced their decision to start a process that would lead to the establishment of long-term Euro-Arab co-operation in all fields, notably economic, technical and cultural co-operation.[2] In the communiqué that was adopted at the end of the meeting, the Community member states expressed their wish to continue the dialogue that had just begun, and to develop from it mutually beneficial co-operation.[3] To provide an organized framework for the co-operation with the Arabs, the Community proposed three initial stages of action, each of which would comprise some of the following specified measures:

(a) exploratory contacts with the 20 member states of the Arab League to specify Arab ideas;
(b) the setting up of a number of joint working groups to examine potential fields of co-operation;
(c) an EEC–Arab conference at ministerial level.[4]

The foreign ministers agreed to authorize Walter Scheel, the West German foreign minister and president of the EEC Council, to undertake the preliminary contacts with the Arab countries. However, although the preliminary contacts were to start immediately, final authorization of the plan was to be subject to the approval of the British government (the political complexion of which was then still uncertain following the elections of 28 February). At the March meeting of the Council, Britain was represented by foreign office officials only.[5]

On the Arab side, the foreign ministers of the League of Arab States met in Tunis during 25–28 March 1974. At the meetings, the ministers agreed to set up a nine-member delegation to start negotiations with the EEC, on matters related to the forms and procedures of the proposed Euro-Arab dialogue.[6]

On 10 June, the foreign ministers of the Nine met in Bonn. The meeting was chaired by Herr Genscher, the German foreign minister and Chairman-in-Office for European Political Co-operation (EPC). The Commission was represented by President Ortoli and M Cheysson. During the meeting, the foreign ministers agreed to go ahead with the long-contemplated dialogue with the Arab countries, after an initial delay due to the differences with the United States over the question of prior consultation.[7] Between 18 and 20 June, there was a preliminary meeting in Cairo between representatives of the European Community and representatives of the Arab League. In the course of the meeting, both sides approved the procedures proposed by the European Community during their meeting on 4 March (initial diplomatic contacts, joint working groups to examine potential areas of co-operation, and then a joint conference at a ministerial level).[8]

On 10 and 11 July, the Political Committee of the European Community held a meeting. It was attended by Commission representatives, and concentrated mainly on the preparations for the joint Euro-Arab ministerial meeting, which had been decided on previously by the foreign ministers at their meeting in Bonn on 10 June.[9]

THE JOINT EURO-ARAB MINISTERIAL MEETING OF 31 JULY 1974

The joint Euro-Arab ministerial meeting was officially opened in Paris on 31 July. The conference included 31 participants, each with one representative. They were: the nine Community members, the twenty Arab League states, and representatives from both the European Community and the Arab League. Each side had co-chairmen speaking on behalf of their respective members.[10] For the European Community, the designated co-chairmen were the French foreign minister (France was occupying the chairmanship of the Community's Council of Ministers in the second half of 1974); the officiating president for Political Co-operation, Jean Sauvagnargues; and the president of the Commission, M Ortoli. On the Arab side, the representatives were Sheikh Sabah Al-Ahmad Al-Jaber, Foreign Minister of Kuwait and President of the League of Arab States; and Mahmoud Riad, Secretary-General of the Arab League.[11]

During the meeting, which was described by M Sauvagnargues as one of 'historic significance', both sides endorsed the Cairo agreement, relating to the procedures of the dialogue, and discussed in detail the future organization of the dialogue. It was decided to form a Permanent General Commission comprised of representatives of all 29 interested states.[12] The General Commission was charged with the responsibility of formulating the theoretical framework of the dialogue, and was to meet for the first time on 26 November 1974, in Paris. In the interim, working committees composed of 'experts' from both sides would meet to study specific areas of potential co-operation between the two regions. The outcome of the experts' deliberations would be made known at periodic plenary sessions.[13]

Also, both sides agreed that the working committees, each in its own field of duties, would form the specialist groups. The members of these groups would also be experts from both sides. The specialist groups would be called in from time to time to study in detail specific technical matters and then submit their reports and advice on them to the working committees concerned. (Up to 1979, the number of specialist groups reached about 30. Examples of the areas covered include petroleum refining industries, petrochemical industries, nitrogenous and mixed fertilizers industries, the electric power generation industry, agro-based industries and animal production.) Finally, the meeting envisaged that these steps, which they had agreed upon, would lead eventually to the convening of a full-scale conference, between all member states of the European Community and the Arab League at the ministerial level. The conference would then assess the final suggestions of the

European–Arab institutions, and sign agreements of economic co-operation between the two sides. Hence, one could say that the institutions of the Euro-Arab dialogue were formally set up in Paris on 31 July 1974.[14]

On 16 September 1974, the ministers for foreign affairs of the European Community met within the context of European Political Co-operation (EPC). During the meeting, the ministers endorsed a document containing details of the structure of European coordination.[15]

In order to pave the way for the first meeting of the General Committee, scheduled for November in Paris, preparatory talks between senior Arab and European officials took place in Cairo on 20 October.[16] At the meeting, the European delegation, composed of representatives from the French presidency and the European Commission, was led by Jacques Tine, diplomatic adviser to the French foreign ministry. The Arab delegation, made up of representatives from the Lebanese presidency (because Lebanon currently held the chairmanship of the League) and the secretariat of the League of Arab States, was led by Mohamed Sabra, Lebanon's ambassador in Cairo.[17] In the course of the meeting, the two sides discussed the essential arrangements concerning the convening of the first meeting of the General Committee. Also, the European delegation presented a working paper related to the organizational and procedural aspects of the meeting. At the end of this meeting, the two parties agreed that it would be convenient for both sides to have the first meeting of the General Committee before the convening of the European summit conference, due to take place in December 1974.[18]

THE ARAB SUMMIT CONFERENCE AND THE
RECOGNITION OF THE PLO AS THE SOLE LEGITIMATE
REPRESENTATIVE OF THE PALESTINIAN PEOPLE

A summit meeting of Arab heads of state (the seventh of its kind) took place in Rabat, Morocco, between 26 and 29 October 1974. The conference was attended by representatives of all member states of the Arab League as well as of the Palestine Liberation Organization. The heads of state of Iraq and Libya did not attend the conference, although both countries had sent representatives to participate in the procedures. The decision to convene the summit meeting had been taken by the Arab foreign ministers who met earlier in Cairo on 1 September. A preparatory meeting of Arab foreign ministers preceded the summit conference. This was opened, also in Rabat, on 22 October by Mahmoud Riad, the secretary-general of the Arab League. The summit conference was officially opened by King Hassan of Morocco as its chairman on 26 October.

At the meeting, various matters were discussed, such as petroleum prices, the question of funds for the armed forces of the front-line of the Arab states, the Euro-Arab dialogue and the Iraq–Iran border dispute. But the most important subject, which dominated the discussions of the conference, was the dispute between Jordan and the PLO over the question of who would be the legitimate representative of the Palestinian people in the occupied territories, especially at the United Nations peace conference scheduled to be reconvened in Geneva to reach a peaceful settlement for the Arab–Israeli conflict[19].

The conference ended with a political victory for the PLO, whose position as the sole legitimate representative of the Palestinian people was recognized, as well as its right to lead the Palestinian people in setting up a national Palestinian authority in any part of liberated Palestine. The communiqué adopted at the end of the meeting confirmed the right of the Palestinian people to return to their homeland and to organize their self-determination. It also 'affirmed the right of the Palestinian people to establish an independent national authority under the leadership of the Palestine Liberation Organization as the sole legitimate representative of the Palestinian people in all liberated Palestinian territory'. The communiqué made it clear that the Arab states, within the context of Arab obligations, would support the Palestine Liberation Organization in undertaking its national and international responsibility.[20]

So the PLO had emerged from October's Arab summit conference as a leading formal actor in the tangled relationships of the Middle East. This role was reinforced and gained political momentum by the formal invitation for the PLO to participate in the United Nations debates, and the speech made by the chairman of the organization, Yassir Arafat, at the General Assembly on 13 November 1974.[21] The invitation for the PLO to take part in the United Nations General Assembly debates had an important impact on international opinion. The Palestinian presence at that session contributed to the PLO being endorsed internationally as the representative of the Palestinian people.

Ironically, these developments on the Palestinian side were seen by the government of the United States and some leaders of the European Community countries as upsetting the balance which they had been labouring to keep with a view to reaching a settlement.[22] Considering the Euro-Arab dialogue, the Rabat summit conference was of great importance. The Arab leaders (after recognizing the PLO as the sole legitimate representative of the Palestinian people) had decided that the Palestine Liberation Organization would take part in the dialogue with the European countries as the 21st member of the Arab League. Moreover the Arab summit conference endorsed the Euro-Arab dialogue and agreed that the dialogue should start in accordance with the principles which had already been laid down.[23]

PROBLEMS ENCOUNTERED IN THE DIALOGUE

The first General Committee meeting postponed

After the recognition of the PLO as the sole legitimate representative of the Palestinian people at the Rabat conference, the Arab League started to prepare for the first meeting of the General Committee, due to take place on 26 November. This meeting, however, had to be postponed because a disagreement arose on the representation of the PLO. The European Community wanted the membership of the General Committee to be restricted to the 29 countries: 20 Arab and 9 European. The Arab countries resisted the proposal and insisted that the Palestinians should be accorded the same status as the 21 Arab League members.[24]

The problem of PLO representation

Palestinian representation in the General Committee was first raised as a problem during the meeting of the representatives of the Arab side in the Euro-Arab dialogue, in Cairo on 12 November 1974. In the course of the meeting, the chairman of the Committee briefed the members that the Arab side had received a protest letter from the European Community. In the letter, the

Community stated its objection to the arrangements of the seats for the members of the delegations at the conference table. The letter referred to all the Arab delegations without mentioning the PLO delegation.

Before this, the European Community suggested that the membership of the General Committee (on the European side), should be open to the Nine and the representatives of the European Commission. The representation of the Arab side to the General Committee was left to a resolution to be adopted by the Arab League. This resolution, when adopted (September 1974), stated that the membership of the General Committee (on the Arab side) would be open to all Arab countries and the Secretariat General of the League, with the co-operation of the Arab organizations and agencies connected with the dialogue. The chairman of the Committee also informed the members that he had contacted the French ambassador, the representative of the Community, and conveyed to him the Arab view that 'a Palestinian delegation must be represented alongside the other Arab delegations and that the ambassador had promised to pass on the Arab point of view (to the Community) and bring the reply to it.'[25]

After this preliminary opening, the representatives of the Arab countries discussed in depth the European position. The outcome of the discussions was that they agreed to insist on Palestine being represented on the Arab side. Among the reasons for Palestinian representation given by the Arab representatives were the following: 'Because Palestine is a member of the Arab League . . . it is impermissible for the European side to interfere in the question of the representation of the Arab delegations . . . because, in fact, the Palestine question is the very basis of the dialogue.'[26] Finally, the representatives agreed that their participation in the meeting of the General Committee was dependent upon Palestinian representation being agreed. At the end of the meeting, the representatives asked the secretary-general of the Arab League to follow up the matter.

The European Community failed to give a proper reply before the date fixed for the General Committee meeting. It therefore had to be adjourned, despite the fact that both sides had prepared for it extensively.[27] The Community members, especially at the beginning, were in fact divided over the Arab demand. It was reported that both the French and Italian governments were, to some extent, prepared to accommodate the Arab request. On the other hand, the British, West German, Dutch and Danish governments insisted that only states would be allowed to have representation at the meeting. Hence they maintained that participation in the dialogue should be restricted to the Nine and the 20 states of the Arab League.

Later, the Community managed to overcome their differences and adopt a unified position. It was decided to reject the Arab demand on PLO participation. The reason given for the rejection was that the PLO did not have legal existence as a state. The European refusal of the Arab demand resulted in the dialogue being suspended for several months. Thus, from the very beginning, the idea of the dialogue was at stake before any official start could be made.[28]

The Dublin formula of 13 February 1975

The Euro-Arab dialogue continued to be at standstill for several months. During this suspension, efforts from both sides intensified in an attempt to overcome the differences, and pave the way for the dialogue to proceed. Examples of those efforts were the regular contacts between the presidency of the European Community and its counterpart on the Arab side. Those contacts culminated in a meeting which took place in Cairo on 18 January 1975.

At the meeting, the European Community delegation was led by representatives from the Irish presidency and the European Commission. The Arab side was led by representatives from the Lebanese presidency and the secretary-general of the Arab League. At the meeting, the European representatives stressed the importance that the Community attached to the Euro-Arab talks. They also expressed their desire to overcome the differences and start the dialogue again. At the end of the meeting, the two sides promised to collaborate and seek ways of continuing with the dialogue. However, despite these efforts, no substantial progress was made. The gap between the two sides, in relation to the PLO, continued.[29]

The stalemate continued until February 1975, when the so-called Dublin formula solved the problem. The formula was called such because the Irish were occupying the presidency of the Community during the first months of 1975. It was worked out during a ministerial meeting which took place in Dublin on

13 February 1975. The meeting was attended by the ministers for foreign affairs of the Nine, together with the president of the European Commission, Francois-Xavier Ortoli, and Ireland's foreign minister and President of the European Council, Garret FitzGerald.[30]

In the course of the meeting, the ministers discussed, *inter alia*, the problem concerning the Euro-Arab dialogue. After long discussions related to the dialogue, the foreign ministers managed to work out a compromise. They proposed to the Arab countries two things, which marked new developments in the Community's position *vis-à-vis* the dialogue. First, the Community suggested that even if the General Commission could not meet soon, it would be possible for the proposed working groups to start the preparatory work. In other words, the Community was proposing that the procedures of the dialogue would be reversed, with the working groups being advanced and the General Commission postponed.

The reason behind the sudden change in the Community's attitude was the feeling that the General Commission would become a forum for political issues. So, to divert attention from the General Commission and concentrate Arab minds on technical matters, while at the same time shifting the onus of responsibility for frustrating the dialogue from the Europeans, the Community proposed that the working groups should start their work.

Secondly, as a way of convincing the Arabs to accept its proposal, the Community kept stressing that the General Commission (because of the problems that had already occurred) was not adequately prepared for the meetings. Hence the Community suggested that the General Committee should be postponed until a proper solution was found. Once the problems of the General Commission had been overcome, it was to meet not on the basis of country delegations but simply as European and Arab delegations. This meant that each side would be free to appoint its delegation members—hiding their national origin in one single delegation. The Community would thus avoid formal recognition of the PLO, while at the same time allowing it to take part in the dialogue. It was agreed that the Irish foreign minister, President of the European Council, Garret FitzGerald, would undertake the responsibility of passing on the Community suggestions to the Arab side.[31]

Following a successful diplomatic effort by Mr FitzGerald in the Middle East, the Arab countries agreed to consider the Community formula. At a meeting on 26 April 1975, the Council of the Arab League (after extensive consultation with the Arab leaders) finally approved the Dublin Formula. The Council then instructed the Secretariat-General to pursue further contacts with the member states of the League. The aim was to hold a meeting of Arab experts, so that they could prepare a joint platform for the imminent Euro-Arab experts' meeting. Member states and the PLO were asked to nominate their experts. At the end of the meeting, it was agreed to set 10 June 1975 as a fixed date for the first Euro-Arab experts' meeting.[32]

THE EEC–ISRAEL AGREEMENT OF MAY 1975

While the preparations for the first Euro-Arab experts' meeting were under way, another obstacle arose which nearly jeopardized the meeting. The crisis concerned the concluding of an association agreement between the European Community and Israel in May 1975. The agreement was the first to be accomplished within the context of the European Mediterranean policy. The essential aim of the agreement was to set up a free trade and economic co-operation between the two sides. In the industrial sector, the agreement provided for the progressive dismantling of all tariff and quota barriers, to be accomplished for all Community imports from Israel by 1 July 1977, for 60 per cent of Israeli imports from the Community by 1 January 1980, and for the remaining 40 per cent by 1 January 1985. Total dismantling of all barriers in this sector would have to be achieved by Israel by 1 January 1989 at the latest.

In agricultural products, the Community made enormous tariff cuts covering about 85 per cent of Israeli's agricultural exports to the Community, mainly traditional products such as citrus fruits and fruit juice. The agreement moreover contained other areas of co-operation such as the stimulation of investment, exchange of technical knowledge, and Israeli participation in scientific and technical ventures between the Nine and other non-member states.

However, the conclusion of the agreement brought an angry reaction from the Arab countries, who protested strongly against it. The Arab governments criticized the Community for not being even-handed and demanded an explanation. They threatened to call off the proposed meeting. Thus, the first Euro-Arab meeting was once again put at risk.[33]

Algeria, Libya and Iraq reacted particularly strongly to the agreement. They led an attempt to persuade other members of the League to suspend the dialogue in protest against the Community's signing of the new trade agreement with Israel.[34] The Kuwaiti deputy foreign minister stressed that the signing of the EEC–Israel agreement would have considerable impact on Euro-Arab relations. In his opinion, the conclusion of the agreement would force the Arabs to review their relations with Common Market countries.[35]

In Brussels, the information committee of the Arab embassies issued a communiqué on 15 May, explaining the Arab position in relation to the Community's agreement with Israel. The communiqué stated that the Arab countries regarded the signing of the agreement as having an essentially political meaning and scope. In their view, the agreement 'has helped Israel to emerge from its international isolation'. It also 'represents both a moral and political encouragement and material and economic support to a country which is occupying by force territories belonging to countries with which the EEC claims to be friends'. This attitude, the communiqué stated, was totally in contrast with the position adopted by the Nine in November 1973. The statement argued that although the Community had only powers in the economic sector, it could 'manipulate the economic argument', and could use its agreements with Israel as a leverage to achieve political concessions for the Arabs. The communiqué cited the example of Greece, when the Community froze its agreement with that country during the colonels' rule. Hence, the Arabs wished that the Community could apply the same method with regard to Israel.[36]

On the more directly economic level, the Arabs inquired whether the Community had made legal reservations as to the territorial field of application of the agreement with Israel, and if the Community had made the necessary provisions to ensure that commodities coming from the occupied Arab areas were not marketed in the Community's market.

The communiqué nevertheless ended by affirming that 'the Arab countries aware of their increasing international responsibilities, remain determined to provide their contribution to the setting up of large-scale co-operation, in the context of a genuine dialogue based on equality, justice, and the interests of all the partners.'[37] However, the spokesman for the Arab League in Brussels stated that this affirmation must not be interpreted as a formal adoption of stance in favour of the opening of the Euro-Arab dialogue on the scheduled date of 10 June. He asserted that the decision on this would be up to the League of Arab States, which would reveal its position at an appropriate time.[38]

Israel's reaction to the agreement, in contrast, was highly positive. The Israeli government considered the accomplishment of the agreement a diplomatic triumph. The Israeli foreign minister, Yigal Allon, stated shortly after the signature that the signing indicated that the Nine were 'not willing to be pushed around'. He added: 'I hope that none of the Nine will individually bow to blackmail.'[39] The foreign minister then suggested that a trade deal which could bring the Arabs and Israelis together within the framework of a common policy would be most helpful economically, psychologically, and politically. 'A little bit of firmness will solve the problem,' said Mr Allon, pointing to the Arab boycott against companies trading with Israel. Mr Allon also affirmed that 'a united Europe cannot be blackmailed, even by oil producers,' stressing that the Community had recovered its nerve since the Arab–Israeli war.[40]

The Community's response to the Arab protest against the agreement with Israel was that the complaint was unjustifiable. In a press conference held on 15 May, M Cheysson, a member of the European Commission, stated that as the Community had already signed an agreement with Israel, it was imperative for the EEC to conclude agreements with the Maghreb countries (Morocco, Tunisia and Algeria) and even with the Mashreq countries (Egypt, Syria, Jordan and Lebanon). In reality, said M Cheysson, the Community Mediterranean policy was in character an overall policy. 'It is a sober political commitment; once the first step has been taken it is urgent and indispensable to take the others, and to overcome existing minor difficulties. I am categorical on this subject,' said M Cheysson.[41]

On this basis, M Cheysson described the critical remarks concerning the conclusion of the agreement with Israel as totally unacceptable. He stated: 'As protests have been made and remarks voiced, l want to put this agreement parallel with what is moreover done with regard to other countries.' He then went on to point out that three Arab League countries (Somalia, Mauritania and Sudan) had signed the Lome Convention with the Community, which offered those countries considerable advantages; two Maghreb countries (Tunisia and Morocco) were associated with the Community, benefiting from a more favourable commercial scheme than that granted to Israel; and the third Maghreb country (Algeria) was offered exemption for all its exports in a substantial part of the Community market (France).[42]

In his statement, M Cheysson stressed that under the new Mediterranean policy, the new agreements to be negotiated with the Maghreb countries would be more favourable than the EEC–Israel agreement. He pointed out that those agreements contained provisions covering financial co-operation as well as the movement of labour. The Nine were 'condemned to succeed' in talks with the Maghreb and had an 'absolute obligation' to negotiate parallel deals with the Arab Mediterranean states. He stated that the agreements to be signed with Egypt, Jordan, Syria and Lebanon would be very much along the lines of the Israeli agreement, although less advantageous than the Maghreb terms.[43] In addition, M Cheysson said that the European Commission had launched exploratory talks with various Arab countries, with the aim of concluding long-term contracts for the supply of foodstuffs that were crucial for those countries. Such contracts would create interdependence. Hence, in his opinion, 'indignation is out of place.'[44]

Explanations also came from Mr FitzGerald, the Irish foreign minister and President of the Community's Council of Ministers, about the EEC–Israel agreement. He defined the scope of the agreement by saying that it did not apply to the occupied Arab territories. Following these clarifications, the crisis concerning the EEC–Israel agreement was overcome. Consequently, the way was open for the Arabs and Europeans to hold the first experts' meeting, scheduled to take place in Cairo on 10 June 1975.[45]

THE EXPERTS' MEETINGS

The Euro-Arab experts' meetings were preceded by a preparatory meeting in Cairo on 15 May 1975. The European Community was represented by Mr E. Gallagher, deputy secretary-general at Ireland's foreign ministry and President of the European Council, and Herr Klaus Meyer, Deputy Secretary-General of the European Commission. The Arab side was represented by Mr Mahmoud Riad, Secretary-General of the Arab League. During the meeting, both sides agreed on 10 June 1975 as a fixed date for the start of the first Euro-Arab experts' meeting.[46]

THE FIRST EXPERTS' MEETING IN CAIRO, 10 JUNE 1975

The Cairo experts' meeting represented a major improvement in the relationship between the Arab world and the European Community. The representatives laid down the objectives and rules of the dialogue. The meeting was also distinguished by the political resolve on both sides to reach, after lengthy preparations, the operational stage of the dialogue. It was attended by a single Arab delegation and one European delegation. The European side was led by Mr Gallagher and Herr Klaus Meyer.[47] The Arab delegation was led by Mr Nihad El-Dajani, representing the Arab presidency, and Mr Mahmoud Riad. During the exchanges of views, each side emphasized the political scope of the dialogue.[48]

In the joint communiqué issued at the end of the meeting, both sides said: 'The Euro-Arab dialogue is the product of a joint political will that emerged at the highest level with a view to establishing a special relationship between the two groups.'[49] It was stated that the dialogue was intended to renew and stimulate the relations between the two regions, eliminate dissension which had caused problems in the past, and place the foundation of future co-operation, embracing a broad area of activities to the benefit of both sides.[50] Furthermore, both sides agreed that the development of economic co-operation between the two regions would contribute towards stability, security and a just peace in the Arab world, and towards world peace and security. It was stressed that setting up such co-operation was inspired by the ties of proximity, common cultural heritage and important complementary interests. Co-operation would lead to the strengthening of existing relations, and to the development of friendship among the states and peoples concerned. It would also open up new horizons in the political, economic, social and cultural spheres.[51] Finally, the two sides agreed to set out the objectives of the dialogue in the following areas of co-operation: agriculture and rural development, industrialization, basic infrastructure, financial co-operation, trade, scientific and technological co-operation, labour and social questions.[52]

THE EUROPEAN PARLIAMENT RESOLUTION OF 10 JULY 1975, CONDEMNING THE PLO MILITARY OPERATION IN JERUSALEM

Two weeks before the second experts' meeting scheduled to take place in Rome on 24 July 1975, the European Parliament on 10 July adopted a resolution threatened to put the experts' meeting at stake. The resolution concerned the military operation launched by the PLO in Jerusalem. On 4 July 1975, a bomb exploded in Zion Square, the main Jewish shopping centre in West Jerusalem. Thirteen people were killed (four were Arabs) and more than 70 injured. Responsibility for the bombing was acknowledged by spokesmen for the Palestine Liberation Organisation in Beirut and Damascus.[53]

In response to the attack, the European Parliament adopted a resolution on 10 July. It was addressed to the parliaments and governments of the member states of the European Community. The resolution condemned the PLO action and expressed the feeling that such a terrorist act would have considerable impact on international peace and security, and on the climate of Euro-Arab relations. Furthermore, it warned against the dangers that might result from such activities. The resolution stated that the house 'condemned all use of force to solve political problems'. The Council of Ministers as well as the European Commission were both instructed to express this sentiment in the Euro-Arab dialogue.[54]

The European Parliament's resolution drew angry reaction from the Arab countries and threatened to create another crisis in Euro-Arab relations. The Arab governments denounced the resolution and regarded the condemnation (by the Parliament) as an attitude that reflected a total partiality to Israel. However, the crisis was overcome at a meeting held in Cairo on 17 July, between the assistant secretary-general of the Arab League (representing the Arab side) and the Italian ambassador (as a representative of the European Community). During the meeting, the representatives discussed the situation in the Middle East and stressed the importance of strengthening the Euro-Arab relations. They also agreed that the second experts' meeting should take place as scheduled in Rome on 24 July 1975.[55]

THE SECOND EXPERTS' MEETING IN ROME, JULY 1975

In accordance with the decision adopted in Cairo on 14 June 1975, a second meeting of Arab and European experts took place in Rome between 22 and 24 July. Although the meeting was at the experts level, the political aspect of the dialogue rose again, when the Arabs reminded the Community of the decision adopted by the European Parliament on 10 July. After a general exchange of views on the state of the dialogue between the two sides, the experts at the Rome meeting concentrated on setting up seven working groups to consider and report in depth on the areas of co-operation agreed upon in the Cairo meeting. Specialized groups, to carry out specific tasks, were set up within the working groups.[56]

At the end of the meeting, both sides restated their common determination to achieve a substantive outcome in the interest of the Arab and European peoples. They agreed that the Rome meeting 'marked the beginning of a more detailed examination of the possibilities of Euro-Arab co-operation and of the exploration of effective channels to advance the dialogue towards its objectives in all fields and to pursue all its purposes'.[57]

THE THIRD EXPERTS' MEETING IN ABU DHABI, 27 NOVEMBER 1975

The meeting opened with a political statement from the Arab side. The Arab representatives blamed the Community for not supporting the United Nations resolution denouncing Zionism. They demanded clarification of the European position with regard to Palestinian rights.[58]

The meeting then took stock of the progress that had been made and the difficulties that had arisen in the areas of co-operation. The working groups (which had met in the meantime) achieved considerable headway in areas related to agriculture, industry and basic infrastructure. In the latter fields some projects had been adopted.[59] They were to be transferred for examination to specialized groups, whose work was to begin after the approval of their mandate and of the related arrangements by the General Committee.[60] In the scientific and technological co-operation sector, both sides exchanged information on matters related to solar and geothermal energy research.

Great difficulties faced the groups dealing with trade, finance and labour affairs.[61] In the field of trade co-operation, the Arab side asked for the signing of a trade convention between the European Community and the entire Arab world. Through this the Community would abolish duties, and all the obstacles to trade, on all Arab exports (without reciprocal concessions from the Arab side), stabilize the earnings of Arab exports, and diversify and promote Arab exports by means of technical assistance, training programmes and trade fairs.[62]

The Europeans did not welcome the Arab demand and argued that the Arabs had already benefited from preference schemes. Somalia, Sudan and Mauritania were members of the Lome Convention; the Maghreb countries (Algeria, Morocco and Tunisia) were negotiating preferential agreements under the Community's overall Mediterranean policy; negotiations were soon to start with the Mashreq countries (Egypt, Jordan, Syria and Lebanon); and the oil-producing countries were in no need of special assistance. The Community argued that the most important Arab exports were covered by the Community system of generalized preferences. Community industry would be damaged if these concessions were given to the Arab countries. Finally, the Community had promised the United States not to extend their preferential system beyond the Mediterranean, and any further expansion would make it difficult for the Community to refuse demands from countries like Iran and Pakistan for similar treatment.[63]

There was also dissension between the two sides regarding financial co-operation. The European Community wanted to encourage Arab investment in Western Europe, whereas the Arab side asked for the protection of their investments from non-commercial risks and refused to offer reciprocal treatment. The European response was not encouraging. Both sides agreed to set up a specialized group to examine possible measures.

The group dealing with labour questions faced considerable problems. The Arab side asked for a convention to safeguard the position of Arab workers in Western Europe, especially their security and social welfare. The European Community was reluctant to discuss the subject at a time of general recession in the West.[64]

With the ending of the Abu Dhabi meeting, the preparatory stage of the dialogue came to an end. In the joint working paper issued at the end of the meeting, both sides agreed that it had 'developed the work done in the previous meetings of Cairo and Rome'.[65] And because they attached great importance to the political aspect of the dialogue, the two sides agreed that it was necessary to convene the General Committee in the near future, at ambassadorial level.[66]

A PRELIMINARY ASSESSMENT

Evaluating this embryonic stage of the dialogue, one can judge it to have been generally successful. Although the achievements were not very impressive, because there were disagreements between the two sides over specific subjects such as trade, finance and labour, some progress was made. The experts from the two sides were well prepared and the meetings proved to be very productive. Many studies on regional projects were discussed in detail. These achievements paved the way for the dialogue to enter a new stage when the two sides (Arab and European) agreed to hold the first meeting of the General Committee at the ambassadorial level in Luxembourg in 1976.

At the political level, the main achievement was the inclusion of the PLO in the Arab delegation, a step which allowed the PLO to play a definite role within the Arab side and sit, for the first time, directly with a European delegation explaining its viewpoint with regard to the dialogue.

THE UNITED STATES ATTITUDE TOWARDS THE DIALOGUE

The United States has never encouraged any independent European role in the Middle East. As a result, its response to the European initiative to open a dialogue with the Arab countries was strong and negative. Antagonisms between the two sides had already reached a climax during the Arab–Israeli war of 1973.

AMERICAN–EUROPEAN DIFFERENCES OVER THE 1973 OCTOBER WAR

During the 1973 October War, the Community refused to coordinate its policies with those of the United States. From the beginning, most of the Community member states made it clear that they did not agree with Washington's assessment of the problem. Hence, in the course of the war, the members of the European Community opposed American policy on two issues: first, the Community members declined to cooperate with the United States in its airlift to Israel; and secondly, they opposed the American decision to put its nuclear weapons on alert on 25 October 1973, without having sought prior advice from its European allies. This matter was crucial for every European country allied with the United States, especially those in which American military bases were situated.[67] They complained that 'they were neither consulted nor informed in advance about the alert.'[68]

Herr Brandt of West Germany wrote to President Nixon explaining that Bonn was not informed in advance about the shipments of arms to Israel through Germany. The West German government, Herr Brandt said, saw this as a threat to its neutral position in the Middle East war.[69] The French prime minister, M Jobert, said that the 'European has been humiliated and treated as a non-person in the US–Soviet Middle East arbitration'.[70] The French ambassador to the United States blamed the United States for excluding the European Community from the efforts to achieve a peaceful settlement.[71] The British prime minister stressed the 'strain' and difficulty besetting the Anglo–American relationship.[72]

In Washington there was an angry reaction to the European response. United States officials complained that most of the European allies, with the exception of Portugal, divorced themselves from American policy of support of Israel in the interest of preserving Europe's flow of oil from the Arab countries. Washington was particularly unhappy that most of the European allies made clear their opposition to allowing American planes bound for Israel either to fly over or to land on their territories.[73] Secretary of State Henry Kissinger stressed his 'disgust' at the European allies,[74] and accused Western Europe of 'acting as though the NATO alliance did not exist'.[75] Defence Secretary Schlesinger raised the idea of withdrawing from Europe: 'West

German protests over the shipment of the US tanks to Israel might force the USA to store the tanks elsewhere.'[76] The State Department spokesman, Robert J. McCloskey, said on 26 October: 'We were struck by the number of our allies going to some lengths in their efforts to separate themselves publicly from the United States.' He stated that United States' support for Israel was just as important for the Western allies as it was for the United States. Mr McCloskey said that the behaviour of the European Community had raised the question of how it can be reconciled with 'their frequent claims of indivisibility in security matters.' He added: 'We are conscious how an oil embargo affects Europe, and are quite aware of the ramifications of that.'[77]

In a major policy speech made in London on 12 December 1973 the US Secretary of State Henry Kissinger spoke of the 'uneasiness' of the United States concerning 'some of the recent practices of the European Community in the political field'. He said: 'To present the decisions of a unifying Europe to us as *faits accomplis* not subject to effective discussion is alien to the tradition of US–European relations.' He went on to say that there was danger of a gradual erosion of the Atlantic Community, which for 25 years had guaranteed peace and prosperity to its nations. Therefore, and in the light of the strains to which NATO had been subjected during the Middle East crisis, the Secretary of State suggested that the revitalization of the Atlantic relationship seemed to be crucial and inevitable.[78] The government of the United States also accused her allies of conducting a 'sycophant' policy in dealing with the Arab countries. It saw the Brussels declaration and the new European initiative as succumbing to Arab 'blackmail', which would hinder the Secretary of State's efforts to achieve a just settlement in the Middle East.[79]

UNITED STATES REACTION TO THE COPENHAGEN STATEMENT

When the European Community agreed in December 1973 on an overall strategy for long-term talks with the Arab countries on economic and energy matters, the United States announced in January 1974 its opposition to the European plan and suggested holding a conference in Washington between the industrialized countries. The aim of the conference was to discuss the energy problem and to find a way to stem the new power of the producer countries. The United States wanted joint multilateral action in which all the industrial countries could coordinate their efforts. This coordination was very important to counteract a new embargo in the future. In the view of Henry Kissinger, joint action by North America, Western Europe and Japan was indispensable to avoid constant crisis and to safeguard the Western world from both the threat of another embargo and the risk of economic collapse. Such a collapse would have a considerable impact on everyone. Wide co-operation would prevent such dangers. It was from this perspective that Mr Kissinger argued that the European Community was too limited a grouping to achieve such a task, whereas the Organisation for Economic Co-operation and Development (OECD) offered a wider and more flexible framework for common action by the developed industrialized countries.[80]

THE WASHINGTON SUMMIT CONFERENCE, FEBRUARY 1974

The initiative to hold a conference was preceeded by a proposal made in London on 12 December by Secretary of State Kissinger. He suggested the establishment of a joint energy action group by the major oil-consuming states to stand against the oil-producing countries. On 10 January, President Nixon sent invitations to eight major oil-consuming countries to attend the so-called Washington conference. These countries were Canada, France, West Germany, Italy, Japan, the Netherlands, Norway and the United Kingdom. Later, invitations were extended to the European Community member states that were not initially approached: Belgium, Denmark, the Irish Republic and Luxembourg.[81]

The main object behind Washington's invitation was to prevent the United States' allies from establishing a dialogue with the Arab world on energy which might lead to the exclusion of the United States.[82]

The European response to the American invitation oscillated between co-operation with OPEC and siding with the United States. The French government rejected the multilateral approach and evinced interest in a bilateral deal with the oil-producing countries. In fact the very idea of the conference was seen by the French government as a clear intervention in its own plan for a special European–Arab relationship. This led the French foreign minister, M Jobert, to describe the United States proposal as only a 'provocation'. The other members of the Community, especially Helmut Schmidt, the foreign minister of West Germany, criticized the 'go-it-alone' policies adopted by some members and favoured joint action with the United States. Herr Schmidt and his government were in complete agreement with Mr Kissinger's view that it was in the best interest of the industrialized countries to have broad measures of consumer co-operation based on a recognition of interdependence. The German government argued that the energy question was a wide issue and had many ramifications. Hence, it was too big to be handled only on a European basis.[83]

Amid this state of crisis which prevailed among the Community member states, the Commission urged the members to try and coordinate their efforts, so that they could agree on a joint reply to the United States' invitation. In mid-January, the Community states concurred that all nine of them should go to the conference, as well as the Community itself being represented by Walter Scheel, then German foreign minister and president of the Council of Ministers. The European Commission was represented by its president, Francois-Xavier Ortoli.

At a meeting on 4 and 5 February, a week before the conference took place, the European Council of Ministers managed to work out a formula based on a joint European position. The formula stressed that the nine foreign ministers had agreed to go to the conference on condition that:

(a) the conference should avoid precipitating a confrontation between the oil producer and consumer countries;
(b) the conference should not be transformed into a 'permanent organism' for international co-operation on energy matters by the industrialized countries;
(c) there should be a commitment to open discussions with the less developed and the producer countries;
(d) the work resulting from the conference should be carried out by means of existing bodies such as the OECD and the IMF.

Within this context, the Nine agreed that they were ready to discuss issues such as the problems of supply, prices, oil-sharing and public control. The Council of Ministers also agreed on a policy of close governmental monitoring of oil movements and prices, a policy which was advocated by the French government. Hence, they moved away from the previous reliance on the oil companies for this information. The coordinated policy adopted by the Nine during this meeting caused the president of the European Commission, M Ortoli, to stress that the United States had managed to push the Community into more European unity on oil in two hours than had been accomplished in the previous ten months.[84]

After the Council of Ministers meeting, the French cabinet issued an official statement on 6 February. It confirmed the French government's position in relation to the Washington conference. It stated that although France had agreed to take part in an exchange of views on the energy crisis, France would by no means support the establishment of 'an organization of oil-consuming industrialized countries independent of other consuming countries, notably developing countries, and of the oil-producing countries'. The statement emphasized the importance that the French government attached to developing a dialogue and co-operation between the producing and consuming countries. Moreover, the statement also confirmed the French government's readiness to engage in both bilateral and multilateral contacts to that end, as for instance between the European Community and the Arab countries.[85]

The conference opened in Washington on 11 February 1974, with the 13 major oil-consuming countries participating. They were represented by their foreign ministers, joined in some cases by their finance ministers and other ministers responsible for energy policy and related questions. The European Community was represented by the president of the European Council and German foreign minister, Walter Scheel, and by the president of the European Commission, M Ortoli, and other Commissioners. The Organisation for Economic Co-operation and Development was represented by its secretary-general, Emil van Lennep.

The conference started with a speech by the American Secretary of State, Henry Kissinger. In the speech, he suggested a seven-point plan for future co-operation on the energy problem. The plan covered conservation, alternative energy sources, research and development, energy sharing, international financial co-operation, the less developed countries and consumer–producer relations.[86]

In the course of the conference, the joint European position which had been adopted during the Council of Ministers' meeting of 4 and 5 February began to fall apart. Wide differences appeared between the French government on the one hand and the rest of the Community members led by the West German government on the other. The French government disagreed with Mr Kissinger's emphasis on a multilateral approach as the solution for the energy problem, and interpreted the prior Council of Ministers' position as clear justification for its refusal to cooperate. The rest of the Community interpreted the Council position as flexible enough to allow support for specific proposals advanced by the United States.

The differences resulted in dramatic personal clashes between the German finance minister, Helmut Schmidt, and Michel Jobert, the French foreign minister. Herr Schmidt emphasized that the energy problem was a broad issue and that Europe alone could not solve it. He referred to political and military links, stressing that the Europeans by themselves 'cannot even maintain a balance on their own continent'. Only the United States had the effective means to accomplish and maintain a settlement in the Middle East.[87]

As a result of these differences, the Washington conference had to be extended for a further day. The outcome was that the conference disregarded the French demand, and the rest of the Community supported the American plan for a broadly-based oil-consumer grouping. The United States, in order to push the Community to accept its energy plan, had started to press hard on security matters (regarded as highly important by most of the Community countries). The Secretary of State and the President of the United States explicitly linked the Community's agreement on the oil issue to the broader question of security and the maintenance of the United States commitment to Europe. In President Nixon's words to the conference, 'Security and economic considerations are inevitably linked and energy can't be separated from either.'[88] Secretary of State Kissinger told the Europeans during the meeting that the United States would reconsider the presence of American troops in Germany if the Europeans did not support the establishment of an energy coordinating group. The strategy of linking security and energy managed to separate the eight Community members from the French and to bring them more closely to the United States position.

The final communiqué of the Washington conference contained not only what the United States had sought (a commitment to conservation, demand restraint, development of alternative energy sources, and co-operation in research and development), but also provided for an emergency oil allocation system in time of future shortages as well as the establishment of a working group to coordinate these measures and present a plan for a cohesive action programme.

The complete text of the communiqué was accepted by all the participating countries except France. The French government protested against the outcome of the conference and characterized the conference as a club representing a group of rich industrialized countries, alienating the Arab oil producers and enabling the reassertion of United States control over Europe. In a radio interview shortly after the conference, the French foreign minister, Michel Jobert, accused the German finance minister of siding with the United States against Europe, adding that only France among the Nine members remained a genuinely European country.[89]

In a statement to the foreign affairs committee of the French national assembly on 21 February, Michel Jobert affirmed that France would not take part in the coordinating group, repeating the view that such a body must not be restricted to the major oil-consuming countries. M Jobert also pointed out that the group's activities would constitute clear intervention in the Community's affairs, because the Community was supposed to be working out its own energy strategy. He stressed that the acceptance of the United States plan by the rest of the Community members amounted to a breach of the mandate for the Washington conference adopted by the Council of Ministers on 4 and 5 February. So when the coordinating group was formally set up at a meeting in Washington on 25 and 26 February, all the original participating countries attended except France, which boycotted the meeting.[90]

UNITED STATES REACTION TO THE COMMUNITY
DECISION OF 4 MARCH 1974

Despite the dramatic outcome of the Washington conference, the French efforts to set up a common European policy to deal directly with the Arab countries did not come to a standstill. The

French government, shortly after the conference, pressed hard for the Community to go ahead with its plan for long-term economic co-operation with the Arab world, which was announced in December 1973 and was overshadowed by the Washington conference. The French efforts bore fruit when, only two and a half weeks after the Washington conference, the EEC Council of Ministers at its meeting on 4 March agreed to a plan for long-term economic, technical, and cultural co-operation between the Community and the Arab states.[91]

The American government's reaction to the Community's decision of 4 March was very vigorous. The United States saw it as a challenge to its energy programme, and an element that might deter its efforts to solve the Middle East problem. Furthermore, the European Council's decision to approach the Arab countries without prior consultation with the United States drew angry reactions from most of the American officials. On 5 March a spokesman of the American State Department stressed that the United States had not conferred beforehand on this plan.[92] The Washington correspondent stated in a dispatch on 12 March that Secretary of State Henry Kissinger had been 'deeply incensed by the European Community's decision to deal directly with the Arab oil-producing countries as a block', stressing the view that this deal had been 'done behind his back'.[93]

In a speech at a press conference in Chicago on 15 March, President Nixon complained that the Community of the Nine had connived against the United States. The president started his press conference by stressing that the European–American alliance was important to the peace of the world. As far as security was concerned, the United States was indispensable to European security—not only through its presence in the continent, but also through its nuclear strength. The Europeans, he went on, could not have it both ways. The day of the one-way street had gone, said Mr Nixon; the United States had been very generous to her allies, and would carry on being so, but whether in the field of trade or any other field, it was crucial that the United States had 'a fair break' for its own producers, just as the United States tries to give a fair break to European producers. He said: 'We cannot have in Europe, for example, confrontation on the economic and political front and co-operation on the security front.'[94] He threatened that if the United States was going to be faced with hostility from the Nine, then he would find it difficult to convince Congress to give full support for a continued American presence at a reasonable level on the security front, adding that the American government 'would no longer permit itself to be faced with a situation where the nine countries in Europe gang up against the United States'.[95] Mr Nixon asserted that the time had come for the United States and Europe to decide whether they were going to go along together or go separately.[96]

Further criticism was also made by the president on 19 March at a press conference in Houston, Texas. In a reference to American–European relations, the president stated, *inter alia*, that discussions about such relations in the economic and political fields had not gone well. This was, he said, because the American allies, at times, had not consulted with the United States fully, or on time, and had in some areas taken a position that was hostile to the United States at a time when the United States provided the security shield for the Community. He said: 'We can at least expect from our European allies that they will consult with us and not work actively against us in the political field or the economic field.'[97]

THE EUROPEAN RESPONSE TO THE AMERICAN CRITICISMS

The European response to criticisms by the United States was one of assurance. At a meeting of Gaullist deputies on 17 March in Nogent-sur-Marne, the French foreign minister commented on Mr Nixon's complaints. M Jobert stressed that there had been 'no lack of consultation with the Americans, both on the bilateral governmental level and between the Common Market and Washington'. France, he said, would carry on this policy and hoped that others would follow suit. He stated that international friendship would exist only if there was 'frankness, flexibility and respect for others'.[98] Moreover, in order to ease American fears, the Europeans continued to stress that the Community initiative in the area would not hinder United States efforts towards a Middle East settlement. In March 1974, the French ambassador in Washington commented: 'It is absurd to imagine that the Euro-Arab project of co-operation could jeopardise the American efforts in the Middle East.'[99] The British foreign secretary, James Callaghan, said in March: 'I assume neither the Community nor the Arab States themselves want that dialogue to hamper Kissinger's efforts to ensure measure of peace in the Middle East.'[100] On 11 March 1974, the West German government stated that it did not see the European initiative as an alternative to the Washington energy committee or as an action in any way likely to undermine Kissinger's search for a Middle East peace settlement.[101]

To reassure the American administration, the West German government suggested in March that a procedure should be set up whereby senior United States officials could be invited to take part in discussions with representatives of the Community, whenever a question affecting United States interests was about to be the subject of a decision by the European Council of Ministers. The proposal was discussed with Mr Kissinger in Bonn on 24 March during his stopover to Moscow. On 2 April the European Council of Ministers took stock of the proposal, but no agreement was reached. The French government opposed the idea of formal consultation with the United States.[102] It insisted that consultation with the United States should take place only after decisions had been taken.[103]

The rest of the Community members, led by the British government, emphasized that the principle of 'prior consultation' between the Western alliance, on everything related to matters of 'major importance', must be respected.[104] The British foreign secretary, Mr Callaghan, told the Council that his government would support the Community's plan for dialogue with the Arab countries only on condition that there would be 'full, frank and reciprocal discussions' with the United States at every stage.[105]

Afterwards the United States stepped up its efforts in the nine countries, in an attempt to persuade the Community to accept the formula of prior consultation. The American pressure achieved results when the question was considered at an informal meeting of the Nine's foreign ministers held at Schloss-Gymmich, near Bonn, on 21 and 22 April at the invitation of Herr Scheel. During the meeting, the foreign ministers consented to a formula according to which consultation with the United States would be accomplished through creating an 'organic consultative relationship'. This would guarantee that the Nine would not pass any important resolutions that might affect United States interests or American policy in the Middle East, without prior consultation with the United States. The agreement on this formula was to be known later as the 'gentlemen's agreement of Gymmich'.

The content of the agreement was given by the German foreign minister, Hans-Dietrich Genscher, at his press conference on 11 June.[106] The ministers, he said, were agreed that in elaborating common positions on foreign policy, there arose the question of consultation with allied or friendly countries. Such consultations, he said, were a matter of course in any modern foreign policy. Hence, they agreed on a pragmatic approach in each individual case, which meant that the country holding the presidency would be authorized by the other eight members to conduct consultations on behalf of the Nine. Therefore, in practice, if any member of the Community raised, within the context of European political co-operation, the question of informing and consulting an ally or a friendly state, the Nine would first discuss the matter. Once agreement was reached, they would authorize the presidency to proceed on that basis.[107] Finally, he said, 'the ministers are confident that this informal gentlemen's agreement will in practice lead to flexible and pragmatic consultations with the United States which will intelligently allow for the interests of both sides.'[108]

The question of prior consultation, as well as the energy problem, were further considered during the Martinique summit meeting in December 1974 (between the French president, Giscard d'Estaing, and the President of the United States). In the course of the meeting, the two sides stressed the importance they attached to prior consultation between the Western allies. During the meeting, the French government also agreed to coordinate its efforts with the Coordinating Working Group that was established during the Washington energy conference. Thus, the United States managed to empty the dialogue of any matter that might affect its interests in such an important area as the Middle East.[109]

NOTES

1. Corrado Pirzio-Biroli, 'Foreign Policy Formation within the European Community with Special Regard to the Developing Countries', in L. Hurewitz (ed.), *Contemporary Perspectives on European Integration*, p. 242.
2. D. Allen, 'The Euro-Arab Dialogue', *Journal of Common Market Studies*, Vol. 16, 1977–1978, p. 328.
3. *The New York Times*, 5 March 1974.

4. *The Times*, 5 March 1974.
5. *Keesing's Contemporary Archives*, 3–9 June 1974, p. 26, 546.
6. S. A. Al-Mani, and S. Al-Shaikly, *The Euro-Arab Dialogue*, pp. 48–9.
7. *Bulletin of the European Community*, 6, 1974, pp. 123–4.
8. H. Maull, *Europe and World Energy*, p. 285.
9. *Bulletin of the European Community*, 7/8, 1974, p. 2,503.
10. P. Taylor, *When Europe Speaks with One Voice: the External Relations of the European Community*, Aldwych Press, London, 1979, p. 96.
11. *Bulletin of the European Community*, 7/8, 1974, p. 2504.
12. *Keesing's Contemporary Archives*, 4–10 November, 1974, p. 26,799.
13. A. R. Taylor, 'Europe and the Arab: How to Bridge the Gap', *Middle East International*, February 1977, p. 11.
14. S. A. Hatem, *The Possibility of Economic Co-operation and Integration between the European Community and the Arab League*, p. 116.
15. *The European Community and the Arab World*, Commission of the European Communities, p. 42.
16. *Eighth General Report on the Activities of the European Community in 1974*, Office for Official Publications of the European Communities, Luxembourg, 1975, p. 253.
17. *Bulletin of the European Community*, 10, 1974, p. 2505.
18. A. S. Al-Dajani, *The Euro-Arab Dialogue*, Research Centre, Palestine Liberation Organization, Beirut, 1981, p. 6.
19. *Keesing's Contemporary Archives*, November 18–24, 1974, p. 26,813.
20. *Ibid*.
21. R. H. Ullman, 'After Rabat: Middle East Risks and American Role', *Foreign Affairs*, Vol. 53, No. 2, January 1975, p. 284.
22. A. S. Al-Dajani, *The Euro-Arab Dialogue*, p. 9.
23. *The European Community and the Arab World*, Commission of the European Communities, p. 43.
24. G. Dhanani, 'The Euro-Arab Dialogue: A Critique', in K. B. Lall, W. Ernst and H. S. Chopra (eds.), *The EEC in the Global System*, Allied Publishers Private Limited, New Delhi, 1984, p. 174.
25. A. S. Al-Dajani, *The Euro-Arab Dialogue*, pp. 7–8.
26. All cited in *ibid*, p. 8.
27. *Ibid*, p. 8.
28. *Keesing's Contemporary Archives*, May 19–25, 1974, p. 27,131.
29. *The European Community and the Arab World*, Commission of the European Communities, p. 43.
30. *Bulletin of the European Community*, 2, 1975, pp. 87–88.
31. D. Allen 'The Euro-Arab Dialogue', *Journal of Common Market Studies*, p. 333.
32. *The European Community and the Arab World*, Commission of the European Communities, p. 43.
33. *Keesing's Contemporary Archives*, p. 27,132.
34. *Keesing's Contemporary Archives*, 13 February 1976, p. 27,571.

35. *Europe*, Agence Internationale d'Information Pour La Presse, Brussels, 12–13 May 1975.
36. *Europe*, Agence Internationale d'Information Pour La Presse, 15 May 1975.
37. *Ibid*.
38. *Ibid*.
39. *Financial Times*, 13 May 1975.
40. *Ibid*.
41. *Europe*, 15 May 1975.
42. *Ibid*.
43. *Financial Times*, 13 May 1975.
44. *Europe*, 15 May 1975.
45. *Europe*, 9/10 June 1975.
46. *Bulletin of the European Communities*, 5, 1975, pp. 97–8.
47. *Bulletin of the European Communities*, 6, 1975, p. 109.
48. *Europe*, 10 June 1975.
49. *The Euro-Arab Dialogue*, Joint Memorandum, Cairo, 14 June 1975.
50. *Trade and Industry*, 5 November, p. 368.
51. *The Euro-Arab Dialogue*.
52. *Bulletin of the European Communities*, 6, 1975, p. 109.
53. *Keesing's Contemporary Archives*, 21–27 July 1975, p. 27,233. Also, *The Financial Times*, 5 July 1975.
54. *Bulletin of the European Communities*, 7/8, 1975, pp. 86–7.
55. A. M. Saied, *Al-hiwar al-arabi al-urubi*, (The Euro-Arab Dialogue), Centre for Political and Strategic Studies, Cairo, 1977, p. 103.
56. *The Euro-Arab Dialogue*, Joint Working Paper, Rome, 24 July 1975.
57. *Bulletin of the European Communities*, 7/8, 1975, p. 111.
58. H. Maull, *Europe and World Energy*, p. 286.
59. *Europe*, 28 November 1975.
60. *Bulletin of the European Communities*, 11, 1975, p. 84.
61. H. Maull, *Europe and World Energy*, p. 286.
62. *Financial Times*, 25 November 1975.
63. *Ibid*.
64. H. Maull, *Europe and World Energy*, p. 286.
65. *Bulletin of the European Communities*, 10, 1975, p. 90.
66. *The Euro-Arab Dialogue*, Joint Working Paper, Abu Dhabi, 27 November 1975.
67. *The New York Times*, 31 October 1973.
68. *International Herald Tribune*, 14 November 1973.
69. *The Times*, 3 November 1973.
70. *International Herald Tribune*, 16 Novemeber 1973.
71. *Daily Star*, 28 March 1974.
72. Ibrahim Sus, 'Western Europe and the October War', *Journal of Palestine Studies*, p. 80.
73. *Keesing's Contemporary Archives*, 14–20 January 1974, p. 26,294.
74. *International Herald Tribune*, 1 November 1973.
75. *Daily Star*, 3 Novemeber 1973.

76. *International Herald Tribune*, 10 Novemeber 1973.
77. *Keesing's Contemporary Archives*, p. 26,294.
78. *Ibid*, p. 26,293.
79. *Guardian*, 7 November 1973.
80. R. J. Lieber, *Oil and the Middle East War: Europe in the Energy Crisis*, p. 40.
81. *Keesing's Contemporary Archives*, 1–7 April 1974, p. 26,429.
82. A. S. Al-Dajani, 'The PLO and the Euro-Arab Dialogue', *Journal of Palestine Studies*, Vol. IX, No. 3, 1980, p. 84.
83. R. J. Lieber, *Oil and the Middle East War: Europe in the Energy Crisis*, p. 22.
84. *Ibid*, pp. 20–1.
85. *Keesing's Contemporary Archives*, p. 26,429.
86. *Ibid*.
87. R. J. Lieber, *Oil and the Middle East War: Europe in the Energy Crisis*, p. 22.
88. *Ibid*, p. 23.
89. *Ibid*, pp. 22–49.
90. *Keesing's Contemporary Archives*, p. 26,430.
91. *The New York Times*, 5 March 1974.
92. S. A. Al-Mani and S. Al-Shaikly, *The Euro-Arab Dialogue*, p. 125.
93. *Keesing's Contemporary Archives*, p. 26,458.
94. *Ibid*, p. 26,457.
95. *The Times*, 16 March 1974.
96. *Ibid*.
97. *The Times*, 20 March 1974.
98. *Keesing's Contemporary Archives*, p. 26,457.
99. *Guardian*, 27 March 1974.
100. *Daily Star*, 20 March 1974.
101. *The Financial Times*, 12 March 1974.
102. *Keesing;s Contemporary Archives*, p. 26,546.
103. *International Herald Tribune*, 11 June 1974.
104. A. S. Al-Dajani, *The Euro-Arab Dialogue*, p. 11.
105. *Keesing's Contemporary Archives*, p. 26,546.
106. Udo Steinbach, 'The European Community and the United States in th Arab World', in H. Shaked and I. Rabinovich (eds.), *The Middle East and the United States*, New Brunswick, New Jersey, and London, 1980, p. 130.
107. *Ibid*.
108. *Bulletin of the European Communities*, 6, 1974, p. 124.
109. For More Details see Panayiotis Ifestos, *European Political Co-operation: Towards a Framework of Supranational Diplomacy?*, pp. 181–3.

IV

THE SUBSTANTIVE STAGE: THE GENERAL

COMMITTEE MEETINGS (1976–1978)

During the experts' meeting in Abu-Dhabi on 27 November 1975, the two parties to the dialogue agreed that the previous meetings had accomplished their objectives, and that it was time to transfer the dialogue into more practical co-operation. Both sides expressed the wish to convene the General Committee in the near future; they agreed that the political aspect of the dialogue should be borne in mind for it to attain its intended objectives.[1] Thus the joint working paper issued at the end of the Abu-Dhabi meeting signalled the completion of the preparatory stage of the dialogue and marked the beginning of a new, operational, stage. This started formally with the first meeting of the General Committee held in Luxembourg between 18 and 20 May 1976.[2] It was agreed to adopt the 'Dublin formula' of the experts' meetings: two delegations, one European and the other Arab, where each side would be free to choose its representatives, hiding their national identities in one single delegation. Moreover, it was agreed that the participants in the General Committee meetings were to be generally of ambassadorial rank.[3]

The first meeting of the General Committee was preceded by preparatory meetings on both sides, Arab and European. The aims of these were to reach a unified attitude towards the forthcoming Committee meeting. The Arab preparatory meeting took place shortly before the General Committee meeting. During it, the Arab representatives agreed on a unified position to be adopted. They also stressed the importance of the political aspect of the dialogue and the need to have a common attitude on this matter. In the course of the meeting, the PLO delegation was very active in promoting concern with the political aspect of the dialogue. The PLO delegation, which was chaired by Al-Dajani, defined the tasks to be performed at the General

Committee as being 'to initiate the political aspect of the dialogue which we have been waiting to discuss for eight months'.[4] The Arab representatives decided to charge the head of the PLO with responsibility for writing the Arab side's speech and chairing the drafting committee which was to agree with the European side on the joint communiqué at the end.[5]

On the European side, the Community position was formulated during the meeting of foreign ministers which took place in Brussels on 3 May.[6] When the European Community conceded that the Arab countries would raise political issues (such as the Arab–Israeli conflict) in the General Committee meeting, the foreign ministers of the Nine decided to reach a position in relation to the political aspect of the dialogue.[7] They agreed that the dialogue in principle would need to have a political scope. But having emphasized that, it was stressed that the dialogue must not develop into a forum to discuss political issues such as the Middle East conflict and the Palestinian question.[8]

THE FIRST GENERAL COMMITTEE MEETING, LUXEMBOURG MAY 1976

The first meeting of the General Committee, which took place in Luxembourg from 18 to 20 May 1976, was regarded by both Arab and European officials as the real start of co-operation between the European Community and the Arab world.[9] Also, it was considered (by Arab and European representatives) very significant because the status of the representatives at the meeting was that of ambassador. Moreover, the Luxembourg meeting paved the way for the political aspect of the dialogue to be accepted by both sides.[10]

The Arab delegation to the meeting was led by Mr Abd Al-Aziz Al-Shamlan, President of the Council of the League of Arab States, accompanied by Mr Mahmoud Riad, the secretary-general of the Arab League, and Dr A. S. Al-Dajani, representative of the PLO. The European delegation was chaired by M Jean Wager, the ambassador of Luxembourg to Rome—the capital of the country occupying the office of President of the European Council—accompanied by Herr Klaus Meyer, Deputy Secretary-General of the European Commission.[11] During the meeting, talks began on both political matters (which some European representatives wanted to avoid) as well as economic issues.

POLITICAL MATTERS

In general the Arabs were preoccupied with the political aspect of the dialogue, whereas the Community wanted to concentrate on the economic and technical sides of the talks. The main objective of the Arab countries was to try and make the Community more committed to the Palestine question. It was reported that the representatives of some specific Arab countries (the radicals) were particularly strongly in favour of this trend. They even threatened that unless the Community adopted a strong political stance they were prepared to allow the meeting to fail. Indeed the Arab countries showed remarkable unity and common interest in the political dimension of the dialogue.[12] In the course of the meeting, a comprehensive political discussion did in fact take place for the first time. There was an exchange of viewpoints between the parties on the Palestine question and the Middle East crisis.

On the Arab side, the participants underlined the importance that the Arab countries attached to the dialogue, and demanded total frankness. They explained the situation in the area after the 6 November declaration, emphasizing the continued Israel occupation of Arab lands, Israel's oppressive policy towards the Palestinian people, and Israel's policy of building up new settlements. The Arabs urged the Community to oppose Israeli occupation, to follow an economic policy which could thwart Israel's expansion, to express their condemnation of Israel's continuing defiance of world opinion on the Middle East, and to stop arms shipments to Israel.[13] Taking into consideration the declaration of the Nine on 6 November 1973, the Arabs stressed the contradiction between this declaration and the Community's behaviour in respect to Israel: specifically the signature of a preferential trade agreement and the opening of discussions for the conclusion of a financial protocol.[14]

The Arab side criticized the European approach to the Arab–Israel conflict, and refused to accept the European view that the policy of the Community was justified inasmuch as this view embodied a policy of balance between Israel and the Arabs.[15] Moreover, the Arabs declared their dissatisfaction with the way the Community dealt with the Palestinian question and its hesitation in adopting a decisive attitude in this matter. 'We ascertain an unjustifiable hesitation to sympathize with the question of the Palestinian people and to call things by their name,' said the PLO representative, Dr Al-Dajani.[16] They demanded full recognition of the PLO and recognition of the right of the Palestinian people to return to their homeland. Dr Al-Dajani asked the European delegation: 'Has not the moment come for the European Community to recognize the PLO which represents the Palestinian people and which directs its revolution?'[17] The Arab side pointed out that force and acceptance of a *fait accompli* were not conducive to stable international relations, and that a just and lasting peace in the Middle East required the following measures to be fulfilled:

(1) withdrawal by Israel from the occupied territories;
(2) recognition of the national rights of the Palestinian people;
(3) participation of the Palestine Liberation Organization, the representative of the Palestinian people, in all international peace efforts.[18]

On the European side, the representatives reaffirmed the four points of the Community's declaration of 6 November 1973, as well as the points embodied in the Community's statement of 10 December 1975. They confirmed that these principles remained the basic foundation for a just and lasting peace in the Middle East, and expressed the firm hope that progress could be made towards this goal. They stressed their readiness to do all in their power to contribute to its accomplishment.[19] The Europeans demonstrated their interest in keeping the Mediterranean region away from the Arab–Israeli conflict and proclaimed that the Palestine question was an urgent problem. They stated: 'The Nine countries believe that the problem at present is of the recognition of the right of the Palestinian people to express their national identity.'[20]

In the joint communiqué issued at the end of the meeting, both sides voiced their concern about the dangerous situation prevailing in the Middle East and its threat to international peace and security. They confirmed their commitment to peace, security and justice, in accordance with the principles of the United Nations Charter. Both sides also expressed their intention to carry on the dialogue in the future and determined some of the specific terms of their co-operation. The two parties affirmed the ties that linked Europe to the Arab world, by virtue of geographical proximity and the interchange between the two civilizations. They agreed that these links, as well as common interests and closer relationships between the two regions, should lead to a better understanding between the two parties to the dialogue. They emphasized that recognition of the legitimate rights of the Palestinian people was an important factor to accomplish a durable, just and lasting peace, and hoped that a Euro-Arab meeting on the level of foreign ministers could take place at the appropriate time.[21]

THE ECONOMIC ASPECT OF THE DIALOGUE: THE ACTIVITIES OF THE WORKING COMMITTEES

It was agreed that improving the economy was a common goal for both sides, and crucial to a successful, dynamic and lasting co-operation between them. To achieve this aim everything possible should be done. In this context, it was agreed to hold regular exchanges of views on economic questions. After approving the recommendations of the experts meetings, the General Committee took stock of the stage reached in the various fields of co-operation. The General Committee, according to the final communiqué, noticed the progress achieved and managed to formalize the priorities laid down at the Rome and Abu-Dhabi meetings. Also, the General Committee took note of a list of important projects proposed by the European side as fields in which early progress was possible. These included the setting up of a widespread spatial and non-spatial telecommunication network connecting a number of Arab countries; the improvement of transport facilities in the Arab countries; rural development of the southern Darfur region of the Sudan; measures of trade promotion; setting up of a polytechnic institute in the Arab world with the aim of preparing middle-level training in a broad range of technical specialties; and the fulfilment of a comprehensive geological survey of the main regions of the Arab world with the aim of improving the future development of natural resources.

In addition, the following projects were proposed by the European side: the setting up of a close working relationship between a wide rank of cultural and scientific institutions in the Arab world and in the European countries; training of researchers, exchange of information and joint research projects in the field of solar energy; the organizing of a symposium on the relations between the two civilizations and of seminars on cultural topics; and the provision of training in a wide number of fields discussed in the working committees.[22] There were also to be studies carried out relating to mutual investments, conditions for the protection of foreign investments and the general outlines of finance contracts.[23]

The General Committee paid special attention to the following sectors:

Trade

The General Committee stressed the importance it attached to promoting and diversifying trade between the two parties. Hence, it instructed the trade working committee to find a proper basis of mutual co-operation in this sector.

Transfer of technology

The General Committee affirmed the importance of the transfer of technology on appropriate terms as an important element for co-operation, and promised to develop a suitable way to deal with it in the framework of the dialogue.

Labour and social affairs

The General Committee took notice of the proposals submitted by the European side concerning the principles governing the living and working conditions of foreign workers. It recommended that the working Committee concerned should study the draft to be submitted by the European side in this respect, for passing on to the General Committee after approval. Furthermore, the General Committee stressed that special attention should be drawn to the questions related to the different aspects of vocational training.[24]

The financing question

The General Committee took stock of the question of financing the activities of the dialogue. It approved the principles of joint financial contributions for the co-operation projects defined in the dialogue.[25]

The structure of the dialogue

The meeting also dealt with the 'institutionalization' of the dialogue so as to ensure that the work would be followed up effectively and on a regular basis.[26] It was agreed to make the General Committee a permanent, supreme and coordinating body for the dialogue. It could meet twice a year at ambassadorial level and might meet at the foreign ministerial level. The working committees were also to become a permanent feature.[27] Finally, the General Committee urged the authorities in the countries concerned to facilitate the work of the different bodies of the dialogue. It also hoped that the Secretariat-General of the Arab League and the Commission of the European Communities would ensure the continuous flow of essential information in order to guarantee the proper functioning of all working bodies of the dialogue.[28]

THE SECOND GENERAL COMMITTEE MEETING, TUNIS FEBRUARY 1977

The second meeting of the General Committee took place in Tunis from 10 to 12 February 1977. Shortly before the meeting, the Arabs and the Europeans made some positive financial commitments in relation to the dialogue. On the Arab side, the Arab ministers of foreign affairs at the meeting of the Council of the League of Arab states on 15 January 1977 agreed to allocate the sum of $350,000 for financing the preliminary feasibility studies and other activities of the dialogue.[29] On the European side the Nine's foreign ministers, during their meeting in Brussels on 8 February 1977, adopted a resolution in which they accepted the principles of co-financing the dialogue and confirmed the Community's financial contribution to the activities of the dialogue. The exact sum of the Community's financial contribution had to be fixed later, due to the differences among Community members on how much they could contribute in this respect.[30] The financial commitments from both sides gave impetus to the dialogue and created optimism that the forthcoming Tunis meeting would result in some tangible achievements.

However, the definition of respective positions in relation to the Tunis meeting occurred, on both sides, shortly before the joint meeting. At a meeting on 8 February 1977, the 'Arab Committee', the organ responsible for coordinating the Arab position in the General Committee, decided to adopt a unified position in the joint General Committee meeting. The Arab side also endorsed the draft communiqué prepared by the leader of the Palestinian delegation, who was charged with the tasks of speaking on behalf of the Arab side in Committee A, which was to debate political issues, and of delivering the final complementary communiqué.[31]

The Community position was formulated during the meeting of the Nine's foreign ministers in Brussels on 8 February 1977. During this meeting, the foreign ministers agreed on a joint position to be adopted in relation to various subjects which were to be discussed in the Tunis meeting. Among the subjects agreed upon special attention was given to trade and social issues.[32]

The composition of the delegations to the Tunis meeting was as follows: the European delegation was chaired by Mr Richard Faber, Under-Secretary of State at the British Foreign Office, and Herr Klaus Meyer, Deputy Secretary-General of the European Commission. The Arab delegation was led by Mr Ismail Khalil, head of the Tunisian mission to the European Communities, and Mr Hussein Khallaf, Assistant Secretary-General of the League of Arab States.[33]

In the meeting, both sides re-stated the importance they attached to the dialogue and confirmed their sincere intentions to strengthen its procedures. An exchange of views took place on all areas of Euro-Arab co-operation in the political, economic, social and cultural fields.[34]

THE POLITICAL ASPECT OF THE DIALOGUE

The Arab statement dealt mainly with the political issues. It gave a detailed exposé of past Zionist policy concerning the building up of new settlements in the occupied lands and the ill-treatment of Arabs in Israel and the occupied territories, assessing at the same time European policy *vis-à-vis* the area. The statement then pointed out that the European states did not manage to put principles into practice.

The European statement, on the other side, underlined the advance that had occurred in the European attitude. In reply to the Arab statement, the European side stressed that the Community would not allow others to determine what kind of relationship the Community should maintain with Israel. The Arabs emphasized that it was imperative to deal with all aspects of Euro-Arab relations, including the Community's relations with Israel, and to put into effect principles endorsed and agreed upon.[35] The Arabs asked the Community again for full recognition of the PLO and to recognize the right of the Palestinian people to return to their own home, urging the Community member states to do their best to ensure the return of the occupied lands from Israel. In the course of the meeting, the Arab side suggested the following measures: setting up a Euro-Arab consultation mechanism in the United Nations, the creation of a committee within the dialogue to discuss political matters, and the participation of Arab countries in the Belgrade Conference (Conference for Security and Co-operation in Europe—the follow-up to Helsinki). The European response to the Arab proposals was only to promise to study the second suggestion carefully.[36]

In the joint communiqué that was issued at the end of the meeting, both sides expressed their worries about security in the Middle East and its threat to the security of Europe and the world in general. The Arab and the European representatives stressed their 'full awareness of the dangers inherent in the persistence of the current stalemate' of the situation in the area. A common interest was expressed for the establishment of a just and lasting peace in the Middle East. The two parties restated that a solution to the Palestine question based on the recognition of the legitimate rights of the Palestinian people, was a decisive factor in achieving a just and lasting peace in the area.[37]

The European side confirmed its belief that the principles embodied in the Brussels declaration of 6 November 1973, as elaborated since then in statements made by the Community, formed the essential elements of a peaceful solution to the Middle East conflict, and that these principles must be taken as a whole. The European representatives reaffirmed their view that the 'solution of the conflict in the Middle East will be possible only if the legitimate right of the Palestinian people to give effective expression to its national identity is translated into fact'.[38] They went on to record the Community's opposition to the occupation of Arab lands by Israel, stressing that the Nine still maintained that the Fourth Geneva Convention was applicable to the occupied areas. The Community registered its refusal to accept any unilateral change to the status of Jerusalem, emphasizing that such alteration would only inhibit the chance for peace. The Community states also confirmed their opposition to the establishment of new settlements by Israel in the occupied territories.[39]

THE ECONOMIC ASPECT: THE ACTIVITIES OF THE
WORKING COMMITTEES

The Tunis meeting made some important headway. The working committees and the specialized groups made considerable progress in special areas. During the meeting, the General Committee reviewed the work done by the different working committees and managed to lay down the guidelines for the future work of the experts. One of the major areas considered was the question of financing the activities of the dialogue. The General Committee agreed to establish an *ad hoc* group. It was charged with the task of working out the procedures necessary for utilizing the financial contributions which both sides promised to make, in order to finance the preliminary and feasibility studies and other activities of the dialogue.[40] The group was to submit its report to the Secretariat-General of the League of Arab States and to the Commission of the European Community by 31 July 1977, so that both sides would be able to examine the report at the following meeting of the General Committee.[41] As regards co-operation in other fields, special attention was paid by the General Committee to the following sectors:

Transfer of technology

A reasonable advance was made in this field. The European side circulated a memorandum that listed the Community's ideas on the best way to deal with this sector. The memorandum suggested the following specific steps:

(1) collaboration in an assessment of the needs of Arab states and regions;
(2) setting up education programmes in European institutions, co-operation with European and Arab institutions, and programmes of sending European experts and teachers to the Arab countries;

(3) exchange of information;
(4) adaptation of technology to Arab needs;
(5) support and assistance in feasibility studies and in the development of research capacities in the Arab world.[42]

The General Committee stressed the importance of the transfer of technology and agreed in principle to establish a Euro-Arab centre for such transfer between the two regions.[43] It also agreed to set up an *ad hoc* group composed, on the Arab side, of the president and the members and experts of the Working Committee on Scientific and Technological Co-operation, and on the European side of the members of the Industrialization Working Committee and members and experts of the Working Committee on Scientific and Technological Co-operation. The *ad hoc* group was charged with the task of drafting a joint declaration on the transfer of technology between the two sides, and of elaborating recommendations for setting up a centre for Euro-Arab transfer of technology. The General Committee instructed the *ad hoc* group to submit its report on this matter to the Secretariat-General of the League of Arab States and to the Commission of the European Communities by 31 July 1977, in order that it could be examined at the following meeting of the General Committee.[44]

Trade co-operation

No tangible progress was achieved in this area. The Arabs reiterated their demand for special preferential trade relations with Europe, through a collective agreement composed of all the Arab countries. The European response was negative. The Nine continued to reject this demand, arguing that the Community already had preferential trade agreements with half of the Arab League countries. Four of these—Somalia, Sudan, Mauritania and Djibouti—had signed preferential trade agreements under the Lome Convention. The Community had also signed preferential trade agreements with Algeria, Morocco and Tunisia in 1976, and with Egypt, Jordan, Syria and Lebanon in 1977. All these agreements were accomplished under the Community Mediterranean policy. The oil-producing countries, the Community stressed, did not need preferential trade agreements because the Community had a trade deficit with them due to its large imports of oil from these countries.[45] Instead the

Community stressed its readiness to conclude individual non-preferential agreements with other Arab countries with whom it had no links at the time.[46]

The General Committee recommended that the Working Committee on Trade should carry on with the aim of finding solutions that would be acceptable to both parties.[47] The European side took note of the Arab demand for the establishment of a 'Euro-Arab Trade Co-operation Centre'. It was therefore agreed that the specific terms of reference for a Euro-Arab trade co-operation would carefully be studied.[48]

Financial co-operation

In the field of financial co-operation progress was limited, because there was disagreement over the question of protection of investments. The European side wanted to encourage the investment of Arab petrodollars in the Community countries. The Arab side demanded that their investments in the Community must be guaranteed against commercial risks such as inflation and falling exchange. This demand was rejected by the Europeans; none of the Nine was even willing to consider it.

In order to overcome the difference of opinion on this subject, the General Committee instructed the Working Committee on Financial Co-operation to lay the groundwork for a Euro-Arab convention between the two sides on the protection of investment against non-commercial risks.[49] The convention would complement the existing and future bilateral agreements between member countries of the Community and of the Arab League. It was stressed that the convention would not prejudice any more restrictive provisions in those agreements. The Sub-Group on Investment Protection was instructed to consider a broad definition of the term 'investment', to include portfolio investments, short-term investments and monetary claims.

In addition, the General Committee asked the Working Committee on Financial Co-operation to first present it with a summary of the conditions laid down by the laws on foreign investment in force in the Arab and European countries. Secondly, it was asked to submit to it a proposal for a decision concerning the dissemination of this information, in order to furnish the investors on both sides with practical information they might need. The General Committee took notice of the monetary risks facing Arab assets in the Community, and recommended that the Working Committee on Financial Co-operation must continue consultation on possible arrangements that could be taken to reduce such risks.[50]

Labour and cultural matters

In the realm of the labour issue, the Community showed interest in raising the standard of living of Arab workers in the Community countries. To this end, the General Committee asked the working committee concerned to specify the principles that should govern the living and working conditions of the Arab workers employed in the Community, and to lay the basis for co-operation on vocational training.[51]

In the cultural sphere, the working committee was directed to provide a list of institutions involved in the study of language, culture and civilization of the other area; to facilitate the exchange of history books to eliminate misunderstanding between the two regions; and finally to draw up a programme for co-operation in the information sector.[52]

Agriculture

A positive result was achieved in this area. It was agreed that the Arabs and Europeans should jointly finance the feasibility studies for four projects to be launched in the Arab countries. These projects were the development of the Juba Valley in Somalia; the Damazine meat development project in Sudan; the Southern Darfur integrated development project in Sudan; and a potato development project in Iraq.[53]

Industrialization

The progress in this area was very limited. The thorny point was the contradictory interests over refinery and petrochemical projects. The Arab countries put strong emphasis on industrialization so that their economies in the future would depend on their indigenous industries. For this reason, the Arabs wanted to expand their petroleum refining facilities as a first step towards wider industrialization.

The European side did not accept the idea, arguing that building up new projects in the Arab world or making progress in these fields would lead in the long term to surplus production and upset the balance between supply and demand. This would create rivalry between the European Community and the Arab world, and could seriously disrupt the European economy. This is true because the availability of low-cost crude oil and surplus capital in some of the Arab countries gives them a competitive advantage. Beyond this there was the fact that already more than 80 per cent of the Community's exports to the Arab world were composed of industrial products, and any drastic increase in Arab industrial capacity would inevitably undermine an essential market for Western Europe.[54]

However, considerable progress was achieved in the standardization of technical norms and contract clauses. In this respect, the General Committee instructed the working committees concerned to finalize their work in mid-1977.

Infrastructure

The Working Committee on Infrastructure made considerable advances. Up to the Tunis meeting it was composed of five working groups (shipping, air transport, land transport, communications and telecommunications, and installations and buildings), with work farthest advanced on port expansion and new overland connections between Arab countries.[55]

THE THIRD GENERAL COMMITTEE MEETING, BRUSSELS OCTOBER 1977

The Brussels meeting was held in an a favourable atmosphere. This was due to the political developments that had taken place between the Tunis and Brussels General Committee meetings, and had paved the way for the relaxed climate. The European Council of Ministers, at its meeting in London on 29 June 1977, had adopted a statement on the Middle East conflict. The statement, which explained the Community's viewpoint on the Arab–Israeli conflict, was regarded by the Arabs as a more advanced attitude than that expressed in the Community statement of 6 November 1973. The text of the European statement received a positive reception from the Arab countries. It was reported that the secretary-general of the League of Arab States, Mr Mahmoud Riad, stated unofficially that the statement of the European heads of government was meeting Arab wishes 'on the understanding that it should be followed by behaviour to match the words'.[56]

THE EUROPEAN STATEMENT OF 29 JUNE 1977

The Community declaration of 29 June 1977 made the following points:

(1) At the present critical stage in the Middle East, the Nine welcome all efforts now being made to bring to an end the tragic conflict there. They emphasize the crucial interest which they see in early and successful negotiations towards a just and lasting peace. They call on all the parties concerned to agree urgently to participate in such negotiations in a constructive and realistic spirit; at this juncture in particular all parties should refrain from statements or policies which could constitute an obstacle to the pursuit of peace.

(2) The Nine set out on many occasions in the past, for example, in their statements of 6 November 1973, 28 September 1976 and 7 December 1976, their view that a peace settlement should be based on Security Council resolutions 242 and 388 and on:
   (a) the inadmissibility of the acquisition of territory by force;
   (b) the need for Israel to end the territorial occupation which it has maintained since the conflict of 1967;
   (c) respect for the sovereignty, territorial integrity and independence of every state in the area and their right to live in peace within secure and recognized boundaries;
   (d) recognition that in the establishment of a just and lasting peace account must be taken of the legitimate rights of the Palestinians. It remains their firm view that all these aspects must be taken as a whole.[57]

(3) The Nine have affirmed their belief that a solution to the conflict in the Middle East will be possible only if the legitimate right of the Palestinian people to give effective expression to its national identity is translated into fact, which would take into account the need for a homeland for the

Palestinian people. They consider that the representatives of the parties to the conflict, including the Palestinian people, must participate in the negotiations in an appropriate manner to be worked out in consultation between all the parties concerned. In the context of an overall settlement, Israel must be ready to recognize the legitimate rights of the Palestinian people; equally, the Arab side must be ready to recognize the right of Israel to live in peace within secure and recognized boundaries. It is not through the acquisition of territory by force that the security of the states of the region can be assured; but it must be based on commitments to peace exchanged between all the parties concerned with a view to establishing truly peaceful relations.

(4) The Nine believe that the peace negotiations must be resumed urgently, with the aim of agreeing and implementing a comprehensive, just and lasting settlement of the conflict. They remain ready to contribute to the extent the parties wish in finding a settlement and in putting it into effect. They are also ready to consider participating in guarantees within the framework of the United Nations.[58]

THE COMMUNITY'S FINANCIAL CONTRIBUTION TO THE ACTIVITIES OF THE DIALOGUE

In addition to the political stance on the Middle East, the Community had reached agreement on the primary amount of money to be contributed to the dialogue. The ministers of foreign affairs of the Nine, meeting in Luxembourg on 5 April 1977, consented to contribute $3.5 million towards the initial cost of the activities of the dialogue.[59] Originally, the European Commission had suggested that the Community's financial contribution should be $5 million. This proposal, however, was not accepted by all member states. Some were reluctant to endorse such a sum that would be spent in its entirety on projects outside the Community, in the Arab states. These differences were finally resolved by adopting a lower compromise figure: $3.5 million.[60] The cash was intended solely for financing the preliminary feasibility studies and other activities of the dialogue, with the exception of the implementation of the projects themselves.[61]

THE PROCEDURES OF THE BRUSSELS MEETING

As already mentioned, the Brussels meeting of the General Committee took place in a politically relaxed climate. The European Council's statement of 29 June as well as the Community's financial contribution helped to create this atmosphere. The delegations to the Brussels meeting were composed as follows: the European delegation was led by Baron Paternotte de Vaillée, Plenipotentiary Minister and head of the Middle East, North Africa and Euro-Arab dialogue section of the Belgian foreign affairs ministry, accompanied by Herr Klaus Meyer, Director-General for Development in the Commission. The Arab delegation was chaired by Mr Taher Radwan, Ambassador of Saudi Arabia in Cairo, accompanied by Mr Mahmoud Riad, Secretary-General of the League of Arab States. Although the pace of the progress in the meeting was limited, it was tangible. The meeting started with exchanges of views between both parties on all the aspects of Euro-Arab co-operation: political, economic, social and cultural.[62]

THE POLITICAL ASPECT OF THE DIALOGUE

Initially, the Arabs hoped that they could accomplish, through the meeting, some advances in the political as well as technical aspects of the dialogue. Their main political demands were these:

(1) the Community states should recognize the PLO as the sole legitimate representative of the Palestinian people;
(2) the European countries should adopt practical measures to incarnate the principles they had announced in condemning Israeli policy in the occupied Arab territories.

The Arab political statement, which was read by the representative of Saudi Arabia, concentrated mainly on evaluating the course of the dialogue. It stressed that the stage at which the dialogue had arrived required an improvement in its political aspect. The statement referred to the events that took place in the Arab occupied areas, and recalled the terms to which both sides had previously committed themselves as regards the Palestinian question and the Arab–Israeli conflict in general. The Arab statement said that issuing declarations concerning any question was a sign of sincere intentions. It was, however, just a beginning that should be followed by another more serious stage, which involved putting into effect the principles and intentions through effective measures. Hence, the statement asked what 'practical and decisive steps—after the issuance of the communiqué—the European countries could take to implement these principles'.

The representative also stressed that exports and imports between the European Community and the Arab world were continually booming, and that the rate of the commercial exchange between them had increased four times in the last four years, with the Community states becoming the Arab world's most important trading partner. The Arab statement emphasized that 'the atmosphere created by the dialogue had affected this growth at the level of bilateral relations'.[63] The Arab side once again urged the Community to recognize the PLO as the sole legitimate representative of the Palestinian people and to desist from supporting Israel economically and militarily.[64]

The European political statement, which was presented by the representative of Belgium, focused on the problem of peace and security in the Middle East. The statement pointed out that the situation in the area was still threatening. Hence it remained the centre of the Community's concern and attention. It explained in detail the contents of the London declaration of 29 June 1977, making it clear that the bases of a settlement were Security Council resolutions 242 and 388, illustrating the principles on which these resolutions were based and confirming the right of the Palestinian people to the effective expression of their national identity, including their right to have a homeland.

The European statement emphasized the Community's readiness to take part in 'any just and studied initiative that could contribute to gradual development towards a real peace', and its concern 'at the illegal measures recently taken by the Israeli government in the occupied territories'.[65] The statement characterized these measures as being in contrast with the principles advocated by the Community states and as hindering the process of negotiation. The Community reviewed the situation in southern Lebanon and demonstrated its concern for the safety of this country. It also stressed that 'the exchange of viewpoints on political questions had certainly helped to remove much misunderstanding', and hoped that 'exchange of viewpoints in all fields would in the future flourish and grow in a manner leading to further results'.[66]

In the joint communiqué issued at the end of the meeting, the two parties to the dialogue accepted the fact that the situation in the Middle East constituted a threat to the peace and security of the area and to international peace and security. Within this context, they restated their belief that the security of Europe was linked to the security of the Mediterranean region as well as the Arab region, emphasizing 'the importance of intensifying efforts in order to achieve a just and lasting peace in the Middle East' and recalling the vote on 27 October 1977 for the General Assembly resolution under agenda Item 126. This resolution, *inter alia*:

(1) determines that measures and actions taken by Israel in the Palestinian and other Arab territories occupied since 1967 have no legal validity and constitute a serious obstruction of efforts aimed at achieving a just and lasting peace in the Middle East;

(2) strongly deplores the persistence of Israel in carrying out such measures, in particular the establishment of settlements in the occupied Arab territories;

(3) calls upon Israel to comply strictly with its international obligations in accordance with the principles of international law and the provisions of the Geneva Convention relative to the protection of Civilian Persons in Time of War, of 12 August 1949;

(4) calls once more upon the government of Israel as the occupying power to desist forthwith from taking any action that would result in changing the legal status, geographical nature or demographic composition of the Arab territories occupied since 1967, including Jerusalem.[67]

The two parties showed their concern about the dangerous situation in Lebanon and hoped to see Lebanon as a united territory. They stressed the importance of holding a Euro-Arab meeting at the ministerial level and consented to consider the measures to be adopted for the preparation of such a meeting.[68] However, the main political achievement of the Brussels meeting was the agreement to create a joint committee for political consultation (the proposal was originally suggested by the Arab side during the Tunis meeting of the General Committee).[69]

THE ECONOMIC ASPECT OF THE DIALOGUE: THE
ACTIVITIES OF THE WORKING COMMITTEES

After reviewing the work that had been accomplished by the different working committees since the Tunis meeting, the General Committee managed to work out guidelines for the future work of the experts in the following sectors:

Financial procedures

One of the essential result of the Brussels meeting as regards co-operation, was the adoption of a code of financing procedures (see Appendix 1). The code was drawn up by the *ad hoc* group set up by the General Committee at its meeting in Tunis in February 1977.[70] Likewise, the General Committee decided to undertake an initial series of practical studies (see Appendix 2), three on agriculture and rural development, four on basic infrastructure and two seminars—one on relations between the two civilizations, and the other on new towns. The studies were proposed by the working committees concerned and accompanied by financial estimates.[71]

The General Committee authorized the Secretariat of the League of Arab States and the European presidency to take the necessary measures to ensure the implementation of the studies in question. In addition, the General Committee took note of the sums allocated by each side of the dialogue (the Arabs $15 million and the Europeans $3.5 million) to finance the preliminary and feasibility studies and other activities of the dialogue. The Arab side proposed that the Europeans should, in due course, participate in the financing of these studies by not less than a third of the total sum allocated from both sides.[72] Moreover, the Arabs proposed that finance of the studies mentioned above should be according to a fixed scale which the Community would contribute at least 30 per cent of the cost of feasibility studies and 50 per cent of the seminars. The Arabs were concerned that the EEC's promotion of the idea of 'triangular co-operation' would mean that the Europeans would contribute only 'know-how'. The Arab proposal was only partly accepted: the Community agreed to contribute 22 per cent of the cost of the feasibility studies.[73]

Transfer of technology

In this sector no progress was achieved because of differences between the two sides. First, there was the problem related to the establishment of the Euro-Arab centre for the transfer of technology. The Arabs wanted the management of the centre to be exclusively an Arab affair[74] and that the centre must be established in an Arab country. Secondly, there was disagreement between the two parties over the text of the joint declaration on the transfer of technology produced by the *ad hoc* group at its meeting in Cairo in June 1977. The Arab side regarded this joint declaration, which contained general issues and indicators, as only an initial step rather than an agreement governing the transfer of technology between the two parties. The European side considered that the points in the joint declaration offered a satisfactory basis for strengthening technological co-operation between the two regions, especially through the activities of the Euro-Arab centre to be established, with no need for a formal agreement. To ease differences, the General Committee instructed the *ad hoc* group to continue its discussions related to the points of its mandate in order to present its recommendations at an early stage.[75]

Industrialization

Limited progress was made in this sector. The General Committee asked the Working Committee on Industrialization to accelerate its work and submit the final reports of its five specialized groups at an early stage. The General Committee also welcomed the 'procedural progress' that the Working Committee on Industrialization adopted for some of its specialized groups, by setting up task forces for the effective preparation of the Group's joint meetings. The General Committee called upon the governments of the member states of both delegations to encourage the work of the Specialized Group on Standardization (see Annex 2).[76]

Basic infrastructure

The pace of the work in this sector was satisfactory. Taking into account the fact that the development and proper adaptation of transport infrastructure was highly important in the development of the economies of the Arab world, the General Committee endorsed the programmes of studies suggested by the working committee in the area of sea transport infrastructures. Also, the General Committee agreed to undertake the following feasibility studies which were proposed by the working committee:

(1) development of the port of Tartous in Syria ($500,000);
(2) development of the port of Basra in Iraq ($500,000);
(3) training project for sea ports, applicable to all Arab countries ($200,000);
(4) information and statistical standardization of data systems for all Arab countries, in the field of maritime transport ($60,000);
(5) holding a Euro-Arab symposium on 'New Towns' ($20,000) (see Appendix 2).

Agriculture and rural development

Considerable progress was achieved in this sector. The General Committee examined and approved a number of study projects, which were proposed by the Working Committee on Agricultural Development. The General Committee hoped that these projects would contribute towards increasing food security in the Arab world. The study projects approved by the General Committee in this field were the following:[77]

(1) studies in connection with the Bardere irrigation scheme as part of the Juba Valley Development project in Somalia ($1,200,000);
(2) feasibility study of an interim operation as part of the Sudan meat project ($50,000);
(3) applied research programme in order to assess the feasibility of potato seed multiplication in Iraq ($1,800,000) (see Appendix 2).

Also, the General Committee asked the working committee to study the project submitted to it by the Arab Centre for the studies of Arid Zones and Dry Lands (ACSAD) concerning an applied agricultural research programme on water resource development and use. The General Committee stressed the considerable impact which the successful outcome of this programme might have on increasing food security throughout the Arab world.[78]

Financial co-operation

The main issue here was the protection of investments. The Arab side restated its demand for the inclusion of protection against currency risks in the convention between the two sides, while the European Community rejected this and emphasized protection against other risks.[79] However, the General Committee instructed the Financial Co-operation Working Committee to continue its work on the scope and content of a multilateral Euro-Arab convention on the protection of different forms of investment. It stressed that the relevant texts which were exchanged for examination at the expert level would help both sides to reach an agreement in good time.[80]

Trade co-operation

In the trade field the Arabs repeated their demand for a preferential agreement. This was rejected by the European Community. The Community representative explained that the Community already had preferential agreements with ten Arab countries while the others were oil-producing countries with huge trade surpluses.[81] Instead, the Community agreed to consider the possibility of making a non-preferential regional agreement between the Arab world as a whole and the Community member states within the framework of the dialogue. This, from the Community viewpoint, would help the Arab countries to increase and diversify their exports. The Arab side took note of the European position while repeating its request for a preferential trade agreement between the two regions.[82]

With regard to the Euro-Arab trade centre, the General Committee instructed the working committee to continue its studies on the establishment of the centre. The European side urged the Arabs to clarify their position in relation to the financing of the centre.

Considering the textiles question, the Arab side raised its concern about the restrictive measures adopted by the

Community in relation to some Arab countries which exported textiles. The Arabs stated that such measures were contradictory to the spirit of the dialogue and of the co-operation agreements accomplished with certain Arab countries. This protectionist measures, the Arabs said, would jeopardize the necessary climate of confidence between the two sides as well as the possibility of establishing special relations between them. Moreover, the Arabs stated that such restrictive measures would create reactions that might damage the development of trade between the two groups of countries. Hence, they asked the Community to lift the restrictive measures, stressing that such action would be in the interest of both sides. [83]

The Community pointed out that the problems which beset the European textile industry had forced the Nine to adopt protectionist measures so as to regain control of the situation. The Community emphasized that its action was in line with existing international obligations and in particular with its co-operation agreements. The European side stressed its readiness to find solutions within the context of the existing co-operation agreements with the countries concerned. The Arab side, however, did not accept the Community statement, and no agreement was reached. [84]

Labour and culture co-operation

Reasonable progress was achieve in this field. The General Committee took note of the work done by the Working Committee on Culture, Social and Labour questions, in particular the drafting of a joint declaration on the principles which should govern the living conditions of the foreign workers resident in the countries participating in the dialogue. The General Committee asked the wWorking committee to carry on its discussions with the aim of finding satisfactory outcomes to both sides concerning the following:

(1) completion of the joint declaration;
(2) setting up of Arab centre for vocational training;
(3) organizing of a colloquium on labour problems.

The Arabs restated their demand for the conclusion of an overall agreement with the countries of the Community. The agreement, the Arabs hoped, would guarantee immigrant Arab workers an improvement in their living and working conditions as well as safeguard their rights. They expressed their concern at measures which had recently been adopted by the Community in relation to foreign workers. Moreover, the Arabs appealed to the Community to avoid any action that might put at stake the right to security of employment and the stability of the Arab workers resident in the Community countries. In reply to the Arab demands, the European side re-confirmed its viewpoint that the adoption of the joint declaration formed a partial response to the repeated demand by the Arab side for an overall agreement.[85]

With regard to the employment question, the Europeans stated that while they understood Arab anxiety, the Community found it difficult in the present economic situation to fulfil all Arab demands concerning the guarantee of security and stability of employment. Both sides agreed to continue the exchange of views in these fields with the aim of reaching solutions that would be in line with the spirit of the dialogue.

In cultural affairs, the General Committee took note of the efforts made by both sides to study and put into practice a number of initiatives. One of these initiatives had involved the holding of a Euro-Arab seminar in Venice in March 1977. The seminar, according to the final communiqué, had contributed immensely towards co-operation in the field of the study and diffusion of Arabic language and literary civilization in Europe. The General Committee emphasized the importance it attached to these activities for the future development of the dialogue.[86] Hence, it asked the respective working committee to:

(1) carry out the recommendations adopted by the Euro-Arab seminar of Venice March 1977, which constituted the first concretization of the dialogue in that field;
(2) continue its efforts to give concrete shape as quickly as possible to the cultural projects that have already been decided on and those that are in the process of being drawn up;
(3) tackle in greater depth the problems of co-operation in the information field on the basis of the working papers already presented, with a view to achieving concrete results.[87]

Both sides expressed their interest in organizing in Hamburg a symposium on the relations between the two civilizations. Subsequently, the General Committee approved the feasibility study related to the symposium and its financial estimate ($250,000) (see Appendix 2).

At the end of the Brussels meeting, the General Committee asked the Secretariat of the League of Arab States and the European presidency to establish contacts in order to envisage possible improvements in the dialogue procedure. The General Committee also stressed that, if appropriate, a small *ad hoc* group (the composition on each side to be decided as each side saw fit) could be established to make suggestions before the end of 1977, for submission to the next General Committee meeting.[88]

NEW POLITICAL DEVELOPMENTS SURROUNDING THE DIALOGUE

After the Brussels meeting the significant development that dominated the political horizon was the Sadat peace initiative, launched by his dramatic visit to Jerusalem on 19 and 20 November 1977. In their evaluation of this initiative, the Arab League countries and the European Community differed to the point of serious contradiction, thus critically damaging the prospects for harmonious dialogue between the two blocs. In order to more fully appreciate this peace initiative, it would be useful to situate the latter in the context of the adoption by President Carter's administration of the 'comprehensive approach' to Middle East peace.

CARTER ADMINISTRATION: TOWARDS A COMPREHENSIVE APPROACH

The 1976 United States presidential election brought in a new American administration, which soon launched a critique of the previous administration's Middle East policy—most specifically of the way that the Nixon administration had dealt with the essential part of the Arab–Israel dispute, namely the Palestinian question.

The new administration described the approach as fruitless and profitless, determined to approach the issue in a different way— seeking to achieve a comprehensive agreement.[89] President Carter's ideas on the solution to the Middle East conflict derived from the so-called Brooking Report, whose full title was

'Towards Peace in the Middle East'. The report was written by a group which was close to Mr Carter at the time, and which believed that peace in the Middle East should come through a comprehensive settlement rather than through the step-by-step approach.[90] So Carter and his team started looking for a means to negotiate a comprehensive agreement and provide the theme for a Geneva conference.[91]

In mid-February 1977, Secretary of State Vance toured the Middle East and met with Israeli and Arab leaders. In the spring of the same year President Carter met with Arab and Israeli heads of states in an attempt to persuade them of his sincere intention to solve the conflict. On 15 March 1977, he spoke during a meeting at Clinton, Massachusetts, about a Palestinian homeland. He defined this in an interview with *Jerusalem Post* correspondent Trude Feldman, on 8 September, as 'a place for people to live'. He also spoke about Palestinian representation at the proposed Geneva conference[92] and about the legitimate rights of the Palestinian people.[93]

In early September, the American administration started to negotiate with the Soviet Union about a common framework for a comprehensive settlement. On 1 October the two super-powers issued a joint statement, which expressed their agreement on the acceptable terms for peace in the Middle East.[94]

In the course of its first year in office, however, the Carter administration began to retreat from its early commitments. There were several reasons for the change: Israel's inflexible position, the pro-Israeli faction in the United States, and strong domestic opposition (especially in Congress) to the idea of including the Soviet Union in any peace process concerning the Middle East conflict. As a result of these factors, the United States (on 5 October) abandoned the US–Soviet joint declaration of 1 October 1977, and regarded it as no longer the *sine qua non* for reconvening and conducting the Geneva conference.[95]

The Carter administration's plan for a comprehensive solution of the Arab–Israel dispute was sabotaged and ultimately terminated by president Sadat's unexpected trip to Jerusalem on 19 and 20 November 1977—an initiative that the United States approved and encouraged. This approbation by the United States effectively implied a return to the earlier step-by-step diplomacy which had been pursued by the former administration and had been criticized by the Carter administration itself. The new policy led to the signature of the Camp David agreement between Egypt and Israel, which in turn brought about the isolation of Sadat's Egypt from the Arab world, a shift in the regional balance of power in favour of Israel, and a situation in which it became difficult to work towards fulfilling the basic legitimate rights of the Palestinian people.[96]

ARAB–EUROPEAN REACTIONS TO THE CAMP DAVID AGREEMENTS

The Arab reaction

The Camp David accords of September 1978 and the Israeli–Egyptian peace treaty of March 1979—both of which were brought about under the auspices of the Carter administration—shocked governments in the Arab world and threw into question the *raison d'être* of the Arab League itself. Turmoil, chaos and confusion characterized the Arab world during the years 1978–79. To discourage any further Egyptian–Israeli rapprochement, the Arab governments reacted strongly from the outset. They viewed Sadat's initiative as a move that involved abandoning the framework of Arab unity in general and the Palestinian cause in particular.[97]

The opposition of other Arab governments to Sadat's policy found expression when, following the circulation of an Iraqi memorandum on 1 October, an Arab summit conference was held in Baghdad on 5 November 1978. It was attended by representatives of 19 members of the Arab League: Algeria, Bahrain, Iraq, Morocco, Jordan, the Palestinian Liberation Organization, the Yemen Republic (North Yemen), Saudi Arabia, Qatar, Syria, Libya, Lebanon, Somalia, the Yemen Peoples Democratic Republic (South Yemen), Tunisia, Djibouti, Kuwait, Mauritania and the United Arab Emirates. Sudan and Oman were not represented. Egypt was not invited to participate in the conference.[98]

During the meeting, the conferees stressed that the Palestine question was a matter of Arab destiny. It was the crux of the conflict with Israel. Hence, the struggle to recover Arab rights in Palestine and the occupied Arab lands was a common national responsibility. All Arabs must join this struggle, in accordance with their standing and their military, economic, political and other resources. The conference affirmed that all Arab countries must lend support to the struggle of the Palestinian resistance in all its forms, via the PLO—the sole legitimate representative of the Palestinian people inside and outside the occupied homeland. It confirmed that all Arab states were committed to safeguard Palestinian national unity and not to interfere in the internal affairs of Palestinian action. Therefore, the conference stated its rejection of any unilateral movement concerning the Palestine question. It pointed out that 'it is not permissible for any single Arab side to act unilaterally with regard to any settlement of the Palestinian question.' It added: 'No settlement is acceptable unless it is adopted by a resolution of an Arab summit conference held specifically for this purpose.'[99]

It was within this context that the conference decided to reject the Sadat peace initiative and his signature of the Camp David agreements. The conferees stated that the agreements were considered to be 'harmful to the rights of the Palestinian people' and 'the rights of the Arab nation in Palestine and the occupied Arab territories'. The conference also stated that these agreements were accomplished outside the framework of collective Arab responsibility. They were in contrast with the resolutions of Arab summit conferences, especially the Algiers and Rabat conferences, and with the Charter of the Arab League and the United Nations resolutions on Palestine. For these reasons, they would not lead to the just peace for which the Arab nations were looking.[100] In addition, the conference adopted a resolution envisaging broad-ranging political and economic sanctions against Egypt if Sadat would not retract and return to the Arab fold.[101]

The European response

When President Carter adopted the comprehensive approach and affirmed the Palestinian right for a homeland as *sine qua non* for a just, durable and lasting solution for the Middle East conflict, the European Council encouraged and approved that step by issuing the London declaration of 29 June 1977. In it, the Community members stressed the importance they attached to giving the Palestinian people a chance to express effectively their own national identity, which implied recognition of the need for a homeland for the Palestinian people. They demanded mutual recognition of the legitimate rights of all parties concerned. The nine members of the European Community also expressed their willingness to contribute to the process if the parties concerned wished to and affirmed their willingness to participate in an international guarantee under the auspices of the United Nations.[102]

Sadat's unilateral initiative demolished Carter's comprehensive approach and faced the Europeans with a new and unprecedented situation. On the one hand, the European Community was confronted with a negative response from most Arab governments. The Community had vast interests in the area, which it had been trying to consolidate since 1973, and so the Community was reluctant to endanger its rather good position in the region. On the other hand, the Community was anxious to seize and exploit the opportunity with a view to fostering a peaceful settlement in the area. The Sadat initiative was seen as constituting the first major hope for such a settlement in the history of the Arab–Israeli dispute.[103]

The initial reaction of the European Community countries was, therefore, cautious, graded and various. France showed signs of reservation and justified its attitude by arguing that the general reaction of the Arab world was extremely hostile, which made any premature statement risky. Raymond Barre, the French prime minister, stated later that 'in the face of an initiative which was the personal initiative of President Sadat, a declaration ran the risk of being premature before knowing exactly how the complex phenomenon could be appraised'.[104]

The governments of Britain, West Germany and the rest of the European Community supported the peace initiative of President Sadat with some vehemence, and approved the mediatory role of the United States. The West German government described the policy of President Sadat as being one that could bring about peace in the Middle East. It viewed Sadat's visit to Jerusalem on 19 and 20 November 1977 as 'an astonishing development for which one can only have the best wishes'.[105]

Of all the member states of the European Community, the British government was the most active, ardent and supportive of Sadat's initiative. It had virtually been involved in the peace process through its regular high-level contact with the parties concerned. Furthermore, the British government was the European country that came closest to the United States in its approach to Middle East affairs, and it exerted great efforts to persuade Jordan to join the peace negotiations. In late December 1977, the British government followed Washington in its initial favourable reaction to the peace plan put forward by the Israeli prime minister, Mr Begin.[106]

THE EEC DECLARATION OF 22 NOVEMBER 1977

In spite of the initial French reservations, France did later modify its position and join the other European Common Market countries in supporting Sadat's initiative. On 22 November 1977, the foreign ministers of the European Community met in Brussels and issued a statement in which they welcomed the 'bold initiative' of President Sadat and the historical and unprecedented dialogue started in Jerusalem.

The initiative was, according to the community, a step that had been undertaken in an attempt to eliminate the mistrust that had prevailed between the two sides of the conflict—mistrust that constituted the main barrier to achieving a peaceful settlement of the Arab–Israeli conflict. The Community stressed the importance it attached to reaching a comprehensive solution that could pave the way for a just, durable and lasting peace for all the peoples in the area—including the Palestinian people. The nine members of the Community made it plain that a comprehensive settlement of this kind should be founded on the principles embodied in the London declaration of 29 June 1977, which were accepted by the international community.[107]

After the statement, the member states of the European Community tried actively to sustain Sadat's initiative and to push the mechanism of the negotiations ahead. Between 26 and 28 November 1977, the French prime minister, Raymond Barre, and his foreign minister, Louis de Guiringaud, visited the Syrian capital Damascus. They made an attempt to persuade President Asad of Syria, if not to join Sadat's initiative, at least to reduce the vehemence of Syrian criticism of Sadat's efforts for peace in the Middle East.[108]

More significantly, on 28 December 1977, Chancellor Helmut Schmidt of West Germany visited Egypt. The aim of the trip was to try to speed up the peace process launched by President Sadat and to bring some encouragement. During his visit Schmidt promised the Egyptian government German aid of 25 billion Marks for 1978.[109]

The EEC statement of 19 September 1978

The Community maintained its support of the peace initiative between Egypt and Israel despite the fact that the Arab countries had virtually unanimously opposed the whole peace process. The negotiations between Egypt and Israel led to the signature of the Camp David agreement on 17 September 1978. The foreign ministers of the nine countries of the European Community, meeting in Brussels on 19 September 1978 issued a statement in support of the agreement. It congratulated President Carter for his great efforts in launching the Camp David meeting and in bringing it to a fruitful, successful outcome. At the same time, the ministers voiced their approbation of the excellent co-operation and help given by President Sadat of Egypt and Prime Minister Begin of Israel. The nine governments of the European Community expressed their wish that the successful result of the Camp David meeting would lead to further steps towards a just, comprehensive and lasting peace. They urged the parties concerned to join the process to that end, and stated their willingness to support all efforts which could bring about peace.[110]

Europe's underpinning of the Camp David agreement was reiterated on several occasions. At the United Nations General Assembly on 26 September 1978, speaking on behalf of the Community, Herr Genscher (the German foreign minister and President of the Council of the European Communities), approved the Camp David Conference and its outcome. The accords, he said, had raised the hopes for a solution of the Arab–Israel conflict that had threatened the stability of the whole world.[111]

During its part-session from 9 to 12 October 1978, the European Parliament adopted a resolution greeting the results of the Camp David summit, and requesting the other parties involved in the conflict to take part in the negotiations. It also called on the European Council and the Commission to design a practical plan for multilateral co-operation between Egypt, Israel and the European Community, aimed at accelerating the economic, technical and social development of the area.[112]

THE FOURTH GENERAL COMMITTEE MEETING,
DECEMBER 1978

The General Committee of the Euro-Arab dialogue held its fourth meeting in Damascus from 9 to 11 December 1978. The meeting took place in an unfavourable atmosphere. The developments that dominated the political arena (Sadat's visit to Jerusalem in November 1977, the signing of the Camp David agreements, together with the split of the Arab world into two camps), helped to create this uneasy climate. To prepare for the meeting, representatives from both sides met in Bonn on 23 and 24 November. During the meeting, the two parties explored the stage of the dialogue and the points that would be discussed on the Damascus agenda. They noted the progress that had been made in some areas of economic co-operation by the working committees concerned, and underlined four 'areas of emphasis' for the agenda of the forthcoming meeting of the General Committee. These areas were: trade co-operation, transfer of technology, protection of investment, and technical assistance for an Arab vocational and teacher training centre.[113]

Shortly before the General Committee held its meeting, two preparatory meetings took place on both sides. The Arab preparatory meeting took place in Damascus on 6 December. During it the Arabs succeeded in coordinating their efforts and agreed to adopt a unified position in the forthcoming meeting of the General Committee. On the European side, the final preparatory meeting also took place in Damascus on 8 December.[114]

The composition of the delegations to the Damascus meeting was as follows: the European delegation was led by Hans Joachim Hille, EEC's special ambassador to the Arab League, accompanied by Manfred Caspari, deputy director-general for external relations at the Commission of the European Community. The Arab delegation was chaired by Rafic Jouejati, director of the western European affairs department in the Syrian foreign ministry, accompanied by Mohamed Riad, Deputy Secretary-General of the League of Arab States.[115]

During the meeting, the delegates pursued the exchange of views on all aspects of Euro-Arab co-operation—political, economic, social and cultural.

The political aspect of the dialogue

As usual, an exchange of views on the Middle East situation continued. The Arab delegates (who showed remarkable unity despite the internal political division created by the Camp David agreements) confirmed their belief that the continued occupation of lands by Israel threatened the security of the Middle East and accordingly the peace and security of the whole world. They stressed that the ideal solution for the conflict was to allow the Palestinian people to establish their own independent state on their territory and to exercise their right to return to their homeland. Condemnation of the measures exercised by Israel was voiced by the Arab representatives. These measures included the settlement policy, changing the status of the Arab lands (including Jerusalem), and the oppression against the Palestinian people in the occupied areas.[116]

Dissatisfaction at the level of political progress achieved in the dialogue was also brought in by the representatives of the Arab countries. They felt that the Community did not respond to the demands of the Arabs put forward at the Brussels meeting, especially that of recognition of the PLO by the Community.[117] For this reason, the Arab delegates repeated their demand for full recognition of the PLO by the European Community, stressing its importance for the progress of the dialogue and expressing their hope 'to receive a positive response to this demand' at the next meeting of the General Committee.[118] The Arabs also emphasized that the stage at which the dialogue had arrived required a joint Euro-Arab meeting at the ministerial level as soon as possible.[119]

As regards the European Community, there was a reticence towards these criticisms. The Europeans confined themselves to restating their view on the desirability of a peace agreement which should be based on Security Council Resolutions 242 and 338, and on the principles embodied in their declaration of 29 June 1977. They stressed that all these aspects must be taken as a whole. They also stated that such a settlement must take into consideration the need for a homeland for the Palestinian people. Within this context, the Community affirmed that the representatives of the parties to the conflict—including the Palestinian people—must take part in the negotiations in a proper framework to be worked out in consultation between all parties concerned.[120]

On the Arab demand for the recognition of the PLO, the Community states consented to consider the request and promised to give their reply at the next meeting of the General Committee.[121]

In the final communiqué issued at the end of the meeting, both sides agreed that the continued Arab–Israeli dispute formed a threat to security and peace in the Middle East and to international peace and security. They confirmed their belief that the security of Europe was linked to the security of the Mediterranean region and the Arab region. Both sides agreed that the Palestinian question was the core of the conflict in the area, and that a peaceful, just and comprehensive settlement of the conflict—including a solution to the Palestinian problem—was not only essential for the Arabs, but also was of great importance for the Community in view of the close relations existing between the two sides.

They also recalled the General Assembly resolution under agenda Item No. 126 of 27 October 1977, which deplored the measures that had been taken by the Israeli government in the occupied territories since its occupation in 1967. They expressed their hope that peace and security could be restored to Lebanon, affirming that national unity among the Lebanese was an urgent need so as to safeguard the independence of Lebanon, its sovereignty and territorial integrity. They stressed their wish that 'the Euro-Arab dialogue might offer a framework for future projects in Lebanon'.[122]

THE ECONOMIC ASPECT OF THE DIALOGUE: THE ACTIVITIES OF THE WORKING COMMITTEES

The General Committee took stock of the work done by the working committees and specialized groups since the Brussels meeting of 26–28 October 1977. There was considerable progress in some areas of economic and social co-operation. The General Committee instructed the working committees to lay special emphasis on certain horizontal approaches to economic co-operation. These involved 'concentration on vocational training in all sectors covered by the dialogue, priority for regional and general studies and schemes, and closer association of private promoters with the dialogue'.[123]

The General Committee also approved a second series of study projects, and fixed the contribution of the Arabs and Europeans to finance these studies and activities. The accomplishment of the studies involved a total financial commitment by the two sides of about $3.7 million. The study projects concerned industrialization, science and technology, and social and cultural matters. Apart from that, the General Committee devoted special attention to the following subjects:[124]

Transfer of technology

In the technological field, reasonable progress was achieved. The General Committee approved in principle the establishment of a Euro-Arab centre for the transfer of technology.[125] It also approved the undertaking of a feasibility study to be carried out by four experts (two from each side). This study should determine the necessary steps for the setting up of the transfer centre. A total sum of about $150,000 was allocated for the study. The General Committee also authorized the co-chairmen of the *ad hoc* group, the General-Secretariat of the League of Arab States, and the Commission of the European Communities to adopt the necessary measures so as to embark on the above-mentioned study. It would then be passed on to the *ad hoc* group on the transfer of technology to prepare a report for submission to the General Committee at its forthcoming meeting.[126]

Industrialization

Considerable headway was made in this sector. The General Committee examined and approved the following study projects (see Appendix 3): setting up of Euro-Arab documentation and information centres for standardization ($450,000), feasibility study on petrochemical industries ($165,000), feasibility study on oil-refining industries ($165,000), and feasibility study on policy and programmes for education and training in the areas of standardization, metrology and quality control ($135,000). The General Committee hoped that the approval of these studies would increase co-operation in the field of industrialization.[127]

Basic infrastructure

Progress concerning basic infrastructure was modest. The preparation for the four studies (approved during the Brussels meeting) related to the port developments on the Syrian and Iraqi coasts, vocational training for port personnel, and the harmonization of statistics continued. Greatest progress was made in the preparation for the symposium on new towns (also approved during the Brussels meeting). Here the General Committee asked the working committee concerned to do its best to organize the meeting in the course of 1979. Moreover, the General Committee recommended that the Working Committee on Basic Infrastructure should, in the future, lay special emphasis on studies of joint interest for the Arab countries in the other basic infrastructure areas. It also underlined the importance of enhancing transport facilities so as to more closely link the Arab world and Europe.[128]

Agriculture and rural development

There was limited progress in this area. The General Committee endorsed the decision adopted by the working committee to set up two sub-groups of experts, one for agricultural mechanization and the other for agro-industries. It also asked the working committee to study the suggestions made by these two sub-groups and to decide how their work could be expanded. Work by the specialized group on the 'Applied Research Programme on Water Resources Development and Use in Rural Areas' continued, and the specialized group produced reports on the progress of its work. As a result, the General Committee asked the Working Committee on Agriculture and Rural Development to pay special attention to the reports presented by the specialized group and to make decisions on the necessary measures for further action. The General Committee underlined the importance for the working committee to specify new areas of co-operation that could increase self-sufficiency in food production and security in the Arab countries, and promote economic integration in the area of agriculture.[129]

Commercial co-operation

Nothing tangible was achieved in this sector. The stumbling block was the disagreement between the two sides over the inclusion of trade agreements. The Arabs wanted a preferential trade agreement, whereas the Community was not willing to grant it. However, the Community did offer a non-preferential trade agreement but the Arabs would not agree, so no substantial progress was made.[130]

Financial co-operation

Progress was reasonable in this sector. The working committee succeeded in elaborating on the principles that were to be the basis for the contents of an agreement on the protection of investments against non-commercial risk. The General Committee approved these principles and recommended that the work on the drafting of the agreement should be accelerated, so as to reach a satisfactory outcome.[131]

Scientific and technological co-operation

Considerable progress was made in this sector. The General Committee stressed the importance it attached to scientific and technological co-operation between the two sides. It examined and approved the following study projects (see Annex 3): the establishment of an Arab institute for water desalination and resources ($600,000), the setting up of an Arab polytechnic institute ($1,000,000), and a survey of scientific infrastructure on marine science in the Arab countries ($160,000). The General Committee hoped that the approval of these studies would open opportunities for more co-operation in this field.[132]

Labour, social and culture affairs

Progress was also achieved in these areas. The most important decision was the adoption by the General Committee of a declaration on the principles governing the living and working conditions of foreign workers and their families of the countries participating in the dialogue. According to the joint declaration, migrant workers and the members of their families should enjoy, in the countries where they legally reside and work, 'equality of treatment as to living and working conditions, wages, economic rights, rights of association and the exercise of the basic public freedoms' (see Appendix 4).

Equality of treatment as to working conditions, wages and economic rights involved the main points of the right for social security benefits and social advantages, assistance from employment exchanges in finding jobs, access to vocational training, access to activities organized for the unemployed, freedom to choose a job in a given country following a period of paid employment, protection as regards industrial hygiene and safety, and equality as regard taxes and contributions relating to his occupation.

Equality of treatment in the exercise of rights of association included freedom to join trade union organizations, the right to vote, and the right to stand for and be appointed to office. Considering the equality of treatment as regards living conditions, it implied (for the children of a migrant worker) access to general and vocational education, and access to welfare and medical services.[133]

In addition, migrant workers and members of their families should enjoy equal rights as regards accommodation (the right to home ownership); the right to exercise the freedoms of speech, association and assembly; legal protection of their person and possessions; and legal aid arrangements. To help migrant workers and members of their families to protect their national identity and cultural values, the declaration emphasized: first, that migrant workers and members of their families must have access to regular information in their own language about both their country of origin and the host country; and secondly, that children of migrant workers must enjoy access to the teaching of their language and culture of origin.

Also, the declaration underlined the importance of facilitating the social integration of migrant workers and of the members of their families in the host countries. This would be accomplished through making the general public in the host country more aware of the problems of migrant workers and their families, and through 'promoting cultural activities for migrant workers and nationals with a view to better mutual understanding'.[134]

Moreover, the General Committee instructed the working

committee concerned to continue the discussion so as to reach a satisfactory outcome to both sides concerning the organization of a colloquium on the problems of vocational training for Arab migrant workers. It also required that the working committee to continue to take stock of some subjects in the social sector such as 'labour statistics, training of the handicapped and social security'.[135]

On the cultural issue, considerable headway was made. The General Committee approved the following studies (see Appendix 3): the publication of the proceedings of the Venice seminar which took place in March 1977 ($20,000); the draft catalogue of cultural and scientific institutions ($6,000); and technical assistance for the setting up of an Arab training centre ($880,000). Also, the General Committee approved the additional amount of money for organizing in Hamburg a symposium on the relationship between the two civilizations ($115,000).[136]

The General Committee underlined the importance for the working committee concerned to: consider the importance of co-operation between young people; establish a specialized group of experts to study the history text books used in both regions; carry on the discussions on co-operation in the field of information so to obtain concrete outcomes; and finally continue its efforts for the 'preparation of the meeting of Rectors/Vice-chancellors of Universities of the two regions, of a seminar for librarians and a seminar on the problems of teaching European languages for academic and higher education purposes'.[137]

CONSEQUENCES OF THE CAMP DAVID AGREEMENT AND THE SUSPENSION OF THE DIALOGUE

When the Camp David negotiations led eventually to the signing of the Egyptian–Israeli peace treaty on 26 March 1979, a shock wave went through the Arab world. The Arab governments decided to take action against Egypt and to put the decisions of the Baghdad summit conference of November 1978 into effect. So on 31 March 1979, a meeting of Arab foreign and economic ministers convened in Baghdad. The resolutions that followed this meeting declared that the government of the Arab Republic of Egypt had overlooked the resolutions of the 9th Arab summit conference held in Baghdad (on 5 November 1978) and had ignored the special demand made by the Arab kings and presidents that Egypt abrogated the Camp David agreement and not to sign any peace agreement with Israel. The Egyptian government had, the ministers stated, deviated from Arab unity, renounced the 'Arab nation's rights, exposed the nation's destiny to . . . challenges' and had 'relinquished its pan-Arab duty of liberating the occupied Arab territories . . . and of restoring the Palestinian Arab people's inalienable national rights, including their right to repatriation, self-determination and establishment of the independent Palestinian State on their national soil'.[138] As a result, the sanctions envisaged at the November Baghdad summit conference were imposed against Egypt.

By the beginning of May 1979, all the countries of the Arab League (with the exception of Oman and Sudan) had severed diplomatic relations with Egypt. Oman and Sudan argued that penalizing Egypt by isolation would not benefit the Arab cause. The membership of Egypt in the Arab League was suspended, and the headquarters of the League transferred from Cairo to Tunis. In early May, Egypt was suspended from the 43-member Islamic Conference and its affiliates, and on 9 May in Fez (Morocco) it was expelled from all the group's activities and financial assistance. In addition, Egypt was debarred from membership of most of the principal Arab financial institutions: the Federation of Arab Banks, the Arab Investment Company, the Arab Bank for Economic Development in Africa, and the Arab Fund for Economic and Social Development.[139]

A wide range of measures were also taken against Egypt in other spheres. The Arab Civil Aviation Organization asked its members to close their airspace to Egyptian planes and to shut down their offices in Cairo. Perhaps of greatest importance was the disbanding of the Cairo-based Arab Organization for Industrialization, which had been set up in Egypt in 1975 by Saudi Arabia, Qatar, the United Arab Emirates and Egypt. The aims of the organization had been to reduce the reliance of Arab countries on imported weapons, to improve Arab military technology and to stimulate the Egyptian economy. The consequences on Egypt of the closing down of the organization included the loss of some 15,000 jobs as well as a source of technology and weapons. In mid-April Egypt was expelled from the Organization of Arab Petroleum Exporting Countries (OAPEC).[140]

Europe's response to the signing of the Egyptian–Israeli peace treaty differed from that of the Arab side. The European Community greeted the treaty in a communiqué issued on 26 March 1979. This declaration stated that the nine members of the European Community greatly respected the desire of President Carter for peace and his consequent personal involvement in the peace negotiations. Similarly they stressed their appreciation of the sincere efforts made by President Sadat and Prime Minister Begin. The treaty was viewed as a proper application of the principles of Security Council resolution 242 to Egyptian–Israeli relations. The Community stressed its belief that the peace treaty between Egypt and Israel was only the first step towards a comprehensive agreement. Such an agreement should include all the parties concerned and must be founded on the principles of Security Council Resolutions 242 and 338, and must take into account the right of the Palestinian people to a homeland.[141]

On 26 April 1979, the Parliament of the European Community passed a resolution on the signature of the peace treaty between Egypt and Israel. The resolution paid tribute to the signatories and endorsed the efforts of both sides which had led to the completion of the peace treaty. It acknowledged the importance of this courageous step, stressing 'that the peace which has just been established will soon take a practical form through the participation of all parties concerned'.[142]

WORK SUSPENDED

The difference in viewpoints between most Arab countries and the European Community over the Camp David agreement, and the differences in their assessment of the whole peace process launched by President Sadat, were aggravated by another obstacle. The European Community was reluctant to deal with the new headquarters of the Arab League in Tunisia, from which Egypt— whose peace policy was approved of and appreciated by the European Community—was excluded. The Community insisted on Egypt being able to participate in the meetings of the Euro-Arab dialogue, despite the fact that Egypt had now been expelled from the League of Arab States.[143]

This combination of factors blocked the dialogue and made it no longer possible for the two sides (the Arab countries and the European Community) to reach any sort of agreement on the procedures of and the conditions for the dialogue. Moreover,

the Arab countries, in their assessment of the dialogue at the end
of the Damascus meeting, felt that the European Community
'stood by what it had declared in the London communiqué, that
it did not respond to the demands of the Arab side . . . and that in
general it was following a policy that fell short of Arab demands
for their rights'.[144] Consequently, in April 1979 the Commission
of the European Community was informed by the secretary-
general of the League of Arab States that the League wanted
now to suspend all activities of the dialogue, at the level of the
General Committee as well as that of the working parties and
specialized groups.[145]

PROGRESS EVALUATION

Generally the pace of work was slow. On the political side, the
dialogue took the form of a forum in which representatives from
both sides, especially from the European Community, used to
repeat statements that had already been issued. The Arabs
hoped to achieve some political goals, such as the recognition of
the PLO and the adoption by the Community of strong action
against Israeli policy in the occupied lands.

Although there was some progress in the European position
towards the Middle East conflict, such as the London statement
of 29 June 1977, and the positive vote by the Community
member states on the General Assembly resolution of 27 October 1977, the European response continued to be cautious,
fluctuating and characterized by a 'wait and see' attitude. It
never reached the point the Arabs sought to achieve: the recognition of the PLO.

The Europeans were unable to satisfy their partners in the
dialogue. This was due to the different attitudes of the Community members towards the Palestinian question, which in the
end confined the Community as a whole and restrained its
movement. As a result, the gap between both sides of the
dialogue continued to widen. It reached a point of extreme
contradiction over the Sadat peace initiative, which in the end
blocked any progress for the dialogue and led to its suspension.

On the economic side, aims for progress towards economic
co-operation was stagnating. Although the economic programme was ambitious and serious, few concrete projects were
actually implemented. There was a contradiction between what

the Arabs wanted and what the Community was ready to offer. This was especially so in the field of financial investment and trade co-operation. The Arabs asked for a multilateral trade agreement on preferential terms, but the Europeans rejected this on the grounds that most of the Arab countries had signed individual preferential agreements with the Community. Similarly, the Arabs demanded the protection of their investment against commercial risks. The Community was unwilling to offer that. The Community argued that in the present economic situation, it was difficult for the Community even to protect its own citizens against such risks.

However, some limited progress was made, especially in the areas of agriculture and rural development (such as the of Juba Valley development in Somalia, the Damazine meat production in Sudan, the southern Darfur integrated development project in Sudan and the potato development project in Iraq); transfer of technology (the agreement on the establishment of a Euro-Arab centre for the transfer of technology); and labour and social affairs (the adoption of a declaration on the principles of the living and working conditions of migrant workers in both regions).

Summing up, one can justifiably term the dialogue's achievements at this stage as only rudimentary, when set against the lofty aims and objectives that had been envisaged at the outset.

NOTES

1. *Bulletin of the European Communities*, No. 5, 1976, p. 8.
2. *Tenth General Report on the Activities of the European Communities in 1976*, Office for Official Publications of the European Communities, 1977, p. 21.
3. *Europe*, Agence Internationale d'Information Pour La Presse, Brussels, 6 January 1976.
4. A. S. Al-Dajani, 'The PLO and the Euro-Arab Dialogue', *Journal of Palestine Studies*, p. 87.
5. *Ibid*, p. 88.
6. *Telex Mediterranean*, 14 May 1976.
7. *Keesing's Contemporary Archives*, 12 November 1976, p. 28,049.
8. H. Maull, *Europe and World Energy*, p. 287.
9. *Telex Mediterranean*, 14 May 1976.
10. *The Euro-Arab Dialogue*, Joint Working Paper, Luxembourg, 18–20 May 1976.
11. *Bulletin of the European Communities*, p. 8.

12. *Europe*, Agence Internationale d'Information Pour La Presse, Brussels, 21 May 1976.
13. A. S. Al-Dajani, *Munazamat al-tahrir al-filastiniya wal-hiwar al-arabi al-urubbi*, (The PLO and the Euro-Arab Dialogue), Research Centre, Palestine Liberation Organization, Beirut, 1979, p. 27.
14. *Telex Mediterranean*, 29 May 1976.
15. A. S. Al-Dajani, 'The PLO and the Euro-Arab Dialogue', *Journal of Palestine Studies*, p. 88.
16. *Telex Mediterranean*, 29 May 1976.
17. *Ibid.*
18. *The Euro-Arab Dialogue*, General Committee, Final Communiqué, Luxembourg, 18–20 May 1976.
19. *Ibid.*
20. A. S. Al-Dajani, 'The PLO and the Euro-Arab Dialogue', *Journal of Palestine Studies*, pp. 88–9.
21. *Bulletin of the European Communities*, pp. 9–10.
22. *Ibid*, pp. 10–11.
23. *Europe*, 21 May 1976.
24. *Bulletin of the European Communities*, pp. 11–12.
25. *Tenth General Report on the Activities of the European Communities*, p. 266.
26. *Bulletin of the European Communities*, p. 9.
27. H. Maull, *Europe and World Energy*, p. 287.
28. *Keesing's Contemporary Archives*, p. 28,049.
29. A. S. Al-Dajani, *Munazamat al-tahrir al-filastiniya wal-hiwar al-arabi al-urubbi*, (The PLO and the Euro-Arab Dialogue), pp. 125–8.
30. *Twenty Fifth Review of the Council's Work (1 January–31 December 1977)*, Office for Official Publications of the European Communities, Luxembourg, 1978, p. 146.
31. A S. Al-Dajani, *Munazamat al-tahrir al-filastiniya wal-hiwar al-arabi al-urubbi*, (The PLO and the Euro-Arab Dialogue), p. 32.
32. *Telex Mediterranean*, 14 February 1977.
33. *Bulletin of the European Communities*, No. 2, 1977, p. 64.
34. *The Euro-Arab Dialogue*, General Committee Meeting, Final Communiqué, Tunis, 1977.
35. A. S. Al-Dajani, 'The PLO and the Euro-Arab Dialogue', *Journal of the Palestine Studies*, p. 89.
36. H. Maull, *Europe and World Energy*, p. 288.
37. *The Euro-Arab Dialogue*, General Committee Meeting, Tunis.
38. *Ibid.*
39. *Ibid.*
40. *Twenty Fifth Review of the Council's Work (1 January–31 December 1977)*, p. 146.
41. *Bulletin of the European Communities*, p. 66.
42. H. Maull, *Europe and World Energy*, pp. 288–9.
43. *European Parliament, Information, Parliament in Session*, Luxembourg: European Parliament, 1977, pp. 9–10.

44. *Bulletin of the European Communities*, p. 66.
45. A. R. Taylor, 'The Euro-Arab Dialogue: Quest for an Interregional Partnership', *Middle East Journal*, Vol. 32, No. 4, 1978, p. 437.
46. *Europe*, Agence Internationale d'Information Pour La Presse, Brussels, 7 January 1977.
47. *Bulletin of the European Communities*, p.66.
48. *Keesing's Contemporary Archives*, 11 November 1977, p. 28,658.
49. A. R. Taylor, 'The Euro-Arab Dialogue: Quest for an Interregional Partnership', *Middle East Journal*, p. 438.
50. *Bulletin of the European Communities*, p. 67.
51. *Ibid*, p. 67.
52. H. Maull, *Europe and World Energy*, p. 289.
53. *The European Community and the Arab World*, Commission of the European Communities, p. 31.
54. A. R. Taylor, 'The Euro-Arab Dialogue: Quest for an Interregional Partnership', *Middle East Journal*, Op.Cit, p. 436.
55. H. Maull, *Europe and World Energy*, p. 289.
56. *Europe*, Agence Internationale d'Information Pour La Presse, Brussels, 14 September 1977.
57. *Keesing's Contemporary Archives*, p. 28,656.
58. *Bulletin of the European Communities*, 6, 1977, p. 62.
59. *Telex Africa*, 25 April 1977.
60. D. Allen, 'The Euro-Arab Dialogue;, *Journal of Common Market*, p. 336.
61. *Bulletin of the European Communities*, 4, 1977.
62. *Bulletin of the European Communities*, 10, 1977, p. 82.
63. A. S. Al-Dajani, 'The PLO and the Euro-Arab Dialogue', *Journal of Palestine Studies*, p. 91–2.
64. *Telex Mediterranean*, 8 November 1977.
65. A. S. Al-Dajani, *Munazamat al-tahrir al-filastiniya wal-hiwar al-arabi al-urubbi*, (The PLO and the Euro-Arab Dialogue), p. 42.
66. *Ibid*, p. 42.
67. *Euro-Arab Dialogue*, General Committee Meeting, Final Communiqué, Brussels, Part One, 26–28 October 1977.
68. *Ibid*.
69. U. Steinbach, 'Western European and EC Policies towards Mediterranean and Middle East Countries', in C. Legum (ed.), *Middle East Contemporary Survey*, Vol. ll, 1977–1978, p. 45.
70. *Twenty Fifth Review of the Council's Work*, p. 147.
71. *Eleventh General Report on the Activities of the European Communities in 1977*, Office for Official Publications of the European Communities, Luxembourg, 1978, p. 253.
72. *Euro-Arab Dialogue*, General Committee, Final Communiqué, Brussels, Part Two, 1977.
73. *Telex Mediterranean*, 8 November 1977.
74. *Bulletin of the European Communities*, p. 83.
75. *Euro-Arab Dialogue*, General Committee, Final Communiqué.

76. *Ibid.*
77. *Ibid.*
78. *Ibid.*
79. *Bulletin of the European Communities,* p. 83.
80. *Euro-Arab Dialogue,* General Committee, Final Communiqué.
81. *Telex Mediterranean,* 11 October 1977.
82. *Twenty Fifth Review of the Council's Work,* p. 147.
83. *Bulletin of the European Communities,* p. 83.
84. *Euro-Arab Dialogue,* General Committee, Final Communiqué.
85. *Ibid.*
86. *Ibid.*
87. *Ibid.*
88. *Ibid.*
89. Nassif Hitti, 'The United States, The European Community and the Arab–Israeli Conflict', in Bichara Khader (ed.), *Co-operation Euro-Arabe,* Vol. 1, Louvain-La-Neuve: Universite Catholique de Louvain, 1982, p. 287.
90. Melvin A. Friedlander, *Sadat and Begin,* Westview Press, Boulder, Colorado, 1983, p. 51.
91. Harvey Sicherman, *Broker Or Advocate? The U.S. Role in the Arab–Israeli Dispute 1973–1978,* Foreign Policy Research Institute, Philadelphia, Pennsylvania, 1978, p. 33.
92. Mohammed K. Shadid, *The United States and the Palestinians,* Croom Helm, London, 1981, pp. 133–5.
93. *The New York Times,* 2 October 1977.
94. Ismail Fahmy, *Negotiating for Peace in the Middle East,* Croom Helm, London, 1983, pp. 233–5.
95. Mohammed K. Shadid, *The United States and the Palestinians,* pp. 136–8.
96. Nassif Hitti, 'The United States, The European Community and the Arab–Israeli Conflict', p. 288.
97. Daniel Dishon, 'The Middle East in Perspective', in Colin Legum (ed.), *Crisis and Conflict in the Middle East. The Changing of Strategy: From Iran to Afghanistan,* Holmes and Meier, Inc., New York and London, 1981, p. 23.
98. Muhammad Shurydi, 'The Baghdad Summit Conference: A Critical Evaluation', in Faith Zeady (ed.), *Camp David: A New Balfour Declaration,* Association of Arab-American University Graduates, Detroit, Michigan, 1979, p. 24.
99. 'Statement Issued by the Ninth Arab Summit Conference, Baghdad, 5 November 1978', *Journal of Palestine Studies,* Vol. VIII, No. 2, 1979, p. 203.
100. *Ibid.*
101. Muhammad Shurydi, 'The Baghdad Summit Conference: A Critical Evaluation', in Faith Zeady (ed.), *Camp David: A New Balfour Declaration,* p. 24.
102. *Bulletin of the European Communities,* No. 6, 1977, p. 62.
103. Ilan Greilsammer and Joseph Weiler, ' European Political Co-operation and the Arab–Israeli Conflict: An Israeli Perspective', p. 140.

104. Harvey Sicherman, 'Politics of Dependence, Western Europe and the Arab–Israeli Conflict', *Orbis*, Vol. 23, 1980, p. 849.
105. Moshe Gammer, 'The Negotiating Process: Attitudes of Interested Parties', *Middle East Contemporary Survey*, Vol. 11, 1977–78, p. 176.
106. *Ibid*, pp. 175–6.
107. *Bulletin of the European Communities*, No. 11, 1977, p. 52.
108. Moshe Gammer, 'The Negotiating Process: Attitude of Interested Parties', *Middle East Contemporary Survey*, p. 176.
109. Harvey Sicherman, ' Politics of Dependence, Western Europe and the Arab–Israeli Conflict', *Orbis*, p. 849.
110. *Bulletin of the European Communities*, No. 9, 1978, pp. 53–4.
111. *Ibid*, p. 103.
112. *Bulletin of the European Communities*, No. 10, 1978, p. 84.
113. *Telex Mediterranean*, 5 December 1978.
114. *Ibid*.
115. *Europe*, Agence Internationale d'Information Pour La Presse, Brussels, December 1978.
116. *Euro-Arab Dialogue*, Fourth General Committee Meeting, Final Communiqué, Part One, Damascus, 1978.
117. A S. Al-Dajani, *Munazamat al-tahrir al-filastiniya wal-hiwar al-arabi al-urubbi* (The PLO and the Euro-Arab Dialogue), pp. 59–60.
118. *Telex Mediterranean*, 19 December 1978.
119. *Bulletin of the European Communities*, No. 12, 1978, p. 20.
120. *Euro-Arab Dialogue*, General Committee Meeting, Final Communiqué, Damascus.
121. *Telex Mediterranean*, 8 May 1979.
122. *Bulletin of the European Communities*, pp. 19–20.
123. *Twelfth General Report on the Activities of the European Communities in 1978*, Office for Official Publications of the European Communities, Luxembourg, 1979, p. 287.
124. *Ibid*, p. 287.
125. *Twenty Sixth Review of the Council's Work (1 January–31 December 1978)*, Office for Official Publications of the European Communities, Luxembourg, 1979, p. 152.
126. *Euro-Arab Dialogue*, General Committee Meeting, Final Communiqué, Part Two, Damascus, 1978.
127. *Ibid*.
128. *Ibid*.
129. *Ibid*.
130. *Telex Mediterranean*, 5 December 1978.
131. *Bulletin of the European Communities*, p. 22.
132. *Ibid*, p. 23.
133. *Bulletin of the European Communities*, No. 3, 1979, p. 140.
134. *Ibid*, pp. 140–1.
135. *Euro-Arab Dialogue*, General Committee Meeting, Final Communiqué, Damascus.

136. *Ibid.*
137. *Ibid.*
138. Yehuda Lukacs, *Documents on the Israeli–Palestinian Conflict: 1967–1983*, Cambridge University Press, 1984, p. 232.
139. M.D. Wormser, *The Middle East*, Washington D.C., 1981, p. 28.
140. *Ibid*, pp. 28–9.
141. *Bulletin of the European Communities*, No.3, 1979, p. 86. See also, *New York Times*, 28 March 1979.
142. *Bulletin of the European Communities*, No.4, 1979, p. 82.
143. Saleh A. Al-Mani and Salah Al-Shaikhly, *The Euro-Arab Dialogue*, p. 65.
144. A. S. Al-Dajani, 'The PLO and the Euro-Arab Dialogue', *Journal of Palestine Studies*, p. 97.
145. 'La communauté Européenne et le monde Arabe', in Bichara Khader (ed.), *Co-operation Euro-Arabe*, p. 68.

V

AFTER THE DEADLOCK: FOCUS ON THE GULF AND THE EEC-GULF DIALOGUE

When the Euro-Arab dialogue reached its deadlock after the signing of the peace treaty between Egypt and Israel, the European Community felt that it was imperative to approach and establish links with the Arab Gulf states, with which the Community had no contractual agreement. For the Community, *rapprochement* between the EEC and the Arab Gulf countries was especially important in view of the intensive economic interaction between the two sides, which increased after 1973. To fully appreciate the European approach to the Arab Gulf countries, it would be useful to know the motivations behind the European move.[1]

THE MOTIVATIONS BEHIND THE COMMUNITY INITIATIVE TOWARDS THE ARAB GULF COUNTRIES

The European Community's approach to the Arab Gulf states stemmed from many elements. Some of these were related to security considerations, others to economic interests.

THE SECURITY MOTIVE

In the late 1970s, the Gulf region was transformed into an area of continuing crisis. A number of factors contributed to the increasing tensions in the area:

(1) the fall of the Shah of Iran in the wake of the Iranian revolution in January 1979;
(2) the Soviet intervention in Afghanistan in December of the same year;
(3) the outbreak of the 'Gulf War' between Iran and Iraq in September 1980.

These factors and their ramifications made the Gulf region politically an explosive area threatened by the risk of direct confrontation between the two superpowers as well as by its internal tensions.[2]

The downfall of the Shah of Iran in 1979 was the most conspicuous cause of the growing instability in the Gulf region. His departure not only added another crisis to the region's long history of tensions and conflicts, but also deprived the Western world—especially the United States and its European allies—of a major military ally in the region. The fall of the Shah meant that the 'two pillars' policy which the United States and its European allies had relied on since the British withdrew from the Gulf region was brought to an end. This, consequently, enhanced the strategic importance of the other Gulf countries, especially the conservative states, and made Saudi Arabia in particular the local key to Western security in the region.

Saudi Arabia had become the only large oil producer in the Gulf region that was constantly pro-Western. Moreover, Saudi Arabia's geography, its influence within OPEC and its wealth made it the only regional power that could work out effective collective security efforts to protect the conservative Gulf states and the Community's primary source of oil imports.[3] This heightened the concern of the European Community and the United States about the conservative Gulf states' security and stability, especially in the face of the growing external and internal threats to these states. The threats manifested themselves on many occasions: the riots and subversion in Bahrain in 1979, immigration problems in Qatar, the growing economic and demographic instability in the United Arab Emirates, the threat of a renewal of the Dhofar rebellion in Oman, and the Grand Mosque uprising and Shiite riots in Saudi Arabia in 1979–80.[4]

The Community's key interest in the Gulf region was obviously to secure access to oil, and not to see the oil supply fall into hostile hands. On this issue the Community's interests were very close to those of the United States. However, the European Community was far more dependent on Gulf oil than the United States, and had greater interest in maintaining its availability. Yet the Community alone was not able to ensure the security of its oil imports. Hence it had to rely heavily on the United States to secure its oil supply.[5]

Oil power and EEC security

To understand how deeply the European Community depended on oil coming from the Gulf region, and how the loss of Gulf oil would result in massive economic and political instability in the Community countries, we need to examine the Gulf countries' position in the world economy. The Gulf countries, especially those of the Gulf Co-operation Council (GCC), occupy a special and unique position. The crucial element is of course their huge and abundant energy resources. Each member of the GCC accounts for an important share of the world energy supply, and the collective share is very substantial. Despite the fact that the Gulf region contains less than one per cent of the world's oil wells, the six countries of the GCC accounted for 42 per cent of the world's proven reserves of crude oil in 1980, and about 63 per cent of the corresponding OPEC total. A decade earlier the GCC share of world proven oil reserves was 18 per cent (about 113 billion barrels). In 1978, the proven reserves had gone up to about 276 billion barrels (see Table 1).

The Gulf Co-operation Council countries also have about 25 per cent of the world's natural gas reserves and are now entering the world's petrochemical industry, which will inevitably lead to an essential change in its structure.[6] Additional new oil and gas fields have been discovered, but are not yet being used. These are the Shuaiba field near the Saudi Arabia and Abu-Dhabi frontiers, and the North Dome gas field offshore from Qatar.[7]

Although the GCC share of crude oil production is not as high as its share of proven reserves, the region is still the world's largest producer of crude oil. In 1980, daily production in the GCC countries stood at 14.1 million barrels. This was equal to 23.5 per cent of the total world production, and more than 52.3 per cent of the total OPEC production (see Table 2). The difference between reserve share and production share is due to the political decisions of the oil consortium, and more recently reflects the conservation decisions of the GCC countries. The allocation in the past of low production rates to the Gulf wells by the oil companies has left the area with a longer production life than would otherwise have been the case. In 1980, the GCC countries' reserves were equal to 53 years of production. By comparison, 1980 the average production life of the OPEC reserves was 44 years, and of total world reserves only 30 years.[8]

Table 1: GCC Proven Crude Oil Reserves, 1973–1980 (millions of barrels)

	1973	1974	1975	1976	1977	1978	1979	1980
Kuwait	72,750	81,450	71,200	70,550	70,100	69,440	68,530	67,930
Qatar	6,500	6,000	5,850	5,700	5,600	4,000	3,760	3,585
Saudi Arabia	140,750	173,150	151,800	153,150	153,100	168,940	166,480	168,030
UAE	25,500	33,920	32,200	31,200	32,425	31,316	29,411	30,410
Oman	1,700	1,600	1,500	1,500	1,800	2,000	2,300	2,400
Bahrain	360	330	310	311	290	270	251	233
GCC	247,560	296,450	262,860	262,411	263,315	275,966	270,732	272,588
OPEC	421,815	484,970	449,870	438,995	439,915	444,936	435,591	434,355
World	627,857	715,697	658,686	636,990	645,848	641,608	641,624	648,525
OPEC/World (%)	67.2	67.8	68.3	68.9	68.1	69.3	67.9	67.0
GCC/OPEC (%)	58.7	61.1	58.4	59.8	60.0	62.0	62.2	62.8
GCC/World (%)	39.4	41.4	39.9	41.2	40.8	43.0	42.2	42.0

Source: Atif A. Kubursi, *Oil, Industrialisation and Development in the Arab Gulf States,* Croom Helm, London, 1984.

Table 2: GCC Crude Oil Production, 1973–1980 (thousands of barrels per day)

	1973	1974	1975	1976	1977	1978	1979	1980
Kuwait	3,020	2,546	2,084	2,145	1,969	2,131	2,500	1,664
Qatar	570	518	438	47	445	487	508	471
Saudi Arabia	7,596	8,480	7,075	8,577	9,200	8,301	9,533	9,901
UAE	1,533	1,679	1,664	1,936	1,999	1,831	1,831	1,702
Oman	293	291	342	366	340	314	295	283
Bahrain	68	67	61	58	58	55	51	48
GCC	13,081	13,581	11,664	13,580	14,010	13,119	14,718	14,069
OPEC	30,989	30,729	27,155	30,738	31,253	29,805	30,929	26,878
World	55,803	56,088	53,384	57,883	59,862	60,143	62,747	59,740
OPEC/World (%)	55.5	54.8	50.9	53.1	52.2	49.6	49.3	45.0
GCC/OPEC (%)	42.2	44.2	43.0	44.2	44.8	44.0	47.6	52.3
GCC/World (%)	23.4	24.2	21.8	23.5	23.4	21.8	23.5	23.5

Source: Atif A. Kubursi, *Oil, Industrialisation and Development in the Arab Gulf States*, Croom Helm, London, 1984.

The major oil producer in the Arab Gulf region is Saudi Arabia. It dominates and holds the largest oil reserve pool, constituting 62 per cent of the total estimate of the proven oil reserves in the region in 1980. Its daily production of this mineral in 1980 reached an average of 9.9 million barrels. This was more than 70 per cent of the total GCC production in the same year (see Table 2). In contrast, Bahrain among the other members of the GCC was the smallest producer in the area, and also had the smallest proven reserves of crude oil.

Most of the oil produced in the GCC countries is for export. As a result, the region as a whole is one of the main crude oil trading areas. In 1979, the six Gulf countries' share of world exports of crude oil accounted for 40 per cent. Their share of total OPEC exports of crude oil was more than 50 per cent in the same year (see Table 3).[9] Among other major economic powers, the European Community is the major consumer of oil from the Gulf. In 1979, the Arab Gulf states as a whole supplied the European Community with more than 50 per cent of its crude oil, and 98 per cent of the Community's imports from the Gulf states were energy products.[10]

In 1981, the Arab Gulf states accounted for more than 70 per cent of EEC imports from Arab League states. Saudi Arabia alone accounted for more than 50 per cent, the United Arab Emirates accounted for more than 6 per cent and Kuwait for more than 4 per cent. The dominant product was of course fuel, comprising more than 98 per cent (see Table 4). Between 1980 and 1983, the European Community was constantly dependent on oil coming from the Arab Gulf countries, especially the GCC states. Table 5 shows that between 1980 and 1983, GCC oil provided 18–68 per cent of British imports of oil, 12–39 per cent of West German oil imports, and 37–58 per cent of those of France. In the same period, Saudi Arabian oil provided 9–48 per cent of British imports of oil, 12–36 per cent of West German oil imports, and 29–52 per cent of French oil imports.

Such trade and energy resources have made the Arab Gulf countries—especially the GCC countries—of crucial importance to the European Community, whose security and economic stability rely on the security of Gulf oil and consequently on the security and stability of the Gulf countries. This was clearly indicated by the German foreign minister, Herr Genscher, on 15 January 1980, when he pointed out that the Gulf region, as the source of half the Community's oil supplies, was vital to Europe.

Table 3: GCC Crude Oil Exports, 1973–1980 (thousands of barrels per day)

	1973	1974	1975	1976	1977	1978	1979	1980
Kuwait	2,642	2,203	1,803	1,791	1,625	1,761	2,083	1,297
Qatar	570	511	428	487	410	480	495	466
Saudi Arabia	7,015	7,922	6,601	8,032	8,606	7,706	8,818	9,223
UAE	1,522	1,690	1,661	1,933	1,990	1,816	1,805	1,697
Oman	292	290	342	368	334	316	295	n.a.
Bahrain	–	–	–	–	–	–	–	–
GCC	12,041	12,616	10,836	12,610	12,968	12,079	13,496	n.a.
OPEC	27,547	27,259	24,064	27,462	27,641	26,089	26,839	22,889
World	31,569	31,344	28,519	32,086	32,315	31,273	33,836	30,617
OPEC/World (%)	87.3	87.0	84.4	85.6	85.5	83.4	79.3	74.8
GCC/OPEC (%)	43.7	46.3	41.6	45.9	46.9	46.3	50.3	n.a.
GCC/World (%)	38.1	40.3	38.0	39.3	40.1	38.6	40.0	n.a.

Source: Atif A. Kubursi, *Oil, Industrialisation and Development in the Arab Gulf States*, Croom Helm, London, 1984.

Table 4: Major Arab League Suppliers of the EEC, 1972 and 1981

EC imports from:	Million ECU 1972	Million ECU 1981	% 1972	% 1981
Total Arab League	9,387	71,231	100	100
Maghreb Countries	1,386	8,515	14.8	12.0
Algeria	765	6,063	8.1	8.5
Mashreq Countries	296	4,636	3.2	6.5
Gulf States and Libya	7,502	57,699	80.0	81.0
Libya	1,676	7,092	17.9	10.0
Iraq	676	2,996	7.2	4.2
Saudi Arabia	2,632	36,832	28.0	51.7
Kuwait	1,599	3,059	17.0	4.3
United Arab Emirates	467	4,643	5.0	6.5
Non-Mediterranean African Countries	202	381	2.2	0.5

Source: *Trade between the European Community and the Arab League Countries,* Commission of the European Communities, Spokesman's Group and Directorate-General Information, Brussels, 1983.

He said that Europe was 'in a state of turmoil, caught between the wave of Islamic fervour and the Soviet invasion of Afghanistan'.[11] So the Community's attempt to open a dialogue with the Gulf countries 'is essentially a political one, representing a contribution by Europe to the maintenance of stability in the region, and illustrates the contention that even a halting dialogue is preferable to total isolation'.[12]

ECONOMIC INTERESTS

The desire of the European Community to approach the Gulf countries for security reasons, did not obscure the economic interest of the Community in the region.

The need for coordinated action on energy matters

One of the Community's economic interests in the Gulf region lay in the need for coordinated action with the Gulf countries on energy matters. First, the Community states wanted to avoid

Table 5: Minimax of Monthly Shifts in Percentage of Western Oil Imports from the Gulf, 1980–1983 (range shown covers period from 1980 'high' to February 1983 'low')

	USA	Canada	Japan	UK	West G.	France
Saudi Arabia	9–23	0–34	36–47	9–48	12–36	29–52
Other Conservative Gulf States						
Kuwait	0–0.5	0–3	0–4	0–11	0–0.2	–
Qatar	–	0	2–4	0	0–1	0–4
UAE	0.4–2	0–2	12–15	9–12	0–2	2–6
Minimax	0.4–2.5	0–5	14–23	9–23	1–3	2–8
Total Conservative Gulf States	9–26	0–39	50–69	18–68	12–39	37–58
Other Gulf States						
Iran	0–0.5	0–10	1–12	0–13	3.6	1–10
Iraq	0–2	0	0–4	?–9	0–3	0–3
Minimax	0–2.5	0–10	1–12	?–13	4–8	0–13
Total Gulf	9–28.5	10–39	60–70	54–77	20–46	38–69
Other Arab						
Algeria	1–4	6–13	1–2	0	5–6	5–6
Egypt	1–2	0	0	0–5	1–3	0–3
Libya	0–11	0–3	0–1	0–1	9–15	0–7
Minimax	2–18	6–13	1–3	0–5	15–24	5–16
Total OAPEC	17–43	13–47	61–73	21–81	38–56	52–70
Total OPEC	32–69	59–73	81–86	45–79	55–65	70–79
Total Imports (in MMBD)	3.4–8.4	0.2–0.7	3.6–6.2	0.6–1.4	2.0–2.8	1.7–2.8
Total Oil Consumption (in MMBD)	14.7–18.8	1.3–1.9	3.6–5.8	1.2–1.8	1.7–2.7	1.2–2.5

Source: Anthony H. Cordesman, *The Gulf and the Search for Strategic Stability*, Westview Press, Mansell Publishing Limited, London, 1984.

disturbances to their respective economies through unpredictable increases in the price of oil, and delivery fluctuations. This objective required that Community oil imports must be available at a reasonable price and be supplied with enough regularity and consistency, so that economic growth and development could go ahead. Moreover, the Community was in need not only of maintaining a total volume of oil shipments, but also of making sure that the Community could rely on a regular flow of the proper types of crude oil without having to buy on the spot market and without causing any minor panics in the world's capital market and oil market, as happened during the Iranian revolution in 1979. This, from the Community's viewpoint, would mean that each of the Gulf oil-producing countries had to the a relatively stable source of oil for the Community.[13] To achieve this goal, the Community decided to approach the Gulf countries in order to conclude direct agreements between the European Community as a whole and individual Gulf countries. In the context of these agreements, the Community hoped that it would be able to secure the Gulf states' approval to provide the Community with 'specific quantities of crude oil at uniform prices with a binding formula to determine price changes'.[14]

Secondly, the Community felt that the bilateral trade-in- exchange-for-oil agreements between individual Community member states and individual Gulf states (in 1979, about 15 per cent of crude oil imports to the European Community was covered by different bilateral agreements, reaching 36 per cent in 1980) were to the benefit of the oil-producing countries. Such bilateral agreements, from the Community viewpoint, could cause an uncoordinated and senseless competition by the Community member states to grant trade preferences. Also, these bilateral agreements 'don't benefit the small member states, which are less well able to keep pace in this race for preferential oil supplies, and undermine the negotiating position of the EEC as a whole'.[15] Therefore, the Community preferred to have close relations with the Gulf countries through agreements coordinated at Community level.

Thirdly, in view of the increasing trend towards government- to- government oil contracts, thus placing oil trading in a more political context, and the fact that these government-to- government deals (according to the Community) were causing high levels of inflation, the Community felt that it was advisable to have close economic co-operation at the Community level with the Gulf States in order to overcome this problem.[16]

Co-operation on petrochemicals

The Gulf economies, like the economies of many other developing countries, suffer from dependence on the export of a single natural resource. For the Gulf states, this is a depletable and unrenewable resource. Therefore, the Gulf states are in an awkward position. They need to diversify their sources of revenue and achieve an industrial economy before the the oil runs out.[17] To achieve this goal, the states have launched an ambitious programme of industrialization based on the development of downstream activities to transform crude oil into oil products and petrochemicals. Petrochemical industries in particular were seen by the Arab Gulf countries as an instrument of change, which could play a crucial role in the Gulf countries' industrialization policies.[18]

There were many reasons for the emphasis on the petrochemical industries in the Gulf region, including the Arab Gulf countries' abundant supplies of hydrocarbons and the substantial financial resources needed for a capital-intensive industry such as petrochemicals. These elements could make the Arab Gulf countries substantial and viable producers of petrochemicals— hence the Arab Gulf countries' huge investments in this sector. Most of the petrochemical complexes in the Arab Gulf were set up, or greatly expanded, in the late 1970s and early 1908s: Yanbu and Jubail in Saudi Arabia, Umm Said in Qatar, Al-Ruwais in the United Arab Emirates, and Al-Zubair in Iraq.[19]

Due to the limited size of domestic markets in the Arab Gulf states (especially in the GCC countries), most of the output of these projects was intended for export, mainly to the Community market—the most attractive, closest and larger market for the Arab Gulf countries.[20] It was this reality that gave rise to the Community's fears that the Gulf-produced petrochemicals could become competitive and threaten the European markets, endangering the Community's own petrochemical industry.[21] For this reason, the European Community needed to set up a dialogue with the Arab Gulf states so as to exchange views and arrange co-operation in this field.

The importance of the Arab Gulf states as export markets

In order to be able to maintain its expenditure on oil imports from the Gulf states, the European Community had to cycle the money back. One of the major ways in which petrodollars could be recycled to the Community was through increasing the latter's exports to the Arab Gulf countries. The Arab Gulf market proved to be an absorptive one, thus offering an attractive market for export from the Community member states. In 1978, EEC exports to the Arab Gulf states accounted for more than 6 per cent of total Community exports, a percentage that almost compared with that of the Community exports to Eastern Europe in the same year.

The bulk of the Community exports to the Arab Gulf countries was composed of processed products (about 88.9 per cent of the total). EEC exports of agricultural produce to the Gulf states in 1978 accounted for nearly five times as much as in 1973.[22] In 1980, the Community exports to the Arab League countries accounted for 15.5 per cent of its total exports. Among the Arab countries, Saudi Arabia headed the list of Arab imports from the Community. In 1980, 3.2 per cent of total EEC exports went to Saudi Arabia, 1.7 per cent went to Iraq and 0.9 per cent went to the United Arab Emirates (see Table 6). In 1981, EEC exports to the six Gulf states accounted for 6.3 per cent of total extra-EEC exports. Most of the Community exports to the GCC states in the same year were manufactured goods (78.6 per cent), agricultural and food products (9.6 per cent) and primary products (4.2 per cent)(see Table 7).

Euro-Gulf trade, in conjunction with general Euro-Arab trade, occupied an important position. Between 1979 and 1981, the Arab countries as a whole represented an impressive expanding market for Community exports. The market of the Arab Gulf states during this period was very important for Community exports. In 1979, Community exports to the Arab Gulf countries accounted for almost 47 per cent of EEC exports to the Arab world. Saudi Arabia alone accounted for about 21.8 per cent of

Table 6: The Arab League's Share of Community Trade

| | EEC Imports | | EEC Exports | |
	Millions ECUs	%	Millions ECUs	%
1976 Total European 9	157,340	100.0	141,300	100.0
1980 Total European 9	271,552	100.0	224,446	100.0
including: USA		16.3		11.8
Saudi Arabia		9.0		3.2
Iraq		2.9		1.7
Libya		2.4		1.8
UAE		1.6		0.9
Algeria		1.5		2.1
Egypt		0.6		1.4
Other Arab League		3.5		4.3
Total Arab League	58,409	21.5	34,716	15.5

Source: *The European Community and the Arab World*, Commission of the European Communities, Directorate-General for Information, Brussels, 1982.

Table 7: European Community Trade with the Gulf States

Breakdown (in %)	1973	1977	1981	1982	1983
EEC Imports	100	100	100	100	100
Energy Products	97	99	98	94	94
Other	3	1	2	6	6
EEC Exports	100	100	100	100	100
Manufactured goods	n.a.	84.9	78.6	81.7	80.2
Agricultural and food products	n.a.	7.1	9.6	8.3	8.8
Primary products	n.a.	1.0	4.2	3.5	1.9
EC imports from Gulf states as %age of total extra-EC imports	7.7	11.4	15.6	6.5	4.5
EC exports to Gulf states as %age of total extra-EC exports	1.3	5.2	6.3	7.4	6.4

Oil (crude)		1982	1983	1984
EC imports from Gulf states (mn tonnes)		122.0	72.0	55.0
% of total extra-EC crude oil imports		38.8	25.8	20.0
Gulf exports (in %) to community	24%			

Source: *The European Community and the Gulf Co-operation Council,* Commission of the European Communities, Directorate-General for Information, Brussels, 1985.

the total, Iraq for 9.1 per cent, and the United Arab Emirates for 6.1 per cent (see Table 8). In 1980, the Community's exports to the Arab Gulf countries constituted more than 45 per cent of the total Community exports to the Arab world (see Table 9). In 1981, this figure jumped to more than 47 per cent (see Table 10).

The increase of the Arab Gulf countries's imports was due to a number of factors: the deliberate policies aimed at speeding up the level of the economic development; the open-door policy which accelerated the imports of consumer goods; arms purchases; the deterioration of the terms of trade which resulted in higher expenditure on imports; and the depreciation of the dollar which resulted in higher prices for goods coming from non-American markets.[23] The rise of the Arab Gulf countries' merchandise imports was most pronounced in Saudi Arabia, where in 1980 imports were worth about $2.5 billion from West Germany, $4.5 billion from the United Kingdom, and $6 billion from Italy.[24] The value of Arab Gulf markets for recycling petrodollars through purchases from the Community was, therefore, very important for the latter. This explains why the European Community had a strategic interest in establishing viable economic relationships with the Arab Gulf states and securing this recycling process.

Co-operation towards recycling Arab Gulf petrodollars

Co-operation in seeking solutions to the 'growing problem in recycling the balance of payment surplus of the Gulf states and to ensure that the Gulf states' resources are not used up prematurely'[25] was also among the motivations behind the Community's approach to the Arab Gulf countries. These countries, especially those of the the GCC, are among the richest in the world in terms of earnings. Due to their continuing large exports surplus, coupled with their limited absorptive capacity, the Arab Gulf states managed to accumulate a substantial financial

Table 8: The EEC's Main Client in the Arab League (Million ECUs and %)

| | ECU Million | | % | |
	1972	1979	1972	1979
Arab League	4,363	29,294	100	100
Maghreb	1,547	6,726	36.1	23.0
Morocco	365	1,677	8.4	5.7
Algeria	938	3,816	21.5	13.0
Tunisia	271	1,233	6.2	4.2
Mashreq	877	4,728	20.1	16.1
Egypt	276	2,324	6.3	7.9
Lebanon	382	819	8.8	2.8
Arab Countries of the Gulf and Libya	1,723	17,108	39.5	58.4
Libya	648	3,387	14.9	11.6
Iraq	217	1,226	5.0	9.1
Saudi Arabia	320	6,392	7.3	21.8
UAE	106	1,790	2.4	6.1
Non-Mediterranean Countries of Africa	190	732	4.4	2.5

Source: *The European Community and the Gulf Co-operation Council*, Commission of the European Communities, Directorate-General for Information, Brussels, 1985.

Table 9: 'EEC 9'—Trade with the Arab League by Country of Destination, 1980 (Million ECUs)

	EEC9	Germany	France	Italy	NL	Benelux	UK	Ireland	Denmark
EXPORT									
Morocco	1,479	171	856	170	80	76	111	5	10
Algeria	4,710	991	1,891	933	191	428	236	21	20
Tunisia	1,541	268	674	379	63	76	50	25	5
Egypt	3,105	736	938	475	154	153	578	31	40
Syria	1,245	324	235	373	83	71	136	8	14
Lebanon	1,032	177	250	340	52	79	118	5	12
Jordan	687	186	142	106	36	36	167	4	10
Libya	4,146	904	484	1,846	120	202	471	95	23
Sudan	473	87	65	36	32	26	208	2	16
Mauritania	52	5	21	–	14	8	4	–	–
Somalia	52	6	6	21	2	7	9	–	1
Djibouti	40	10	6	9	4	1	9	–	1
Iraq	3,816	1,298	778	684	180	245	538	8	85
Saudi Arabia	7,283	1,694	1,051	1,499	790	378	1,746	23	102
Kuwait	1,474	356	214	294	74	48	426	8	55
Bahrain	323	33	31	33	15	10	192	1	8
UAE	2,079	341	336	311	132	78	835	12	34
Oman	394	61	28	20	35	20	218	2	9
Qatar	392	67	68	45	21	10	170	1	10
North Yemen	340	54	112	48	43	9	61	2	11
South Yemen	53	3	9	4	20	2	6	–	8
Total Arab League	34,716	7,772	8,195	7,626	2,141	1,583	6,289	253	473
EEC/Arab League trade balance	–23,693	–3,701	–7,398	–5,690	–3,784	–2,640	–1,029	–31	+201

Source: The European Community and the Arab World, Commission of the European Communities, Directorate-General for Information, Brussels, 1982.

surplus. In 1980, the Arab Gulf countries experienced a massive capital inflow, worth $489.1 million a day. Saudi Arabia alone received a daily average of about $350 million in oil revenue, or well over $100 billion a year. This income gave Saudi Arabia an annual surplus on its current account of roughly $50 billion in 1980. Subsequently, Saudi Arabia managed to increase its overseas investments to about $150 million (see Table 11).

This oil surplus caused concern for the European Community. First, the Community feared that if the oil surplus were to be invested as in the past (short term), it would cause serious disturbances and fluctuations for the currencies of the EEC member states. Investment could be switched from one currency to another in a period of high international liquidity. Secondly, from the Community's viewpoint, recycling of surplus for investment could be uneven among the member states, depending upon the attractiveness of money and capital markets existing in individual Community countries.

Table 10: The EEC's Major Client in the Arab League, 1972 & 1981 (Million ECUs and %)

| | ECU Million | | % | |
EC Exports to:	1972	1981	1972	1981
Arab League	4,338	51,180	100	100
Maghreb	1,574	9,252	36.3	18.1
Morocco	365	1,745	8.4	3.4
Algeria	938	5,583	21.5	10.9
Tunisia	271	1,924	6.2	3.8
Mashreq	851	8,379	19.6	16.4
Egypt	276	4,265	6.3	8.3
Lebanon	382	1,254	8.8	2.5
Jordan	67	1,379	1.5	2.7
Syria	126	1,481	2.9	2.9
Arab Countries of the Gulf and Libya	1,723	32,517	39.7	63.5
Libya	648	8,081	14.9	15.8
Iraq	217	7,083	5.0	13.8
Saudi Arabia	320	10,442	7.3	20.4
UAE	106	2,684	2.4	5.2
Non-Mediterranean Countries of Africa	190	1,032	4.4	2.0

Source: *The European Community and the Gulf Co-operation Council,* Commission of the European Communities, Directorate-General for Information, Brussels, 1985.

Table 11: Capital Resources of the Gulf States in 1980

	Nominal Current Value of Oil Production at Average OPEC Price of $35 per barrel ($ millions)		Capital Holdings in investment in the West ($ billions)		Total Trade Surplus on A/C (1980 in $ bns)	Trade with US ($ billions)		
	Daily	Annual	Total	In US		Exports	Imports	Balance
Saudi Arabia	350.0	127.8	110–150	40–60	50	5.8	13.3	–7.5
Other Conservative Gulf States								
Bahrain	1.6	0.6	54.9	–	–	–	–	–
Kuwait	52.5	19.2	–	–	14	0.9	0.5	+0.4
Oman	17.5	6.4	–	–	–	–	–	–
Qatar	10.8	4.0	–	–	3	0.1	0.3	–0.2
UAE	56.7	20.7	–	–	8	1.0	2.1	–1.1
Subtotal	139.1	50.9	–	–	25	2.0	2.9	–0.9
Total Conservative Gulf States	489.1	178.7	–	–	75	7.8	16.2	–8.4
Other Gulf States								
Iran	56.7	20.7	–	–	0	0.0	0.4	–
Iraq	21.0	7.8	–	–	6	0.7	0.4	–
North Yemen	0	0	–	–	–	–	–	–
South Yemen	0	0	–	–	–	–	–	–
Subtotal	77.7	28.5	–	–	6	0.7	0.8	–0.1
Total Gulf	566.8	207.2	–	–	81	8.5	17.0	–8.5
Total OPEC	738.5	296.6	–	–	107	17.8	54.8	–8.5

Source: Anthony H. Cordesman, *The Gulf and the Search for Strategic Stability*, Westview Press, Mansell Publishing Limited, London, 1984.

There would thus be no inflow of capital to countries with weaker economies to offset their deficits, and recycled funds would instead be concentrated in the major financial centres. This would inevitably lead (especially in the countries with weaker economies) to 'protectionist moves and a general tendency for trade and economic activity to contract, resulting in unemployment and a decline in development aid'.[26] So as to avoid a fall in growth and greater unemployment, the Community was interested in opening a dialogue or concluding agreements with the Gulf states that would deal, *inter alia*, with the terms and procedures for setting up smooth recycling of oil revenue surpluses.

The need to help the Gulf states to develop their industrial economies

The Gulf countries' economies suffer from dependence on a single product, oil. To overcome this problem, the Arab Gulf states have invested huge sums in the diversification of their industries. But the Arab Gulf countries also suffer from a shortage of qualified workers and a general shortage of indigenous labour. Hence 'co-operation in training and joint ventures to promote industry offer a further chance of co-operation between the ECC Member States and the Gulf States'.[27]

The need for a coordinated approach to prevent economic collapse in the developing countries

The non-oil-producing developing countries, because of the high price of the oil imports, were faced with a difficult problem. Their balance of payments deficits continued to worsen as the oil bills became higher. In 1981, it was estimated that the combined current account deficit of the oil-importing developing countries reached $80,000 million. The direct result of this deficit was a drastic cut-back in development projects in these countries.

Also, the oil-importing countries, in order to be able to pay their oil bills, were forced to reduce their other imports. This caused concern for the European Community. First, the European Community did not want to see the developing countries, upon which it depended for strategic materials, collapse because of their oil problems. Secondly, the Community feared that it might lose important markets in the developing countries because the latter had to pay for their oil bills. This, from the Community's viewpoint, would lead to higher deficits in the exporting Community member states. The European Community had, therefore, a strategic interest in approaching the Gulf countries and establishing a stable 'three-way relationship' involving the Community member states, the Gulf oil-producing countries, and the Third World oil-importing countries. Through this approach, the European Community hoped to persuade the Gulf countries to relieve the oil-importing developing countries from part of the financial burden and help them find a financial solution to funding their oil imports.[28]

The European initiative towards a limited, specifically economic dialogue with the Arab Gulf states has, then, to be understood in the context of (1) the deadlock which had been reached in the Euro-Arab dialogue (as shown in the previous chapter), and (2) the increased economic importance of the Gulf states and the extensive interaction with the EEC (which was analysed above). Having examined the background, let us now take a closer look at this EEC–Gulf states dialogue.

THE EEC–GULF STATES DIALOGUE

The German initiative

The first attempt by the European Community to open a dialogue with the Arab Gulf states came through the so-called German initiative. In December 1979, the German minister for economic affairs, Count Lambsdroff, visited the Gulf states and held talks with their governments about close co-operation with the Community. He then presented the European Council of Ministers with a proposal for bilateral agreements with the Arab Gulf states.

This attempt was then followed up by the German foreign minister, Herr Genscher, who strongly advocated the idea of having close economic co-operation with the Arab Gulf states. At a meeting in Brussels on 15 January 1980, Herr Genscher brought up his proposal for discussion in the European Council of Ministers. In the proposal, he suggested that bilateral co-operation agreements be concluded with the Arab countries in the Gulf region: Kuwait, Bahrain, Qatar, Oman, United Arab Emirates, Saudi Arabia and Iraq. The co-operation agreements, he suggested, would cover co-operation in the energy sector (exchanges of information on world supply and demand forecast, Community energy policies, and so on), encouragement and protection of investment, economic and industrial co-operation to diversify the Arab Gulf states industries, and technical and scientific co-operation.

Also, the co-operation agreements would include granting the Arab Gulf countries 'most-favoured' nation states. It was suggested that in formal terms the co-operation agreements with the Arab Gulf countries would be signed in accordance with the same procedures as the ASEAN agreement (the co-operation agreement between the EEC and the five members of the Association of the South-East Asian Nations, which aimed to strengthen and diversify economic relations between the two sides).[29]

On 5 February 1980, the European Council of Ministers approved the German proposal and agreed in principle to hold negotiations with the countries concerned in order to conclude co-operation agreements. Hence the European Council directed the European Commission to make the necessary preparations for sounding out the seven countries 'on the possibilities for following up the Community initiative'.[30] As a result, technical missions of the European Commission were sent to the region to identify the interests of the individual Arab Gulf states. One of these missions visited Oman in June 1980, while the others were scheduled for the autumn of the same year. The mission that visited Oman confirmed that to some extent Oman was in favour of the Community initiative.[31]

However, the European Community initiative to have close economic co-operation with the Arab Gulf states did not go far enough because it was blocked by the European Council of Ministers. In September 1980, the European Council decided to suspend the work. It believed that any move to have a dialogue with the Arab Gulf states was premature and inopportune. The reason given was the war between Iran and Iraq.[32]

REACTIONS TO THE GERMAN INITIATIVE

The reactions of both sides to the initiative were generally passive. On the European side some of the Community member states (especially France) were reluctant to accept the proposal. The French government justified its reservation by explaining that, in view of the existence of the Euro-Arab dialogue, moribund though it might be, there would be no justification for such an initiative. In addition, the French government argued that the initiative might be viewed as an attempt by the European Community to divide the Arab countries. These reservations from some of the Community member states could also be seen in the light of the tendency of certain of them to adopt purely national policies over their oil supplies.[33]

On the Arab side, while Bahrain, the United Arab Emirates and Oman gave a positive response to the initiative, Iraq, Kuwait and Saudi Arabia expressed their doubts and reservations. These initial reactions were confirmed at a meeting held in Brussels on 4 June 1980, between the rapporteur of the European Parliament's Committee on External Economic Relations and representatives of the Arab Gulf countries that had expressed reservations. During the talks, the representatives justified their reservations by arguing that the Community initiative towards the Gulf states was a short-term offer 'made only because of the EEC countries' present uncertainty about their oil supplies and one which totally disregarded the other aspects of co-operation'; hence 'this co-operation would be forgotten as soon as the oil question had been resolved with some degree of certainty'.[34]

The representatives stressed the importance their governments attached to having closer co-operation with the Community. But having emphasized that, they asserted that the European Community should adopt a clear position in the Middle East, since the economic issues could not be separated from political matters. This was clearly indicated by the representative of Iraq when he stated (during the talks) that 'it was ridiculous to try to disregard the political problems which had already blocked the Euro-Arab dialogue in a direct EEC–Gulf states dialogue'.[35] He went on to stress that if negotiations between the EEC and the Arab Gulf states took place, the same problems would appear again. For this reason, making separate arrangements would bring the European Community no political advantage. The representatives therefore confirmed that they would prefer to develop their relations with the European Community through the Euro-Arab dialogue and did not want to be deflected from the solidarity being achieved in this dialogue.[36]

THE ESTABLISHMENT OF THE GCC, AND RELATIONS WITH THE NEW GROUP

The official creation of the Gulf Co-operation Council took place between 4 February and 26 May 1981, when six Gulf states (Saudi Arabia, Kuwait, Bahrain, Qatar, Oman and the United Arab Emirates) agreed to establish a co-operation council among their states, to set up a secretariat-general for this aim, and to hold periodic meetings at the summit as well as at foreign ministers' level. According to a statement issued on 4 February, and read by the Saudi foreign minister, Prince Saud al-Faisal, the creation of the Gulf Co-operation Council was due to many considerations such as 'special relations, joint characteristics, joint creed, similarity of regimes and unity of heritage' among the Gulf states, and their 'desire to deepen and develop co-operation and coordination among them in all fields in a manner that brings good, development and stability to their peoples'.[37] In addition, it was stressed that the creation of the Gulf Co-operation Council was in accordance with the framework of the Arab League Charter, which encouraged regional co-operation. Mr Abdallah Bishara, the secretary-general of the GCC, stated in a press conference on 27 May that the Gulf Co-operation Council had an important role to play in the world and that it was not exclusively a political body. Priority was given to economic affairs.[38]

The creation of the Gulf Co-operation Council was welcomed by the European Community. At the meeting of the European Council on September 1981, the ministers of foreign affairs discussed the relations between the European Community and the newly established Gulf Co-operation Council. It was decided to initiate informal preliminary contacts with the secretariat of the GCC in order to examine the scope of the proposed co-operation with the GCC.[39] As a result, informal contacts with the secretariat of the Gulf Co-operation Council were established by the Commission's departments.

Subsequently, a visit was paid by the secretary-general of the GCC, Mr Bishara, to the European Commission on 9 and 10 June 1982.[40] The visit aimed to 'acquaint the Secretary-General with the aims, functioning and structure of the European Communities with a view to his institution benefiting from the Community experience'.[41] Also, during the visit, Mr Bishara held talks with the Community representatives. It was decided that more contacts on a technical level between the two sides should take place in order to 'identify specific subjects on which concrete co-operation could be developed, including the dispatch of personnel for training'.[42]

In response to an invitation from the Gulf Co-operation Council, representatives from the European Commission later paid a visit to Saudi Arabia (where the headquarters of the GCC are situated) from 20 to 22 March 1983. Its principal goal was 'to find out more about the objectives and the functioning of the Gulf Co-operation Council'.[43] During the talks, which took place in Riyadh, it was agreed to 'inaugurate a technical co-operation programme in the areas of statistics, customs, information and energy'.[44]

On 29 and 30 March 1984, Dr Abdallah El-Kuwaize, Assistant Secretary-General (Economic Affairs) of the Gulf Co-operation Council, visited the Commission of the European Communities and held discussions with representatives from the Commission's departments. The outcome was an agreement 'on a continued and expanded programme of technical co-operation between the GCC Secretariat and the European Commission'.[45] On 7 and 8 November 1984, informal contacts between representatives from the European Commission and the Gulf Co-operation Council took place in Bahrain.[46] The aim was to 'explore the possibility and make preparations with a view to launching negotiations to conclude a co-operation agreement'[47] between the European Community and the GCC as a whole. Also, it was agreed to hold more exploratory meetings (for this purpose) at the beginning of 1985.[48]

The exploratory talks between the representatives of the European Commission and the Gulf Co-operation Council continued at the beginning of 1985. On 11 and 12 February, the secretary-general of the Gulf Co-operation Council, Mr Abdullah Bishara, visited the European Commission, where he met M Cheysson, the member with special responsibility for Mediterranean policy. The aim of the visit was 'to discuss preparations for the forthcoming exploratory talks—scheduled for the beginning of March in Bahrain—on the possibility of a co-operation agreement'.[49] On 1 and 2 March 1985, another round of exploratory discussions took place in Bahrain between representatives of the Gulf Co-operation Council and the European Commission. The principal goal of the discussions was 'to explore further the possibilities for formal negotiations on a co-operation agreement between the two regions'.[50]

After the talks, both sides issued a joint communiqué in which they stated that they 'agreed that it was in their mutual interest to aim to conclude a comprehensive, mutually beneficial, all-embracing agreement to foster the broadest possible commercial and economic co-operation between the GCC and the European Community'.[51] The joint communiqué went on to stress that such an agreement between a developing and a developed region would be of considerable importance and a clear indication of the economic interdependence which existed between the GCC states and the European Community. Both sides emphasized that by coordinating their efforts on matters of common interest within the framework of an agreement, they would be able to improve their relations. They recognized that the co-operation agreement should take due account of the developing nature of the GCC region and of the objectives and priorities of its development plans and programmes. Also, the two sides agreed that the co-operation agreement should be of an evolutionary nature, taking into account the changing circumstances in the two areas. It was suggested that the proposed region-to-region co-operation agreement between the GCC countries and the European Community would include areas such as access to markets, energy, scientific, technological and industrial co-operation and training, investment and financial co-operation.[52]

However, among the subjects which proved to be a major source of friction between the European Community and the GCC states was the issue of access of GCC exports to the Community market. The GCC states demanded preferential treatment for their industrial products—especially petrochemical products—in the Community market. The European Community declined to grant them such treatment. Instead, it offered a non-preferential agreement. The GCC countries rejected the offer as unacceptable and no agreement was reached on this subject.[53]

DISAGREEMENT OVER THE PETROCHEMICALS ISSUE

The disagreement between the European Community and the Gulf Co-operation Council states over the petrochemical issue lay mainly in the terms of entry granted by the Community for GCC petrochemicals. The European Community, in order to protect its own petrochemical industry, insisted on imposing tariffs on the Gulf countries' petrochemical products once the duty-free ceiling under the Community's Generalized Scheme of Preferences was exceeded.[54] The Community imposition of tariffs angered the petrochemical producers in the GCC countries, who viewed the action as a direct threat to their infant petrochemical industry. 'When some developed nations meet our entry into the petrochemical market with calls for protectionism, we can only warn that this is a threat as much to the world economic system as a whole as to Saudi Arabia,' said Mr Ibrahim Salamah, the chairman and managing director of the Saudi Arabian Basic Industries Corporation (Sabic).[55]

Subsequently, the GCC countries refused to accept the Community protectionist measures and demanded that their industrial products, particularly petrochemicals, should enter the Community market if not free, then at a reduced rates of duty as 'applied to most dutiable goods imported into the Gulf'.[56]

The GCC countries justified their demand by arguing, first, that EEC exports entered the GCC countries either duty-free or at very low customs duties (between 4 to 7 per cent).[57] In 1984, most Community sales to the GCC countries, which were worth 22,759 million ECUs, entered the region duty-free. Hence, the GCC governments expected comparable treatment from their European trade partner: 'We expect that our industries would find freer access to the Community markets in the same manner in which European industries flow into our markets,' said Shaikh Sabah Al-Ahmad Al-Jaber, the Kuwaiti foreign minister.[58]

Secondly, the GCC countries emphasized that the petrochemical products produced in the GCC countries were mainly basic petrochemicals. When exported they became feedstocks for the manufacture of final petrochemicals, which were in turn exported back from the European Community to the GCC countries.

Thirdly, the most-favoured nation clause accorded by to the developing countries by the United Nations Conference on Trade and Development (UNCTAD) meant that the industrial exports of the developing countries should find outlets in the advanced countries' markets. This should be done without obliging the developing countries to grant the same concessions on imports from the industrial countries. The GCC governments stressed that in the case of the GCC and the European Community, the situation was reversed.

Finally, the GCC countries asserted that failing to reach agreement on this subject might lead the GCC states to consider imposing similar customs duties on imports from the European Community.[59]

The European Community's response to the GCC countries' demand was negative. The Community stated clearly that there was no possibility of removing the extra tariffs it had imposed on Gulf petrochemical exports to the Community market. The Community states justified their position by arguing, first, that customs duties in the European Community were routinely applied in accordance with the legal regulations followed by the Community within the context of the Community's international obligations. Therefore, according to the Community, it was not possible to offer preferential treatment to the products coming from the GCC countries without offering the same treatment to all exporters, in compliance with the provisions of GATT.

Secondly, the low cost of raw materials in the GCC countries gave those countries an 'unfair' advantage over the Community petrochemical producers, who already had excess capacity. This excess capacity would continue even though, for example, the Community's methanol capacity had been cut down.

Thirdly, the competitive position of the GCC petrochemical products, especially Saudi petrochemical products, would allow those countries to compete with other products within the Community market, even after the imposition of the customs duties. The Community stressed that even after paying the tariffs and duties, the GCC sales price—especially the Saudi sales price—was unbeatable.

Fourthly, the European Community was concerned that if the GCC petrochemical products were allowed to enter the EEC market without customs duty, the EEC petrochemical industry would suffer serious disruption, bearing in mind the geographical proximity of the Arab producers to Europe. This would be further intensified 'by the loss of the European producers' market in the Middle East and Africa for these products, as a result of competition from the new producers. This might cause the closure of European factories, aggravating the unemployment situation in EEC countries.'[60]

In June 1984, at the instigation of the Netherlands the European Community imposed its first 13.5 per cent tariff on Saudi Arabian exports of methanol to the Community market. (For more information on the capacity and output of Saudi petrochemical plants, see Table 12.) The reason given by the Community for its protectionist move was that Saudi Arabia had exceeded the ceiling limiting its exports of methanol to the Community as specified by the Community's Generalized Scheme of Preferences. (Sabic first started exporting in April 1983, with a shipment of 33,000 tonnes of methanol destined for Japan.)[61]

The response of the GCC countries, especially Saudi Arabia, to the Community's move to impose restrictions on Saudi petrochemicals was one of anger. Shaikh Abdul-Aziz Al-Zamil, Saudi Minister of Industry and Electricity, described the Community protectionist measure as an 'unjustifiable' action and said: 'While we have always called for free trade, it is the very people who preached these ideas who started to put obstacles in front of us.'[62] The Council of Saudi Chambers of Commerce and Industry in Riyadh expressed its concern about the Community tariff on Saudi Arabian petrochemical products.

Also, the Arab-European Chambers of Commerce (at the request of the Arab-British Chamber of Commerce's secretary-general and chief executive, Mr Abdul Karim Al-Mudaris, in his capacity as liaison and coordination officer of these chambers) held an emergency meeting in Paris on 5 December 1984. The meeting was attended by the secretaries-general of the Arab-European Chambers and by Dr Burhan Dajani (Secretary-General of the General Union of Chambers of Commerce, Industry and Agriculture for Arab countries), Mr Abdullah Al-Dabbagh (Secretary-General of the Council of Saudi Chambers of Commerce and Industry) and Mr Saad Al-Sayyari (Vice President, Sabic Marketing Company).

During the meeting, the participants discussed the Community's protectionist measures against Saudi Arabia petrochemical products. The secretaries-general of the joint Euro-Arab chambers of commerce expressed their deep concern over the Community measures which contradicted the concept of free trade and put unjustifiable barriers in the way of Arab-European economic co-operation in general.[63]

After the meeting, the secretaries-general issued a statement in which they made public their dissatisfaction with the

Table 12: Capacity and output of Saudi petrochemical plants

Name	Partner	Feedstocks	Products	Capacity (,000 t/y)
Saudi Petrochemical Co (Sadaf)	PectenArabia, subsidiary of Shell Oil Co	Ethane Salt Benzene	Ethylene Ethylene dichloride Styrene monomer Crude indust. ethanol Caustic soda	656 454 295 281 377
Saudi Yanbu Petrochemical Co (Yanpet)	Mobil Oil Corp	Ethane from East-West pipeline	Ethylene Linear low density polyethylene High density polyethylene Ethylene glycol	455 205 91 220
Al-Jubail Petrochemical Co (Kemya)	Exxon Chemical Co	Ethylene from Sadaf	LLDPE	270
Saudi Methanol Co (Ar-Razi)	Japanese consortium headed by Mitsubishi Gas Chemical Co	Methane	Chemical grade Methanol	600
National Methanol Co (ibn-Sina)	Celanese (25%) Texas Eastern (25%)	Methane	Chemical grade Methanol	650
Arabian Petrochemical Co (Petrokemya)	100% Sabic owned	Ethane	Ethylene	500
Eastern Petrochemical Co (Sharq)	Japanese consortium headed by Mitsubishi	Ethylene from Petrokemya	LLDPE Ethylene glycol	130 300
Al-Jubail Fertiliser Co (Samad)	Taiwan Fertiliser Co	Methane	Urea	500

Source: R. Wilson, *Euro-Arab Trade: Prospect to the 1990s*, EIU Publications, London, 1988.

Community protectionist measures against Saudi Arabian petrochemicals. These measures, according to the statement, contradicted the principle of free trade which had always been endorsed by the Community and applied by Saudi Arabia. The statement declared 'that such measures work against the interests of the EEC, and called upon the European parties concerned to reconsider their protectionist measures against Saudi Arabian petrochemicals'.[64]

Relations between the European Community and GCC countries were further strained when the European Commission on 3 August 1985, imposed a tariff of 13.4 to 14 per cent on imports of Saudi Arabian polyethylenes. The European Commission justified its decision by stressing that the kingdom's exports of linear low-density polyethylene (LLDPE) had reached 15 per cent of total Community consumption. Commission officials stated that in the first half of 1985, the European Community imported 40,000 tonnes of Saudi polyethylenes, worth 28 million ECU against a 6.1 million ECU duty-free GSP ceiling.

Saudi Arabia did not accept this explanation and reacted strongly against the Community tariffs. On 5 August 1985, the Saudi Arabian Basic Industries Corporation (Sabic) issued a strongly worded condemnation of the Community action of imposing tariffs on Saudi polyethylenes. Sabic stated that the Community move 'was based on exaggerated data and unfounded fears regarding the purported impact of Saudi exports on EEC countries'.[65] Sabic went on to stress that Saudi polyethylene exports to the European Community in general constituted less than 1 per cent of the combined Community polyethylene consumption of 5.5 million tonnes a year. This amount was 'certainly not a threatening level that could injure EEC industry', Sabic said.[66]

The disagreement over the Community action against Saudi polyethylene reached its peak when the GCC countries threatened that they might take retaliatory action. On 7 August 1985, the Jeddah English-language daily newspaper, the *Saudi Gazette*, quoted an unidentified GCC official as saying that the six member states of the GCC might consider imposing an 'across-the-board' tariff on 25 per cent of Community products.[67]

The Community protectionist measures did not help the ongoing exploratory talks on an EEC-GCC co-operation agreement. In fact it poisoned the negotiations between the two sides and made it impossible for them to reach an agreement on the terms of the economic co-operation pact. The exploratory talks 'have shown that there are still a number of difficulties to be overcome,' said M. Poos, Luxembourg's foreign minister.[68] To break the impasse of the negotiations, the Community decided to launch a manoeuvre aimed at soothing the discontent of the GCC countries, especially that of Saudi Arabia, and reactivating the talks for an eventual co-operation agreement between the two sides. Thus on 1 September 1985, the West German foreign minister, Herr Hans-Dietrich Genscher, visited Kuwait and held talks with the emir, the crown prince, prime minister and the foreign minister. He also held an unpublicized meeting with GCC Secretary-General, Mr Abdullah Bishara, the GCC's main negotiating representative. Before leaving Kuwait, Herr Genscher stated that the talks between the GCC and the Community needed a 'political push'. He described the EEC and the GCC as 'two regional organizations sharing close interests complementary to each other'.[69]

After Herr Genscher's visit, M Cheysson, the member of the Commission with special responsibility for North–South relations, paid a visit to Saudi Arabia on 8 and 9 September 1985. During the visit, M Cheysson held discussions with Prince Saud (Minister of Foreign Affairs), Mr Al-Zamil (Minister of Industry and Electricity), and Mr Abdullah Bishara, Secretary-General of the Gulf Co-operation Council. The talks focused on the development of co-operation between the GCC countries and the Community, and on the possibility of holding a joint EEC/GCC minsterial meeting in order to give political impetus to the negotiations between the two sides. Following M Cheysson's visit to Saudi Arabia, the way was open for holding a joint ministerial meeting between the European Community and the GCC countries.[70]

SEARCH FOR PROGRESS AT NEW HIGH-LEVEL TALKS: 1985–6

A ministerial meeting between the European Community and the Gulf Co-operation Council was held in Luxembourg on 14 October 1985. The participants on the Arab side were Shaikh Sabah Al-Ahmad Al-Jaber (Deputy Prime Minister and Minister of Foreign Affairs of Kuwait, as well as Chairman of the GCC

Ministerial Council) and Mr Abdullah Bishara (Secretary-General of the GCC), representing the Gulf Co-operation Council. On the European side the participants were M Jacques Poos (Deputy Prime Minister and Minister of Foreign Affairs of Luxembourg, and President of the EEC Council of Ministers) and M Claude Cheysson (Member of the Commission of the European Communities), representing the European Community.[71]

In the joint communiqué issued at the end of the meeting, the Community representatives welcomed the rapid development of the Gulf Co-operation Council as a regional organization aimed at achieving coordination and integration between its member states in all fields. The Community representatives also recognized the successful outcomes achieved by the Council in strengthening and consolidating relations, ties and the scope of co-operation between the people of the Gulf in various fields: political, cultural, economic and commercial.[72]

The GCC representatives acknowledged the important role played by the European Community as a factor of economic and political stability and as an element of balance in international relations. They welcomed 'the outward-looking character of this integration as exemplified by the determination of the Community to cooperate with regional organizations and particularly with the GCC'.[73]

Both sides reaffirmed the friendly and traditional relationship between the two regions. They emphasized the economic and political importance they attached to the future development of their relations, and their common will to deepen and strengthen this relationship. In addition, the two sides stressed their satisfaction with the improvement of their economic relations, and determined to deepen and consolidate these in the future.[74] They declared that the discussions should move to a more vital stage 'with a view to the conclusion of a comprehensive, mutually beneficial agreement to foster the broadest possible commercial and economic co-operation between the two regions'.[75]

The agreement, according to the joint communiqué, must cover various aspects of future development such as energy, industrial co-operation, investment, transfer of technology and training.[76] Both sides affirmed that early conclusion of such an agreement was essential in order to create a framework within which the two sides could work together in a relaxed atmosphere, thus announcing 'the opening of high-level discussions which would explore in depth the substantive issues to be covered in negotiating the Agreement between the Community and the GCC'.[77] The representatives of the two sides agreed that the Luxembourg meeting constituted a step forward in the relations between the Gulf Co-operation Council states and the European Community, and that it was useful for the two sides.[78]

However, despite the exchange of platitudes, the Luxembourg meeting failed to solve the thorny trade dispute, especially the petrochemical issue, between the European Community and the GCC countries. In fact hardly any discussions took place on this subject during the meeting. It seemed that the two sides had decided to avoid raising the issue. Hence there was no agreement on the trade issue and the deadlock over the trade question continued.[79]

Yet efforts to bridge the gap between the two sides continued. On 6 December 1985, senior EEC and Gulf Co-operation Council officials met in Paris. The meeting was part of a new round of high-level talks agreed at the ministerial meeting between the Community and the GCC. The talks aimed at overcoming differences and speeding up negotiations towards a comprehensive region-to- region economic and commercial co-operation agreement. Little progress was achieved.[80]

This round of talks was followed by another. On 3 and 4 March 1986, M Cheysson, the member of the Commission with special responsibility for North–South relations, visited the United Arab Emirates, where he had discussions with Mr Rashid Abdullah (Minister for Foreign Affairs), and Mr Manaa Ben Said Al-Otaiba (Minister for Petroleum and Mineral Resources). M Cheysson then visited Kuwait on 5 and 6 March 1986, where he had talks with Shaikh Sabah Al-Ahmad Al-Jaber (acting Prime Minister and Minister for Foreign Affairs), Mr Jassim Al-Kharafi (Minister for Finance and the Economy), Shaikh Ali Al-Khalifa (Minister for Oil and Industry), and Mr Ahmad Al-Saadoun (Speaker of the National Assembly).

In addition, M Cheysson had a meeting with Mr Ali Attiga (Secretary-General of the Organization of Arab Petroleum Exporting Countries). He also had talks with Mr Mamoun Kurdi (Deputy Minister for Foreign Affairs of Saudi Arabia and coordinator for the Gulf Co-operation Council's relations with the European Community). The talks centered on the terms of access to European markets for Gulf industrial exports, particularly petrochemicals, and on progress towards the conclusion of

Table 13: Arab petrochemicals listed as sensitive under the EC's generalised scheme of preferences (GSP), 1986 and 1987 (ECU ,000)

Product	1986 GSP system Fixed amount at '0' duty	Ceiling[a]	1987 GSP system Fixed amount at '0' duty	Ceiling[a]
Liquid ammonia	Libya 5,475	Saudi Arabia, Bahrain, Kuwait, UAE 5,913	Bahrain, Libya 5,920	Saudi Arabia, UAE, Kuwait, Qatar 5,920
Caustic soda		non-sensitive 330		Saudi Arabia 800
Styrene		Saudi Arabia, Kuwait 3,285	Saudi Arabia 7,000	Kuwait 7,000
Dichloroethane (ethylene dichloride)		non-sensitive		Saudi Arabia 1,000
Methanol	Libya 2,000	Saudi Arabia, Bahrain 3,300	Saudi Arabia, Bahrain 5,500 Libya 1,000[b]	
Ethylene glycol		Saudi Arabia, Kuwait 1,095	Saudi Arabia 2,500	
Diethylene glycol		Saudi Arabia 340	Saudi Arabia 700	
Melamine		Saudi Arabia, Kuwait 449	Saudi Arabia 600	Kuwait 600
Polyvinyl chloride (PVC)		non-sensitive 4,600		Saudi Arabia, Libya 4,650

[1] The fixed amount at '0' duty or ceiling applies to each country.
[2] A specific quota rather than a fixed amount at '0' duty.
Source: R. Wilson, *Euro-Arab Trade: Prospect to the 1990s*, EIU Publications, London, 1988.

a co-operation agreement between the two sides. It was decided to move to formal negotiations at an early stage.[81]

On 26 and27 April 1986, Commission representatives visited Riyadh in Saudi Arabia and held discussions with representatives of the Gulf Co-operation Council. The talks covered all aspects of the pending co-operation agreement, including trade, energy, industrial co-operation, investment, transfer of technology and training. It was agreed that the high-level talks 'had now finished and that both sides would be making recommendations to their respective authorities with the intention of opening formal negotiations at an early date'.[82]

However, the high-level talks between the two sides revealed that there were still divergent views over finding a solution to the terms of access for Gulf petrochemical products entering the Community market. In 1986 alone the Community re-imposed tariffs on nine petrochemical products originating in the Gulf countries, when low Community ceilings had been reached.[83] (For more information on the GCC petrochemical listed as sensitive under the EEC's GSP, see Table 13.)

In justifying its action, the Community stressed that the Gulf countries must have a better understanding of the EEC's Generalized System of Preferences (GSP), through which the Community offered the developing countries, including those of the Gulf countries, tariff concessions on a limited volume of their exports. The Community confirmed that the GSP system worked autonomously and that it could not be changed or altered for the sake of one beneficiary.[84]

The states of the Gulf Co-operation Council believed that the only solution to the trade problem with the European Community was through concluding a free trade co-operation agreement.[85] The European Community preferred an ASEAN type of co-operation agreement based on the most favoured nation clause. The GCC countries refused to accept the ASEAN type of agreement and insisted that they should be treated on equal terms with the other states in the region, citing Israel and the Arab Mediterranean countries as an example. The Community declined to offer the GCC countries either an Israeli-style agreement or the Arab Mediterranean type, and insisted on an ASEAN-style agreement.

Nevertheless, despite the fact that the Community was opposed to the idea of concluding a free trade agreement with the Gulf countries, there was a school of thought in the

European Commission that was sympathetic to the Gulf demand for a free trade agreement, and considered it as ultimately inevitable. This school argued, first, that the interests of the Community petrochemical industry would be best served by concluding an agreement of the type the GCC countries desired (a free trade agreement). It stressed that if the GCC countries felt that they were rebuffed, this might lead to a retaliatory measures being taken by the GCC countries against the Community, such as increasing tariffs on EEC exports or awarding major contracts outside the Community.

Secondly, it was argued that by concluding a free trade agreement between the EEC and the GCC countries, the Community would stand to gain more from the abolition of barriers than the GCC countries, given the fact that petrochemical products constituted only a small proportion of GCC exports to the Community. The vast bulk of GCC countries exports to the Community consisted of crude oil and refined petroleum, which entered the Community market duty-free.

The task of convincing the Community member states of the advisability of concluding a free trade agreement with the GCC countries proved to be difficult, given the concern over the petrochemical industry and the strong petrochemical lobby within the Community. Some of the Community member states, moreover, were concerned about possible American reaction if the Community concluded a free trade agreement with the GCC countries. This was true despite the fact that the European Commission received assurances from the United States confirming that if the eventual agreement between the EEC and GCC countries was in tune with GATT, the United States would have no objections over it.[86]

THE EUROPEAN PARLIAMENT AND THE APPROVAL OF AN EEC–GCC CO-OPERATION REPORT

Within the European Parliament, a tendency favourable towards concluding a free trade agreement with the GCC countries also emerged. In December 1986, the European Parliament's Committee on External Economic Relations adopted a report on EEC–GCC economic and trade relations. The report recommended a free trade co-operation agreement as an option. It also suggested a number of areas for co-operation: transfer of technology; energy; science and technology; vocational training; after sales service and maintenance; agriculture and agro-industry; control of refuse and waste water; plants for desalination and the conveyance of sea water; urban public services and transport infrastructure; joint participation in co-operation and assistance programmes for developing countries; and tourism. In addition, the report suggested that the oil supply for the EEC should be guaranteed through direct agreements between the EEC and the GCC on behalf of the oil-producing countries. The report proposed that the ECU should be used as a reference currency for price fixing and as a means of payment for commercial oil transactions between the Community and the GCC countries.

However, the report did not win the Community's consent. The European Commission criticized it, stressing that it lacked the precise definition as to what shape a EEC–GCC trade agreement should take.[87]

THE SECOND EEC–GCC MINISTERIAL MEETING

At the request of the GCC countries, a second ministerial meeting took place in Brussels on 23 June 1987. The aim of the meeting was to accelerate the negotiations between the two sides, and to give further political impetus to work on the projected co-operation agreement. The Community was represented by M Leo Tindemans (Belgian Foreign Minister and President of the Council), and M Claude Cheysson (Member of the Commission with special responsibility for North–South relations). Mrs Lynda Chalker (United Kingdom Minister of State, Foreign and Commonwealth Office), and Mr K.E. Tygesen (Denmark's State Secretary for Foreign Affairs), were also present. The Gulf Co-operation Council was represented by its president, Shaikh Rashid Abdullah al-Nuaimi (Minister of State for Foreign Affairs of the United Arab Emirates), Prince Saud al-Faisal bin Abdul Aziz (Minister for Foreign Affairs of Saudi Arabia), Mr Yusuf bin Alawi bin Abdullah (Minister of State for Foreign Affairs of Oman), and Mr Abdullah Y. Bishara (Secretary-General of the Gulf Co-peration Council).[88]

In the joint communiqué issued at the end of the meeting, the participants recalled their first ministerial meeting and confirmed their mutual agreement on almost all the proposed fields of co-operation (energy, investment, industrial co-operation, technology and training). Both sides expressed their desire to conclude a mutually beneficial agreement to foster the widest possible economic and commercial co-operation between the two sides. They stated their willingness to promote and improve trade to the mutual benefit of both areas. Within this context, the Gulf Co-operation Council states renewed their demand for the type of agreement the Community had concluded with certain Mediterranean countries, such as Israel and the Arab Mediterranean countries. The Community response was negative. It did not agree to offer such an agreement. Instead, the Community promised to take note of the Gulf states' request. Finally, the representatives from the two sides consented to recommend 'their respective authorities to take the necessary steps to open official negotiations on a co-operation agreement as soon as possible'.[89]

FROM THE 1987 MANDATE TO THE 1988 CO-OPERATION AGREEMENT

On 8 October 1987, the European Commission sent the European Council of Ministers a draft decision which would authorize it to negotiate a co-operation agreement with the Gulf Co-operation Council states.[90] On 23 November, the European Council of Ministers approved directives authorizing the European Commission to start negotiations with the GCC countries with a view to concluding a co-operation agreement.[91] Subsequently, representatives from the European Community and the Gulf Co-operation Council states met in Brussels on 7 December 1987. During the meeting, the representatives held a broad exchange of views on various fields of mutual co-operation which would be included in the forthcoming co-operation agreement. After the meeting the way was open to the conclusion of the agreement.[92] Thus on 24 March 1988, representatives from the European Commission and Gulf Co-operation Council states initialed a co-operation agreement between the Community and the Gulf states. The agreement set a contractual relationship between the Community and the GCC countries. It was intended to provide co-operation in the following fields: economic affairs, agriculture and fisheries, industry, energy, science, technology, investment, the environment and trade.[93]

On economic co-operation, the two sides agreed to facilitate the transfer of technology through joint venture and to encourage co-operation on standards. As regards energy, they agreed that they would 'promote co-operation between firms, training and joint studies on trade in oil, gas and petroleum products'. They also consented to promote appropriate investment protection and a reciprocal improvement of investment conditions.

In the case of trade co-operation, which was a major issue between the two sides, a compromise was reached. Initially, it was decided that both sides would continue to accord each other most-favoured nation treatment. As soon as the agreement was signed, it was agreed to start negotiating a second agreement, the aim of which would be to improve access for exports to their respective markets and liberalize mutual trade, on condition that both sides could find solutions for their sensitive sectors. To ensure the smooth application of the agreement, a joint council was set up which would meet at least once a year or at the request of one of the parties.[94]

The agreement was officially signed in Luxembourg on 15 June 1988. Herr Genscher, President of the European Council, and M Cheysson, Member of the Commission with special responsibility for North–South relations, signed the agreement on behalf of the European Community. Prince Saud al-Faisal bin Abdul Aziz, the Saudi Arabian Minister for Foreign Affairs and President of the Ministerial Council of the GCC, and Mr Abdullah Bishara, Secretary-General of the GCC, signed on behalf of the GCC countries.[95]

Following the signing of the agreement, a joint political statement was issued on 15 June 1988. In the statement, both sides stated, *inter alia*, 'their determination to take necessary steps to ensure the early entry into force of the co-operation agreement . . . and to pursue with vigour its subsequent implementation'.[96]

CONCLUSION

For the first time, the European Community and the Gulf countries had reached a contractual agreement. Despite the fact that the negotiations to conclude the agreement were difficult and protracted, the agreement (at least for the GCC countries) did not solve the major issue which had embittered EEC–GCC relations, namely the petrochemical problem. The agreement stipulated that until a second agreement (dealing with trade issue) has been signed, there would be no change in the status quo of the trade relations between the two sides. This meant that the Community would still have the right to impose tariffs once the ceilings limiting the Gulf exports were exceeded. Hence the Community could still ensure the protection of its petrochemical industry. By comparison, the GCC countries achieved no short-term gain in the trade sector from the agreement. Their exports of petrochemicals (which were essential for their economic development) would still have to face barriers and obstacles in entering the Community market. Ironically, most Community exports entered the GCC countries duty-free.

It may have been preferable that the agreement was accomplished within the framework of the Euro-Arab dialogue, not outside it. One justification for having a separate agreement, bearing in mind that the GCC countries were members of the Arab League, currently conducting a dialogue with the EEC, was that the GCC countries form a smaller and less divided unit. However this additional dialogue served to increase the fears of some Arab governments regarding the European approach to the Gulf countires, suspecting it as a means to divide the Arab world.

NOTES

1. Colette Cova, *The Arab Policy of the EEC*, pp. 107–110.
2. Mohamed Al-Rumaihi, 'Factors of Social and Economic Development in the Gulf in the Eighties', in Klaus Jurgen Gantzel, Helmut Mejcher (eds.), *Oil, the Middle East, North Africa and the Industrial States*, Paderborn, Schoningh, 1984, p. 207.
3. Anthony H. Cordesman, *The Gulf and the Search for Strategic Stability*, Westview Press, Mansell Publishing Limited, London, 1984, pp. 1–2.
4. For more details, see *ibid*, especially pp. 568–620.
5. Olivier Carre, 'The Future for the Gulf/Europe/America Relationship: A European View', in B.R. Pridham (ed.). *The Arab Gulf and the West*, Croom Helm, London, 1985, p. 324.
6. Atif A. Kubursi, *Oil, Industrialization and Development in the Arab Gulf States*, Croom Helm, London, 1984, p. 41.
7. John Townsend, 'The Extent and the Limits of Economic Interdependence', in B.R. Pridham (ed.), *The Arab Gulf and the West*, p. 55.
8. Atif A. Kubursi, *Oil, Industrialization and Development in the Arab Gulf States*, pp. 41–2.
9. *Ibid*, p. 42.

10. Wieczorek Zeul, *Trade Relations between the EEC and the Gulf States*, 2nd edn, European Parliament, Luxembourg, 14 August, 1981, p. 10.
11. Eric Meyer, *Euro-Arab Relations*, European Commission (London Office), March/April, 1980, p. 7.
12. *Ibid.*
13. Anthony A. Cordesman, *The Gulf and the Search for Strategic Stability*, p. 63.
14. Wieczorek Zeul, *Trade Relations between the EEC and the Gulf States*, p. 7.
15. *Ibid*, pp. 14–15.
16. Eric Meyer, *Euro-Arab Relations*, p. 7.
17. Ali M. Jaidah, *An Appraisal of OPEC Oil Policies*, Longman, London, 1983, p. 69.
18. Yannis A. Stournaras, 'Is the Industrialisation of the Arab Gulf a Rational Policy?', *The Arab Gulf Journal*, Vol. 5, No. 1, April 1985, p. 21.
19. *OAPEC: Fifth Annual Report*, Secretary General, Kuwait, 1978, p. 51.
20. Fereidun Fesharaki and David T. Tsaak, *OPEC, the Gulf, and the World Petroleum Market: A Study in Government Policy and Downstream Operations*, Croom Helm, London, 1983, p. 210.
21. *Middle East International*, 11 January 1985.
22. Wieczorek Zeul, *Trade Relations between the EEC and the Gulf States*, p. 10.
23. Abbas Alnasrawi, 'Arab Oil and the Industrial Economies: The Paradox of Oil Dependency', *Arab Studies Quarterly*, Vol. 1, No. 1, winter 1979, p. 19.
24. Anthony H. Cordesman, *The Gulf and the Search for Strategic Stability*, p. 23.
25. Wieczorek Zeul, *Trade Relations between the EEC and the Gulf States*, p. 5.
26. *Ibid*, p. 12.
27. *Ibid*, p. 11.
28. *Ibid*, pp. 13–14.
29. *Ibid*, pp. 9–10.
30. *Twenty Eighth Review of the Council's Work (1 January–31 December 1980)*, Office for Official Publications of the European Communities, Luxembourg, 1981, pp. 167–8.
31. *Twenty Ninth Review of the Council's Work (1 January–31 December 1981)*, Office for Official Publications for the European Communities, Luxembourg, 1982, p. 167.
32. Colette Cova, *The Arab Policy of the EEC*, p. 109.
33. *Ibid*, p. 108.
34. Wieczorek Zeul, *Trade Relations between the EEC and the Gulf States*, 1st edn, European Parliament, Luxembourg, 9 February, 1981, p. 8.
35. *Ibid*, pp. 8–9.
36. *Ibid*, p. 9.
37. R. K. Ramazani, *The Gulf Co-operation Council: Record and Analysis*, The University Press of Virginia, USA, 1988, p. 1.
38. *Ibid*, pp. 1–2.
39. *Twenty Ninth Review of the Council's Work (1 January–31 December 1981)*, p. 167.
40. *Thirtieth Review of the Council's Work (1 January–31 December 1982)*, Office for Official Publications of the European Communities, Luxembourg, 1983, pp. 159–60.

41. *Bulletin of the European Communities*, No. 6, 1982, p. 78.
42. *Ibid*, p. 78.
43. *Bulletin of the European Communities*, No.3, 1983, p. 65.
44. *Ibid*.
45. *Bulletin of the European Communities*, No. 4, 1984, p. 54.
46. *Bulletin of the European Communities*, No. 11, 1985, p. 55.
47. *Thirty Second Review of the Council's Work (1 January–31 December 1984)*, Office for Official Publications of the European Communities, Luxembourg, 1985, p. 174.
48. *Ibid*.
49. *Bulletin of the European Communities*, No. 2, 1985, p. 60.
50. *Bulletin of the European Communities*, No. 3, 1985, p. 62.
51. *The European Community and the Gulf Co-operation Council*, Commission of the European Communities, Directorate-General for Information, Brussels, 1985, p. 3.
52. *Ibid*.
53. *Telex Mediterranean*, 18 June 1985.
54. *Telex Mediterranean*, 22 October 1985.
55. R. Wilson, *Euro-Arab Trade: Prospects to the 1990s*, EIU Publications, London, 1988, p. 88.
56. *Telex Mediterranean*, 2 July 1985.
57. *Telex Mediterranean*, 24 September 1985.
58. *Telex Mediterranean*, 22 October 1985.
59. R. Wilson *Euro-Arab Trade: Prospects to the 1990s*, pp. 89–90.
60. *Ibid*, p. 90.
61. The Arab-British Chamber of Commerce, 'Saudi Arabian Petrochemicals Exports: The EEC Protectionist Measures and Sabic's Prospects', *The Arab Gulf Journal*, Vol. 5, No. 1, 1985, pp. 9–12.
62. *Ibid*, p. 11.
63. *Ibid*, pp. 16–17.
64. *Ibid*, p. 17.
65. *Telex Mediterranean*, 24 September 1985.
66. *Ibid*.
67. *Ibid*.
68. *Telex Mediterranean*, 22 October 1985.
69. *Telex Mediterranean*, 10 September 1985.
70. *Bulletin of the European Communities*, No. 9, 1985, pp. 62–3.
71. *Meeting between the European Community and the Gulf Co-operation Council, Final Text*, Luxembourg, 14 October 1985.
72. *Ibid*.
73. *Ibid*.
74. *Ibid*.
75. *Bulletin of the European Communities*, No. 10, 1985, p. 64.
76. *Ibid*.
77. *Thirty Third Review of the Council's Work (1 January–31 December 1985)*, p. 155.

78. *Meeting between the European Community and the Gulf Co-operation Council.*
79. *Telex Mediterranean,* 22 October 1985.
80. *Telex Mediterranean,* 17 December 1985.
81. *Bulletin of the European Communities,* No. 3, 1986, pp. 57–8.
82. *Bulletin of the European Communities,* No. 4, 1986, p. 83.
83. *Telex Mediterranean,* 1 July 1986.
84. *Telex Mediterranean,* 21 January 1986.
85. *Telex Mediterranean,* 6 May 1986.
86. R. Wilson, *Euro-Arab Trade: Prospects to the 1990s,* pp. 96–7.
87. *Ibid,* p. 97.
88. *Bulletin of the European Communities,* No. 6, 1987, p. 87.
89. *Ibid,* p. 87.
90. *Bulletin of the European Communities,* No. 10, 1987, p. 62.
91. *Bulletin of the European Communities,* No. 11, 1987, p. 71.
92. *Bulletin of the European Communities,* No. 12, 1987, p. 91
93. *Bulletin of the European Communities,* No. 3, 1988, p. 93.
94. *Ibid.*
95. *Bulletin of the European Communities,* No. 6, 1988, p. 97.
96. *Ibid,* p. 119.

VI

THE ACCEPTANCE OF THE POLITICAL
DIMENSION IN THE DIALOGUE: THE NEW
STAGE

THE WAY TO THE VENICE DECLARATION

The year 1979 saw the escalation of tension throughout the Middle East, often threatening the stability and security of the region and also of the whole world. Key events included the Egyptian–Israeli peace process, the Iranian revolution, the Grand Mosque incident in Saudi Arabia and the Soviet intervention in Afghanistan. These events also had a significant impact on the European Community. The member states of the Community feared that the events would have enormous repercussions on their interests in a region of great importance to them. This situation prompted the Community to coordinate its efforts and launch initiatives aimed at gathering diplomatic momentum in the region and preventing the situation from deteriorating further.

The Community's efforts in the Middle East resulted, however, in its issuing the Venice Declaration. This in turn paved the way for the resumption of the Euro-Arab dialogue, which had been at a standstill since the signing of the Camp David agreements.

THE MIDDLE EAST IN 1979

In order to assess the significance of events in the Middle East in 1979 for European efforts in the region, the events themselves need to be analysed briefly.

The pace of the peace process

The peace process initiated by President Sadat, despite having led to the establishment of diplomatic relations between Egypt and Israel, had lost most of its impetus by the end of 1979.[1] On the one hand, President Carter of the United States was now busy in his presidential election campaign. The Israeli lobby was playing its usual role in the election, such that Carter sought to avoid antagonizing or putting pressure on Israel at a time when his political opponents were expressing their strong support for that country. By mid-September 1979, he even decided to abandon the whole issue of Palestinian autonomy and leave it in the hands of Sadat and Begin. Later on, when his re-election campaign was in full gear, he relinquished totally his 1977 commitment to a homeland for the Palestinian people.[2]

On the other hand, there was no chance of achieving any sort of progress within the Camp David peace process in relation to self-rule for the Palestinian people on the West Bank and Gaza Strip. Each side (Egypt and Israel) insisted on its own viewpoint as to what 'autonomy for the Palestinian people' should mean. The Israeli government demanded, first, that the Jewish settlements which had been established should remain, and that settlers should be permitted to carry on building settlements on the West Bank and the Gaza Strip. Secondly, it insisted on Israel's right to keep control over the land and water of the occupied territories. Thirdly, it was unwilling to give up the right to take security measures to control violence and maintain order in these areas.

The Egyptian government, for its part, emphasized the need for a completely independent state for the Palestinians, for recognition of the Palestinian Liberation Organization and finally for the dismantlement of the Jewish settlements. Conflicting views between Egypt and Israel over Palestinian autonomy on the West Bank and Gaza Strip led to deadlock when the Israeli parliament announced, in mid-1980, that Jerusalem was the eternal capital of the Jewish State. The situation was aggravated further by the determination of the Israeli government to stick to its hard line on settlement policy, despite the Egyptian and Carter administrations' objections.[3]

The Iranian revolution

The revolution in Iran started with the eruption of protests and violence during the summer of 1978. Tensions mounted and culminated in the departure of the Shah Mohammed Riza

Pahlevi for an 'extended holiday' on 16 January 1979. This ended at least half a century's rule by a harsh, dominating and repressive regime.[4] The fall of the Shah of Iran and the take-over of power by revolutionary forces brought to an end the West's privileged position in Iran.[5]

Following the Iranian revolution, two separate but interconnected developments exacerbated and complicated the situation in the region. First, the rise in the oil price, due to the reduction in Iranian oil production; and secondly, the seizure of the American embassy in Tehran, with its personnel as hostages. The oil crisis began in the summer of 1978, when militant elements of the opposition to the Shah threatened the foreign technicians who were in charge of running the Iranian oil industry and requested that they withdraw. Soon the administration of the oil fields was in anarchy; oil production dropped to less than half normal by December 1978, and was completely at a standstill, due to a strike in the oil fields, from the end of December 1978 to mid-March 1979.[6] The repercussions on the world oil market and on the price of oil were severe, especially on the spot market where between January and March 1979 the price increased by more than 40 per cent. The predicament escalated further when, in early April, Saudi Arabia decreased its production to the level of December 1978. This was done at a time when the shortages of Iranian production were still affecting the global distribution system. The price of oil rose from 12.70 dollars a barrel during 1978 to 13.34 dollars in January 1979, then to 14.55 dollars in April and finally it soared to 41 dollars in November 1979. In short, the summer of 1979 saw the second oil crisis, with consumers propelled to buy whatever oil they could get and at any price they could pay.[7]

The seizure of the staff of the American embassy as hostages constituted another setback to the influence of the United States and other Western countries in the Middle East. It had a considerable impact on the United States policy in the area, occupying the attention of American public opinion as a whole—in addition to that of the President. It was clear that the government success or failure in solving the problem would have repercussions on President Carter's chances of re-election.[8]

The embassy siege began on 4 November 1979, when a group of militant students occupied the embassy and 'arrested' 63 of the American staff, most of whom were diplomats. The initial response of the American government to the incident was a series of punitive measures: freezing Iranian assets in the United States (estimated at around eight to nine billion dollars); calling for American companies to halt their purchases of Iranian oil and demanding that Western allies follow suit; sending two carrier task forces to the Arabian sea; cancelling a half-billion dollar contract for spare parts and also all trainee programmes for Iranian personnel in the United States.[9] In addition, the President of the United States demanded in December 1979 that the United Nations call for collective economic sanctions against Iran. A resolution following from the latter demand was vetoed by the Soviet Union. On 7 April 1980, the United States broke off diplomatic relations with Iran. In the absence of any progress towards the release of the hostages, on 24 April 1980 the United States launched a mission to rescue them. This resulted in a further setback for the Carter administration and escalated the impasse on the hostages issue.[10]

The countries of the European Community supported the United States on the issue of the hostages and initiated diplomatic efforts in an attempt to find an early solution to the problem. France and Britain endorsed and voted for the Security Council resolution on 13 January 1980, which called for the imposition of an embargo on exports to Iran except for medicine and food, the prohibition of new contracts and new credits, and the reduction of Iran's diplomatic personnel stationed abroad.[11]

On 2 April 1980, the heads of government of the European Community, at their meeting in Luxembourg, confirmed their support for the United States and agreed upon a sanctions policy to be implemented in two stages. The first stage was to reduce the number European diplomatic personnel serving in Iran, as well as of Iranian diplomats in Europe, to reinstitute the visa requirements for Iranians wanting to visit Europe, and to stop arms sales to Iran. The second stage was to impose trade sanctions against Iran if by 17 May no progress was made to release the hostages.[12] The deadline passed without any progress having been made towards the hostages' release; hence the foreign ministers of the European Community, meeting in Naples (Italy) on 17 and 18 May, approved the implementation of trade sanctions against Iran. They exempted contracts which had been signed before 4 November, the date the American Embassy siege began.[13] The repercussions of the Iranian revolution on the Western bloc were enormous. The collapse of the Shah meant the deterioration of the Western position in the area, which had since 1971 been based on a friendly relationship with the Shah of Iran. Up to 1971, the security of the region had been upheld by the British military presence. After the British departure, the Shah of Iran, with Western help and assent, effectively took responsibility for being the policeman and the guardian for Western interests in the region.[14]

The Iranian revolution created a vacuum because neither Saudi Arabia nor the smaller emirates were capable of fulilling the same role. The confused situation in Iran spurred Western fears of a possible Soviet intervention in the country, which would increase pressure on the pro-Western Gulf states and once more threaten Western oil supplies. Moreover, it was feared that a country like Japan, with its nearly total dependence on oil coming from the Gulf region, might reach an accommodation with the Soviet Union instead of running the risk of having its oil supply cut off.[15] There were additional fears that an Iranian-style revolution might recur in other Middle Eastern countries with similar social and economic conditions. This could lead to further conflict within the area and cause even more disturbance to oil supplies.[16]

The Iranian revolution was also a setback to the arms industries of the United States and Western Europe. After the revolutionary forces had seized power, they abandoned the Shah's long-term project that had been initiated in the mid-1970s and was intended to make Iran a regional power by the mid-1980s. It was based on purchasing arms from the United States and other Western countries. With the coming of the Iranian revolution all this vanished.

Finally, the handling of the Iranian crisis threatened to sour, if not openly wreck, Western diplomacy throughout the Middle East. It raised doubt in the minds of many local countries about the credibility of American guarantees for these states in the long term.[17] This was the reason for the new emphasis given to the special relationship between the United States and Saudi Arabia, and the promise from the United States for a more active American role in the region.[18]

The Mecca Mosque incident in Saudi Arabia

The occupation of the Grand Mosque in Mecca in late November 1979 by a group who were opposed to the Saudi monarchy, was an ominous incident. It raised questions as to the loyalty of the Saudi National Guard—some of whom apparently gave support to the rebellion—and as to the stability of the Saudi regime in general. It threw into question the Al Saud family's ability to stay in power.[19]

As a result, the political outlook for the ruling family of Saudi Arabia, as well as that of the shaikhs of the smaller Gulf states, began to look rather uneasy. By the same token, the foreign and oil policies of the Western bloc—the United States and West Europe—which were based on the continuation of the Saudi monarchy and the Gulf shaikhs for more than half dozen years, appeared to be rather reckless.[20]

Soviet intervention in Afghanistan

The Soviet Union's intervention in Afghanistan on 27 December 1979 was viewed in Washington and Western Europe as an important development in the Gulf region. The Soviet Union had deployed its troops outside the eastern bloc for the first time since World War II.[21] The Soviet action helped to change the direction of United States foreign and defence policies. President Carter announced on 23 January 1980 that any Soviet attempt to gain a foothold in the Gulf region would be met by any means necessary, including military force. He also initiated the building up of a Rapid Deployment Force, and increased defence expenditures.[22] Furthermore, the United States government called for the United Nations Security Council to meet; on 7 January a resolution co-sponsored by five Third World members of the Council condemned the Soviet military intervention in Afghanistan and called for the immediate withdrawal of Soviet forces. At the request of the American government, the General Assembly in a special emergency session on 14 January passed a resolution calling for the immediate withdrawal of Soviet troops from Afghanistan.[23] In addition, the Carter administration took stringent measures against the Soviet Union: a grain embargo, the restriction of high-technology sales to the Soviet Union, and finally the boycotting of the summer Olympic Games in Moscow in June 1980.[24]

The Soviet intervention in Afghanistan brought Soviet

military forces nearer to vital Western interests and placed them in an advance position to interfere in Iran, if they wanted to, across the eastern border of that country. It also increased the potential pressure which the Soviet Union could exert on Pakistan, reviving Western fears concerning the supposed Soviet desire to reach the warm waters of the Indian Ocean. The importance of Pakistan in relation to Western strategy pushed the United States to reassess its moribund relations with Pakistan. The United States government expressed its willingness to secure that country and supply it with advanced weapons, even at the cost of creating strain with India.[25]

EUROPEAN MIDDLE EAST INITIATIVE

The developments mentioned above increased the European feeling of vulnerability. Against this background, the members of the European Community realized that some kind of peace initiative should be launched, to break the impasse of the Middle East situation and prevent the diplomatic momentum from collapsing altogether.

The first step of the Community in this respect was the foreign ministers' statement issued in Paris on 18 June 1979. This statement showed the change which had taken place in the European position. The European Community did not extend any further endorsement to the peace initiative between Egypt and Israel. Instead the Community member states gave further emphasis to the position they had taken in the Community statement of 26 March 1979, which expressed the Community belief that a just and lasting peace in the Middle East could come about only through a comprehensive arrangement, to be based on Security Council resolutions 242 and 338 and on the principles set out by the Nine in their statement of 29 June 1977. The Community also condemned certain Israeli policies which they considered to be a major barrier to the pursuit of peace in the Middle East. These policies were the establishment of Jewish settlements in occupied Arab territories and the Israeli reiteration of its ultimate sovereignty over the occupied lands.[26]

In a parallel development, the Community of the Nine took the initiative towards reactivating the Euro-Arab dialogue, which had been in abeyance since the signing of the Camp David agreements. At the Community ministerial meeting on political co-operation, which was held in Dublin on 11 September 1979, the European foreign ministers discussed, *inter alia*, the Euro-Arab dialogue. Following the meeting, Mr O'Kennedy, the Irish foreign minister and President of the Council of Ministers stated in a press conference that the nine members of the European Community attached great importance to the Euro-Arab dialogue and would continue to uphold it. Mr O'Kennedy stressed that the Community viewed the dialogue as a means to strengthen the 'internal solidarity of the two regions' as well as to improve the co-operation between both groups. Consequently, the dialogue should be developed with the whole group of the Arab countries and should be applicable to all countries on each side. Mr O'Kennedy also explained that the foreign ministers of the European Community wished that circumstances would soon exist which could pave the way for the dialogue to be launched again.[27]

Another step came when Mr O'Kennedy, in an attempt to lay the ground for the resumption of the Euro-Arab dialogue, reiterated at his press conference—following the meeting of the foreign ministers of the Nine in Brussels on 20 November 1979—what had been said in his previous statement of 11 September 1979. He stated that the nine member states had confirmed that special efforts should be undertaken to follow up the progress that had already been made in some areas of the dialogue. Mr O'Kennedy explained that the European Community had suggested a meeting to be held with the secretary-general of the Arab League, in order to explore possible ways to resume the dialogue.[28] After that statement, representatives of the president and of the Commission of the European Community met with Mr Klibi, Secretary-General of the League of Arab States, on many occasions (in London on 4 December 1979, in Tunis on 7 February 1980, and in Rome on 6 March 1980).[29]

The outcome of these preliminary contacts between the two parties revealed that the Arab side was eager to resume the dialogue 'at a more political level'. However, it was not until the Venice Declaration of the European Council of Ministers on 13 June 1980 stressing the need to develop the political dimension of the dialogue, that the resumption of the Euro-Arab dialogue was seriously considered.[30]

EUROPEAN DIPLOMATIC EFFORTS IN THE MIDDLE EAST,
AUTUMN 1979 TO SPRING 1980

The European Community, in order to establish a position from
which to launch its peace initiative and reach a common understanding with the Arab countries, sought to engage in a broad
diplomatic manoeuvre. Relevant initiatives can be divided into
(a) the declarations made in the name of the EEC itself; (b)
individual governments' statements or initiatives, which we
deem to be directly related to the creation of a joint European
position; and (c) extra moves on wider European and international scenes.

Declarations made in the name of the EEC itself

In a statement at the United Nations General Assembly on 26
September 1979, Mr O'Kennedy—speaking on behalf of the
EEC—gave details of a proposed European peace plan for the
Middle East. This included the right of the Palestinian people to
a homeland and to participate, through their representatives, in
any future negotiations for a comprehensive settlement. He
stressed the importance the Community attached to the acceptance of the United Nations Security Council resolutions 242 and
388 by all the parties concerned, including the Palestinian Liberation Organization. Mr O'Kennedy made it clear on behalf of the
EEC that the Community did not accept any unilateral change in
the status of the holy city of Jerusalem.[31]

On 1 March 1980, the nine members of the EEC voted for a
resolution in the United Nations General Assembly which condemned Israeli settlements in Arab occupied territories, including Jerusalem. (The United States representative voted in favour
of the resolution, but later on the American government withdrew its support for the resolution on the ground that there was
a misunderstanding.)[32]

Individual governments' statements or initiatives

Concurrently, the way was being prepared for the forthcoming
EEC peace initiative by individual governments, both in declarations of a general nature and in statements about which

elements would have to be taken into account. It seems clear that these individual steps were part of a more-or-less coordinated move. France under President Giscard d'Estaing appear to have played a major role in this process, cajoling the others towards a more pro-Palestinian posture. Already in July 1979, the French foreign minister M Jean-Francois Poncet had met Farouk Kaddoumi, his equivalent in the PLO. During the meeting M Poncet emphasized that France took the PLO seriously. The French president went further, however, and used his six-month incumbency in the EEC Presidency to press other European governments to recognize Europe's interests in meeting some of the Arabs' demands. The most important subjects of this pressure were no doubt the British and West German governments, the two other 'heavyweights' in the European Community. (In most cases the EEC policies tended to follow the consensus of the 'big three': France, Britain and West Germany.)[33]

Giscard's major step emerged during his trip to the Gulf states between 1 and 9 March 1980, when he stressed in the various capitals the right of the Palestinian people to self-determination (a code-word in Middle East diplomacy which implied an independent Palestinian state—to which both the United States and Israel were opposed).[34]

After the president's return to France, the French government issued a final communiqué on the issue (on 11 March 1980) which stated, *inter alia*, that a just and lasting settlement for the conflict in the Middle East must be founded on two main principles characterized as having been 'universally accepted', to whit: the right of every state in the region, including Israel, to live in peace within secure and recognized boundaries; and the right of the Palestinian people to self-determination within the framework of a comprehensive agreement. The statement also made reference to the necessity of the participation of the PLO in any negotiations on this basis.[35]

As for Britain, the Conservative party which had come to power enlisted on August 1979 government support for the Camp David agreement, but at the same time the Conservatives expressed their intention to work for a wider agreement which could satisfy all the Arab countries which did not participate in the Camp David process.[36] In early February 1980, British Foreign Secretary Lord Carrington stressed that the need for a European initiative in the Middle East had become extremely urgent, as the Camp David negotiations had reached dead-lock.[37] On 17 March 1980, he issued a statement to the effect that he found it very hard to believe that the PLO 'is a terrorist organization as such'.[38]

Five days previously, on 12 March (i.e. only a day after the French communiqué), the West German foreign minister, Hans-Dietrich Genscher, approved the French recognition of the right of the Palestinian people to self-determination, and called on other European countries to follow suit. The West German government had in fact been the first government in Europe to use that terminology. It had employed it in 1974, and in 1979 had been followed in this by the Belgian and Irish governments.[39]

Initiatives on wider European and international scenes

In addition to the above moves by the EEC member states—and providing a background to them—there were some significant developments on the wider European and international scene. Opinion in at least some sections of the international community appeared to shift decisively in favour of the Arab position. Two major examples of this come from, respectively, the beginning and the end of the period under consideration—one international, the other an individual country's plea for a fresh European initiative.

In July 1979, former West German Chancellor Willy Brandt and Austria's Chancellor Dr Bruno Kreisky met PLO leader Yassir Arafat under the auspices of the Socialist International, to explore ways of mediating in the Arab-Israeli conflict.[40] And on 4 June 1980, Ole Algard, Norway's highly respected delegate to the United Nations, expressed his (and Norway's) conviction that, as the Camp David talks between Egypt and Israel had reached deadlock on the question of Palestinian autonomy, the time was ripe for a new approach. A solution for the Palestinians should be the central concern; they, and particularly the West Bank Arabs, had to be brought into the negotiating process. Nobody, Algard argued, could 'lay claim to be more repre-sentative [of the Palestinians] than the Palestinian Liberation Organization'. Algard, and Norway, herewith supported a fresh European initiative on the Middle East, in strong oppo-sition to the views of the Carter administration.[41]

It is against this background, and with the benefit of feedback rom these people and their collective moves and statements, that the European Middle East initiative was to emerge. It took the form of an EEC attempt, firstly, to try to modify United Nations Security Council resolution 242 in such a way as to replace the word 'refugees' by 'Palestinians'. Secondly, it attempted to confirm the legitimate right of the Palestinian people to self-determination. And thirdly, it sought to recognize the PLO as the legitimate representative of the Palestinian people in future talks.[42] In a nutshell, the nature of the European initiative as it was conceived may best be described in the words of the French foreign minister, M Poncet. He characterized it as a 'balanced approach' or an equal offer from the European Community to both parties concerned, the Arabs and the Israelis. This approach, he said, 'should provide for Israeli security and for Arab self-determination'. (The term self-determination refers to the right of the Palestinians to have their own separate state on what is now the occupied West Bank of the River Jordan and in the Gaza Strip.)[43]

THE ARAB, AMERICAN AND ISREALI RESPONSES

The response of the different parties to the proposed European initiative in the Middle East, not surprisingly, varied considerably.

The Arab world

When the European Community started its efforts in the Middle East, the Arab response was in general positive. From the beginning, all Arab countries welcomed the courageous European initiative. Arab foreign ministers encouraged the member states of the EEC to become more involved in the search for Middle East peace, and to have their own role in the Arab–Israeli conflict. 'This year is the year of the West European states' recognition of the PLO', said Dr Ahmed Sidki al-Dajani member of the PLO Executive Committee.[44] Syrian officials in the foreign ministry expressed their wish that Europe would be able to move the entire Middle East question back from the Camp David fold to the more fruitful ground of the United Nations, 'where circumstances are favourable'.[45] The leader of the PLO, Yassir Arafat,

urged the European Community to extend its present commitment to 'Palestinian rights' and 'a homeland for the Palestinian
people' so that the European Community would also recognize
the 'Palestinian right to self-determination'.[46] The European
role, in the Arab view, needed to be plain, clearly defined and
distinct from that of the United States.[47]

The United States

The United States resisted strongly this European activity on the
Middle East and did its best to stop the European Community
from launching an initiative in the region. The President of the
United States, Jimmy Carter, exerted considerable pressure on
the EEC countries, particularly those which had special links
with the United States. He demanded that the Europeans wait,
for the time being, and not involve themselves in Middle East
diplomacy or interfere with the Camp David peace process.[48]
President Carter warned the European Community that the
United States would not allow any step in the United Nations
that would change the status of Security Council resolution 242.
He reminded the Community that the United States held a veto
power, and that this would be used if need be to protect the
Camp David process from collapsing.[49] In the President's
words:

> We will not permit in the United Nations any action that would
> destroy the sanctity of and the present form of UN Security Council
> resolution 242. We have a veto power that we can exercise if necess-
> ary to prevent this Camp David process from being destroyed or
> subverted and I would not hesitate to use it if necessary.[50]

Mr Donald F. McHenry, the United States delegate to the United
Nations, said that the opportunity must be given for the Camp
David process to break through. It provided that Egypt and
Israel negotiate a measure of limited self-rule for the Palestinian
people in the West Bank and Gaza strip. 'This is the only politically viable avenue available,' said Mr McHenry; 'no-one has
been able to come up with a workable alternative.'[51] At a meeting at the French embassy, between the french foreign minister,
Jean-François Poncet, and the American Secretary of State,
Edmund S. Muskie, on 13 May 1980, Mr Muskie demonstrated
vigorously his opposition to the European initiative. He
informed M Poncet that the American administration viewed

the autonomy talks between Egypt and Israel, whose deadline had passed on 26 May 1980, as being still alive, and that if the European Community determined to go ahead with its initiative, they would certainly damage the Camp David process.[52] On 9 June 1980, Mr Muskie called for a 'constructive' initiative that would not undercut the American-sponsored peace initiative. He explained that the United States would not oppose an eventual European initiative, provided that it was constructive and not prejudicial to the Camp David process.[53] The American administration, in an attempt to safeguard the Camp David process and hinder European efforts in the Middle East, kept giving the impression of movement in the negotiations between Egypt and Israel.'We are actively pursuing the resumption of the talks,' said Edmund Muskie in an interview on the NBC News programme 'Meet the Press' in June 1980. 'I expect the talks to resume,' he said, but added, 'I cannot put a time frame on it.'[54]

American resistance to the European initiative in the Middle East stemmed from several factors. First, the United States regarded the Camp David process as the essential part of its Middle Eastern policy. This essential part gained currency, with the collapse of the Shah of Iran, in the context of the strategy of confrontation with the Soviet Union in its global and regional dimensions.[55] Secondly, the United States believed that negotiations could produce a dynamic influence of their own that would open the way for a gradual solution of the major conflicting issues, in contention between the Palestinians on the one hand and the Israelis on the other.[56] Thirdly, the American administration was very busy with its campaign for re-election. President Carter regarded the Camp David agreement as a major asset in his re-election strategy, and he was therefore prepared to veto the revision of Security Council resolution 242.[57]

Israel

The Israeli government, for its part, undertook a major diplomatic initiative in order to impede further European involvement. The prime minister, Menahem Begin, declared in the Knesset on 2 June 1980 that any European initiative based on the rights of the Palestinian people to self-determination would be totally unacceptable to Israel. He delivered a copy of the PLO charter to all European capitals. On the eve of the EEC meeting in Venice, he dispatched Foreign Minister Yitzhak Shamir to some of the European capitals in an attempt to persuade European governments to abandon the initiative completely, or at least to gain a pledge from those countries that there would be no real European initiative.[58]

Abba Eban, the spokesman of the Labour opposition party, stated on 13 June 1980 that over the previous seven years of active work to reach a compromise in the area, the European contribution had been nil. He stressed that although Europe had the right to pursue its own interests, this should not be at the expense of Israel's survival.[59]

THE EEC INITIATIVE TO AMEND RESOLUTION 242 ABANDONED

American and Israeli pressure eventually brought results. The European Community, under the threat of the American veto, yielded and decided not to go ahead with its initiative to amend Security Council resolution 242. Instead, the governments of the Nine decided to issue a collective statement at their forthcoming summit meeting in Venice on 12 and 13 June 1980. Shortly before this meeting took place, the Community assured the government of the United States that the statement the Community was to issue in Venice would neither recognize the PLO nor characterize the PLO as the sole legitimate representative of the Palestinian people.[60] The Venice statement, the European Community said, would try to explain accurately the term 'self-determination of the Palestinian people' as well as define the role of the PLO in any future talks about peace settlement.[61]

On 12 June 1980, the Italian foreign minister, Emilio Colombo, was sent by the European Community as special deputy to the government of the United States to assure it of the 'identity of views which exists between the United States and Europe on a series of international issues'.[62] Mr Colombo stressed that the Community did not wish to present a European initiative which could be viewed as an 'alternative in contradiction with the Camp David formula'.[63]

Furthermore, in an interview with the foreign press on 12 June 1980, Hans-Dietrich Genscher, the West German foreign minister, assured the governments of the United States and Israel that the statement which the European Council of Ministers intended to adopt in Venice would not recognize the PLO as the sole legitimate representative of the Palestinian people. He stressed that the declaration would simply emphasize 'the right to self-determination of the Palestinian people and the importance of Jerusalem'.[64] Herr Genscher affirmed that the European Community had no intention of suggesting a change in the United Nations Security Council resolution 242, stating that the term 'European Initiative' had given rise to misunderstanding, notably in the United States.[65] Probably the best description of the European initiative in the Middle East was the one given by Lord Carrington, the British Foreign Secretary. He explained that the European initiative was 'moribund but few of the Nine want to upset President Carter further'.[66]

THE VENICE DECLARATION AND REACTIONS OF THE PARTIES CONCERNED

The Venice Declaration

The most cohesive and coordinated European initiative in the Middle East emerged from the meeting of the heads of state and government of the nine countries of the European Community at Venice on 12 and 13 June 1980. The Venice Declaration started by registering the Community's support for Security Council resolutions 242 and 388 and reiterating the Community's position outlined in the statements issued on various occasions by the Community (29 June 1977, 19 September 1978, and 26 March and 18 June 1979). The declaration also confirmed the right to existence and security of all states in the region (including Israel), and the need for justice for all the people—which implied recognition of the legitimate rights of the Palestinians.

However, the essential part of the Venice Declaration was the European Community's emphasis on the right of the Palestinian people to self-determination, and the need to associate the PLO in any peace talks in the region. The Nine declared their readiness to participate 'within the framework of a comprehensive settlement in a system of concrete and binding international guarantees, including guarantees on the ground'. Furthermore, the governments of the European Community expressed their willingness to launch a new initiative in the Middle East. To that end M Gaston Thorn, Foreign Minister of Luxembourg and President of the EEC Council and of the European Political Co-operation, was appointed to chair a so-called 'fact-finding mission' and instructed to consult all the parties concerned. In response to the findings of the mission, the Community would then formulate the structure of a European peace initiative in the region.

Concerning the Euro-Arab dialogue, the Venice Declaration stressed the importance that the Community attached to the Euro-Arab dialogue at all levels (political, economical and cultural), and the 'advisability' of holding a meeting between both sides—Arab and European—at the political level. In this way, the Community could contribute towards improving mutual understanding between the Arab world and the European Community.

The Venice Declaration was the strongest, clearest and most advanced position adopted by the Community on the Middle East question. To understand fully its significance, it is important to quote the text as it was issued by the heads of state and government of the Community at their meeting in Venice on 12 and 13 June 1980:

(1) The right to existence and to security of all the states in the region, including Israel, and justice for all the people, which implies the recognition of the legitimate rights of the Palestinian people.
(2) All of the countries in the area are entitled to live in peace within secure, recognized and guaranteed borders. The necessary guarantees for a peace settlement should be provided by the United Nations by a resolution of the Security Council and, if necessary, the basis of other mutually agreed procedures. The Nine declare that they are prepared to participate within the framework of a comprehensive settlement in a system of concrete and binding international guarantees, including (guarantees) on the ground.
(3) A just solution must finally be found to the Palestinian problem, which is not simply one of refugees. The Palestinian people, who are conscious of existing as such, must be placed in a position, by an appropriate process defined within the framework of the comprehensive peace settlement, to exercise fully their right to self-determination.

(4) The achievement of these objectives requires the involve-
    ment and support of all the parties concerned in the peace
    settlement which the Nine are endeavouring to promote in
    keeping with the principles formulated in the declaration
    referred to above. These principles apply to all the parties
    concerned, and thus the Palestinian people, and to the PLO,
    which will have to be associated with the negotiations.
(5) The Nine recognize the special importance of the role played
    by the question of Jerusalem for all the parties concerned.
    The Nine stress that they will not accept any unilateral
    initiative designed to change the status of Jerusalem and that
    any agreement on the city's status should guarantee free-
    dom of access for everyone to the Holy Places.
(6) The Nine stress the need for Israel to put an end to the
    territorial occupation which it has maintained since the con-
    flict of 1967, as it has done for part of Sinai. They are deeply
    convinced that the Israeli settlements constitute a serious
    obstacle to the peace process in the Middle East. The Nine
    consider that these settlements, as well as modifications in
    population and property in the occupied Arab territories, are
    illegal under international law.
(7) Concerned as they are to put an end to violence, the
    Nine consider that only the renunciation of force or the
    threatened use of force by all the parties can create a climate
    of confidence in the area, and constitute a basic element for
    a comprehensive settlement of the conflict in the Middle
    East.
(8) The Nine have decided to make the necessary contacts
    with all the parties concerned. The objective of these con-
    tacts would be to ascertain the position of the various parties
    with respect to the principles set out in this declaration and
    in the light of the results of this consultation process to
    determine the form which such an initiative on their part
    could take.

With regard to the Euro-Arab dialogue, the Nine noted the
importance they attached to the dialogue at all levels, and the
need to develop the advisability of holding a meeting of the two
sides at the political level. In this way, they expressed their
intent to contribute towards the development of co-operation
and mutual understanding between Europe and the Arab
world.[67]

THE REACTIONS OF DIFFERENT PARTIES TO THE VENICE
DECLARATION

The response of interested parties varied. The government of
the United States expressed its satisfaction with the European
statement, because it did not clash with the Camp David process
or undermine it. The Israeli reaction, on the other hand, was
brutal and rejectionist. Arab reaction was generally wary and
guarded.

The United States

The American reaction to the European plan was one of considerable relief. The Secretary of State, Mr Muskie, expressed his
appreciation to the nine members of the European Community
for the 'midline position' they had adopted and the 'sense of
restraint' they demonstrated. He added that the European declaration did not appear to endanger American efforts towards
achieving advancement in the talks between Egypt and Israel on
Palestinian autonomy.[68] The government of the United States,
he said, considered the EEC declaration 'as a European effort to
be helpful in the Middle East situation'. He added: 'I don't see
anything in it that challenges the Camp David process or seeks
to divert the parties to the Camp David process from their
work.'[69] He stated that no change would occur in the American
commitment to Israel, a commitment that had been achieved
through a memorandum of understanding between the United
States and Israel in 1975.[70] According to this memorandum, the
United States had pledged not to embark on negotiations or
dealings with the PLO until it recognized Security Council resolution 242. 'We are not trying to keep the PLO out', said Mr
Muskie, 'we are trying to make clear to the PLO that until it
changes its position with regard to Resolution 242 which it has
never supported, and recognizes Israel's right to exist, we will
not deal with it.'[71]

President Carter, for his part, commented that the United
States government had successfully managed to keep the
European Community away from interfering in the Middle
East peace process. 'We have made good progress in staying
the European allies from interfering.'[72] In an answer to a
question about the European declaration (specifically as to the

recommendation that the PLO should be associated with the peace process), Mr Muskie replied that there could be no dealing with the PLO until the latter recognized Israel's right to exist. 'The ball is in the PLO court,' Mr Muskie said. He went on to say: 'Anybody unacceptable to either of the two parties the United States is trying to bring together—Egypt and Israel—must be disqualified.'[73]

Israel

Israel's reaction to the Venice Declaration was very hostile. Denunciation of the European initiative came from both the government and the opposition. The Israeli government viewed the European initiative as a step designed to intrude into the peace process and abort the Camp David agreement in return for a continuous, secure and stable supply of Arab oil.[74]

In response to the Venice Declaration, the Israeli cabinet approved, on 13 June 1980, a communiqué in which it explained its position. Prime Minister Begin himself read out the statement, which took the form of a major attack on the European countries. First, the communiqué characterized their statement as a 'Munich surrender', with the nine members of the European Community being described as 'cynical and unprincipled'. Secondly, the communiqué accused them of having collaborated with 'Vichy France and Fascist Italy' in expelling the Jews to German concentration camps, and held the European countries, with the exception of Denmark, responsible for failing to exert satisfactory efforts to save the Jews.[75]

The Israeli prime minister expressed—through a cabinet statement—his rejection of the European appeal for the PLO to be associated with the peace negotiations. He also rebuffed the European bid for security guarantees, pointing out that it was no better than the empty promise given to Czechoslovakia in 1938. He stated:

> For the peace that would be achieved with the participation of that organization of murderers, a number of European countries are prepared to give guarantees, even military ones. Anyone with a memory must shudder, knowing the results of that guarantee given to Czechoslovakia in 1938.[76]

He argued that Europe's 'background of co-operation with the Nazis' placed the Community in a position of having no right to make recommendations to Israel on security matters. He went on stressing that 'since *Mein Kampf* was written, no words were ever more explicit for all the world to hear, Europe included, on the striving to destroy the Jewish state and nation.'[77]

Mr Begin blamed the European Community for trying to interfere with the status of the 'eternal and indivisible' capital of the Jews and with their right to stay and settle in 'Eretz' Israel (the original territory of Palestine, which includes the West Bank). In Begin's view, this right constituted 'an integral part of our national Security in the face of enemies and aggression'.[78] Finally the Israeli statement stressed that 'nothing will remain from the Venice resolution but its bitter memory.'[79] According to the leader of the opposition Labour party, Shimon Peres, the Venice Declaration had resulted not in an enhancement of European influence in the region, but in the deterioration of European prestige. It 'damages Europe first of all and reduces European influence on Israel and Middle Eastern countries which truly seek peace'.[80]

The anger of the Israeli government, especially that of Prime Minister Begin, was rooted in two substantial factors. First, there was disappointment at the ineffective role played by the countries in the EEC that were considered to be friendly with Israel: the Netherlands, Denmark and West Germany. These countries had failed to stop the Venice Declaration from being passed. Secondly, the reaction of the United States towards the European statement was disappointing from the Israeli point of view.[81]

The Arab reaction

Arab reaction towards the Venice Declaration was generally favourable, but it differed from one state to another. 'Moderate' Arab countries, such as Jordan and Saudi Arabia, supported the European statement and appreciated the European efforts at finding a solution to the Middle East conflict. King Hussein of Jordan, during his trip to Paris at the end of June 1980, praised the positive step that had been taken on the European side, saying that this was certainly in the right direction. Prince Fahd of Saudi Arabia stated at the end of August 1980 that the European initiative in the Middle East constituted the final opportunity for the Arab–Israeli conflict to be settled, before the Arab countries use all the means they have at their disposal.[82]

Egypt was the only Arab participant in the Camp David process. Its attitude towards the Venice Declaration was ambiguous. On the one hand, Sadat did not publicly approve or support the European statement. On the other hand, he did not formally reject it. He preferred to wait and see. If negotiations between Egypt and Israel over Palestinian autonomy led to some result, he would neglect the European initiative. If (as indeed happened) the negotiations with Israel reached a deadlock, Sadat would then endorse and encourage the European efforts. The Egyptian government's stand over time thus leaned towards favouring the European initiative. This tendency was to be strengthened after the assassination of President Sadat and his replacement by President Hosni Mubarak.[83]

As for the PLO, the official response was a rather uneasy one, despite the fact that the PLO made some gains. In a statement issued in Damascus on 15 June 1980, the PLO greeted the European declaration but it mentioned that it was obscure, unclear and full of contradictions. The Venice Declaration, stated the PLO communiqué, constituted a positive step forward, but it did not live up to the PLO's expectation as regards recognition of the PLO as the sole legitimate representative of the Palestinian people. It was, rather, a product of American pressure, said the PLO official, and an attempt to persuade some of the Arab countries to join the Camp David process.[84] The PLO communiqué stressed that Europe had a major political and moral role. It should force the aggressors to end their aggression. A plain and firm stance by Europe would be of great help to the Palestinian people under Israeli occupation and would help to put an end to Israeli 'arrogance, intransigence, expansion and occupation'.[85]

Yasir Abed Rabbo, a member of the PLO's Executive Committee and spokesman for the Democratic Front for the Liberation of Palestine, said that the Venice Declaration constituted only a 'limited step forward'.[86] Mr Kaddoumi, head of the PLO's Political Bureau, speaking at the UN General Assembly in July 1980, stressed that the Venice Declaration of the European Community contained a glance of hope, but it was inadequate and unsatisfactory.[87]

The European position

Broadly, there was widespread relief among the European Common Market governments as a result of the Venice Declaration. They regarded it as a major step in the process of shaping a European foreign policy. The Italian prime minister, Francesco Cossiga, stated that the Venice Declaration was neither support for the Camp David peace process nor did it put Europe on a collision course with it; it was 'alongside the Camp David' accords. The French president, Valéry Giscard d'Estaing, described the declaration as 'a clear text that does not evade the issues, but offers a just and balanced point of view'.[88]

Despite the fact that the Venice Declaration did not recognize the PLO as sole legitimate representative of the Palestinian people, and did not go beyond the Camp David framework to modify Security Council resolution 242, it did establish a plain, strong and distinct European policy in the Middle East.[89] This policy was 'necessary because of the need to give the Arabs something they can support in the absence of a comprehensive agreement' for the Middle East question.[90]

THE RESUMPTION OF THE DIALOGUE

The Venice Declaration removed a major barrier and facilitated the renewal of the dialogue. The emphasis on the importance of such a resumption was received with widespread relief and comfort in the Arab world.

Soon after the Declaration, contacts between the League of Arab States and the European Community were made, in an attempt to work out a common understanding on how to resume the dialogue. A meeting was held in Brussels on 22 July 1980, between the secretary-general of the League of Arab States, Chedli Klibi, and the foreign minister of Luxembourg and President of the European Council, Gaston Thorn. During the meeting, the two sides took stock of the state of the dialogue and its future prospective, and agreed to resume the dialogue officially. They also stated their willingness to hold another two preliminary meetings, to take place in Tunis on 30 July and 18 October 1980. These two preliminary meetings were to pave the way for a major political meeting between the two sides in Luxembourg on 12 and 13 November 1980.[91]

THE LUXEMBOURG MEETING, NOVEMBER 1980

The meeting between the representatives of the European Community and the Arab League, which took place in Luxembourg on 12 and 13 November 1980, was characterized by two features. First, it was the first occasion on which the dialogue was held at a political level. Secondly, the Arab side at the Luxembourg meeting was chaired by a Palestinian, Dr Ahmad Sidki Al-Dajani, who was at that time President of the Arab League.[92] The meeting was held according to the so-called 'Troika formula', that is to say, it was composed of representatives of the past, present and future presidencies of both the European Community and the League of Arab States.[93]

At the meeting, the European delegation was led by M Helming, State Secretary for Foreign Affairs of Luxembourg, representing the Presidency of the European Council, and representatives of Italy and the Netherlands (past and future presidencies of the Community). M Claude Cheysson, representative of the European Commission, also attended the meeting.

As we have seen, the Arab delegation was chaired by Dr Ahmad Sidki Al-Dajani, member of the Executive Committee of the PLO, representing the presidency of the League of Arab States, and delegates from Oman and Qatar, representing respectively the previous presidency and the country next in line for the presidency of the Arab League. Mr Adnan Omran, Assistant Secretary-General of the League of Arab States, was also present.[94] The essential aim of the Luxembourg meeting was to try to establish guidelines and rules for the resumption of the dialogue, covering all aspects of co-operation between the two neighbouring regions—political, economic, technical, financial, social and cultural. Both sides agreed that a Euro-Arab meeting at foreign ministers' level should take place in June or July 1981, after precise preparation by select working group.[95]

In the course of the meeting, explanatory statements were made by both sides. These dealt with political problems, as well as economic, financial and cultural co-operation. In the political section, the European explanatory statements, which were presented by M Helminger and M Claude Cheysson, referred to the Venice Declaration issued by the heads of state and government on 13 June, in which the latter stressed the importance that the Community attached to the dialogue at all levels and the need to improve and develop the political aspect of it. The statements referred to the declaration as a basis for the special role the Community intended to play in the Middle East conflict. To this end, the statements referred to M Thorn's mission to the Middle East as a part of the Community efforts in this respect.[96]

The explanatory statement of the Arab side was read by Dr Ahmad Sidki Al-Dajani. In it, the Arabs drew attention to the resolution adopted by the 10th Arab Summit Conference which took place in Tunis in November 1979, in which the heads of the Arab states emphasized the need to increase co-operation with the Community member states and to improve the mutual interest of the two sides. The Arabs laid stress on the dangerous situation prevailing in the Middle East and the threat it formed to the security and prosperity of both Arab and European regions. The Arab side asked the European Community to put into practice the UN resolutions concerning Arab occupied territories and the national rights of the Palestinian people, including their right to return and their right to self-determination.

The Arabs also urged the Community to use its leverage to put an end to Israeli policies in the Arab occupied lands, such as the establishment of settlements, the annexation of Jerusalem, the annexation of the Golan Heights, and the acts of aggression against the Palestinian and Lebanese people. They confirmed their demand for the Community to recognize the PLO as the sole legitimate representative of the Palestinian people. They stressed that such recognition would constitute a crucial step in the efforts made to establish a just and lasting peace in the area.

In the economic, financial and cultural sectors, both sides reaffirmed the importance they attached to the dialogue in these fields. They recalled the Cairo joint memorandum of 14 June 1975, establishing special links between the two communities, as an indication of a common political will at the highest level. They reiterated the desire, stated in the joint memorandum, to 'discover, renew and strengthen the existing links between these two neighbouring regions and the desire to foster close co-operation over a wide range of activities to the mutual benefit of the two sides'.[97] In addition, both sides expressed the wish to achieve a concrete outcome as early as possible, in the form of joint projects and common institutions. They agreed to widen the range of their co-operation in other economic aspects of mutual interest.[98]

The parties also recalled the invitation issued to the working groups by the General Commission at its meeting in Damascus on 9 and 11 December 1978, to concentrate their efforts on projects of a general interest in the Arab world. They therefore marked the resumption of the activities of the working groups. They instructed the co-chairmen and the rapporteurs of all the working groups to meet as soon as possible, so that they could decide the date, venue and agenda of their meetings. The aims were to obtain concrete outcomes subject to finalization by the General Committee meeting, which would immediately pre-cede the Euro-Arab meeting at ministerial level. Both sides agreed to entrust the Coordinating Committee with the re-sponsibility for examining the methods and the procedures ap-plied hitherto in the dialogue, with the aim to making the dialogue procedures more effective.[99]

THE MINISTERIAL MEETING POSTPONED

As noted earlier, during the Luxembourg meeting both sides had agreed to hold a Euro-Arab meeting of foreign ministers in the summer of 1981. They had also agreed to form a special *ad hoc* group to be responsible for the preparation of the meeting, and had left the *ad hoc* group with responsibility for suggesting the venue, agenda, arrangements of the meeting and its precise date.[100]

The *ad hoc* Euro-Arab group responsible for preparing this ministerial meeting met four times in 1981: in the Hague (Febru-ary), Tunis (April), the Hague again (May) and London (Oc-tober), attempting to draw up an agenda which covered political, economic, financial and cultural matters.[101]

This *ad hoc* group formed another specialist group, a kind of task force, and was charged with the responsibility for preparing the economic content of the future ministerial meeting. The task force met in Tunis on 13 and 14 November 1981. It designated the themes which the working groups should concentrate on in order to arrive at a decision when the ministerial meeting should take place. These themes were: a centre for European-Arab commercial co-operation, a Euro-Arab convention on the pro-motion and protection of investment, a Euro-Arab centre for the transfer of technology and the general conditions relevant to European Arab contracts.[102]

In the view of the European Community, the ministerial meeting should widen the dimension of co-operation between the two sides under the dialogue to cover three further fields. These were: hunger in the world and the security of food supply; energy saving and new and renewable sources of energy; and co-operation between the European and Arab development aid organizations.[103]

However, the ministerial meeting scheduled for the beginning of summer 1981 had to be postponed twice. It did not take place. This was because of disagreement over the Palestinian question, exacerbated by changes that had taken place in the political context of the area. Political developments had occurred in the Middle East arena which worked against the possibility of holding a ministerial meeting. On the Arab side, disagreements among the Arab countries themselves had been intense since the signing of the Camp David agreement, and were now aggravated further by the outbreak of the Iraqi–Iranian war. They reached their peak when the Fahd peace plan was put forward in August 1981.[104]

The Fahd plan, masterminded by King Fahd of Saudi Arabia, was the first peace plan in the history of the Arab–Israeli conflict to be initiated by the Arab side. It embodied the following points: withdrawal of Israeli military forces from all Arab occupied territories captured in 1967, including the Arab sector of Jerusalem; demolition of all Israeli settlements established in the Arab lands since 1967; freedom of religion for all people in the city of Jerusalem; the right of the Palestinian people to have their own independent state, with East Jerusalem as the capital; compensation for Palestinians who did not wish to return to their homeland; the right of all the states in the region to live in peace; the commencement of a transitional period in the West Bank of Jordan and Gaza Strip under United Nations supervision for a duration not exceeding a few months; finally, the implementation of these principles should be guaranteed by either the United Nations or some of its member states.[105]

On 6 October 1981, President Sadat of Egypt was assassinated. His death created confusion in the Middle East, indicating the shaky ground on which the Egyptian–Israeli peace treaty was constructed.[106] A few days later, on 25 November 1981, an Arab summit conference convened in Fez, Morocco. At this conference the Fahd peace plan was presented, but it did not gain the approval or the endorsement of all Arab countries. This was because of the strong objections to the plan by Syria, Libya, Algeria, South Yemen and the PLO. President Asad of Syria refused even to attend the conference. Consequently, the Fez summit conference had to be adjourned; it suspended its work a few hours after its opening.[107]

On the European side, there were also important developments. As noted earlier, one of the essential points of the Venice Declaration was that the European Community would establish contacts with the parties concerned in the Middle East question. Accordingly, the Community appointed Gaston Thorn, who was the president of the European Council of Ministers for the second half of 1980, to chair the so-called fact-finding mission to the Middle East. The mission's tour lasted from 30 July until the end of September 1980. During it, M Thorn visited the headquarters of the League of Arab States in Tunis, as well as seven Arab Mashreq countries and Israel. He met with the parties concerned and listened to their points of view, repeating the European position which had been declared in the Community's various statements.[108]

After M Thorn's mission, the Dutchman Chris Vander Klaauw, who took over from Thorn as president of the European Council of Ministers, was charged with the task of conducting another fact-finding mission in the Middle East. Mr Klaauw decided to keep as low a profile as he could. Accordingly, during his tour to the Middle East (which lasted from 22 February to May 1981), he confined himself to listening to the parties concerned, and repeating what his predecessor had said. This constituted the beginning of the policy of delay and marked the turning point in the European efforts towards a Middle East peace initiative. Following Mr Klaauw's mission, the withdrawal of European diplomatic efforts became clear with the changes that took place in the French presidency. The defeat of President Giscard d'Estaing, the strong supporter of the Arab world, weakened French efforts to mediate in the Arab–Israeli dispute. It also eliminated any prospect for a collective European role or initiative in the Middle East.[109] Claude Cheysson, the French foreign minister and member of the European Commission, clearly explained this trend when he said: 'Since we are not countries in the region, we have neither a plan nor an initiative to propose. There will be no French plan nor any French initiative; there will not, whilst we are in government, be any European plan nor any European initiative.'[110]

Furthermore, on 24 November 1981 the ten members of the European Community took a decision to participate in the international peace-keeping force in the Sinai. This indicated—at least in the view of the Arab countries who opposed the Camp David agreement—that the Community still associated itself with the Camp David peace process. The Community stated that it regarded its efforts in this respect as an attempt to pave the way in the direction of a global solution.

On the Israeli front, there were also some developments, which helped to hinder any prospect for Euro-Arab ministerial meeting. Prime Minister Begin went ahead with his hard-line policy in the Arab occupied territories. On the external front, moreover, in April 1981, the confrontation with Syria over the deployment of missiles in the Bekaa Valley reached its peak, after the Israelis managed to shoot down two Syrian helicopters. This was followed by the bombing of the Iraqi nuclear reactor in June of the same year. On 17 July 1981, the Israeli air force bombed West Beirut and caused considerable casualties among Palestinians and Lebanese. After that came the annexation of the Golan Heights in December 1981.[111]

This escalation of provocation coincided with the arrival of a new American administration, which tended to deal with the Middle East conflict from the point of view of its global strategic conception. More attention was paid to the superpower role in every conflict, whether regional or local, and allies were expected to follow suit.[112] Henry Kissinger (even though he was speaking on his own behalf) threatened that the European Community must act in tune with the United States. He stressed that it was illogical to have a common policy in the field of defence while at the same time having conflicting views over foreign policy.[113]

The combination of these events made it impossible for the two parties of the dialogue to hold their prospective ministerial meeting or even to achieve anything tangible. On the contrary, during this period the dialogue entered a time of stagnation.[114] This situation continued throughout 1982, owing mainly to the events that took place in Lebanon (the Israeli invasion of Lebanon in June 1982). Amid this impasse and in order to push the mechanism of the dialogue ahead, the Arab side proposed, at the end of 1982, that the General Committee of the dialogue should hold a meeting. Europe's response was positive, and after intensive efforts both sides agreed that the fifth meeting of the General Committee should take place in Athens in December 1983.[115]

The fifth General Committee meeting, December 1983

After a long interval, The General Committee managed to hold its fifth meeting in Athens on 14 December 1983. It was quite different from earlier meetings in that it ended in complete failure. The two sides could not reach agreement over the final communiqué, which should have covered political, technical and economic aspects of the dialogue. As a result the meeting was adjourned with only a joint press statement, issued on 15 December 1983.[116] In it the two sides mentioned that they had exchanged their points of view on different aspects of the dialogue. Ironically, the statement insisted that the meeting was fruitful. It said: 'This exchange of views, which provided the opportunity to set forth a wide spectrum of common positions, has proved very useful.' The statement ended by stressing that both sides had intended to increase their 'diplomatic contacts as regard subjects of mutual interest'.[117]

ACTIVITIES OF THE WORKING COMMITTEES

Up to the Luxembourg meeting of 1980, the working groups were in suspension. When the Luxembourg meeting took place, the working committees were asked to resume their activities.

Among the various working groups, only the cultural, labour and social affairs group actually managed to achieve something tangible. It succeeded in holding a symposium on the relations between the two civilizations, in Hamburg on 11 April 1983. The symposium was officially opened by Klaus Von Dohnanyi, the Mayor of Hamburg, Hans-Dietrich Genscher (the German foreign minister) and Chedli Klibi (Secretary-General of the League of Arab States).[118] The main purpose of the gathering was to take a look at the problems concerning the history of both civilizations, the present condition of their cultural co-operation, and the possibility of increasing such co-operation in the future.

The work of the symposium started with a preliminary survey presented by Dr Mohi Eldine Saber, General Director of the Arab Organization for Education, Culture and Science. There followed ten public sessions, each covering a special subject determined in advance. The discussions included a review of historical events, and an assessment of present problems of both civilizations and the prospect of their mutual development.[119] Finally, three workshops were held on the following topics: the possibility of an extension of cultural exchanges; the social and cultural consequences of the migration of workers and intellectuals; and co-operation in the field of language teaching. Each of the three workshops was led by two co-organizers, one Arab and the other European, and assisted by a number of experts participating in the symposium. The symposium ended with a paper presented by Gunter Diel of the West German foreign ministry, and the participants at the conclusion of the symposium stressed their satisfaction with the outcome of the discussions.[120]

STATUS OF THE DIALOGUE IN THE AFTERMATH OF THE ATHENS MEETING

Attempts to revive the dialogue

It was hoped that the fifth General Committee meeting would reduce the gap between the two parties of the dialogue and give new impetus for it to go ahead. That did not happen, although both sides, at the end of the meeting, did express their 'sincere intentions' to continue contacts with each other in order to find ways to increase their co-operation. The dialogue, once again, reached deadlock after the Athens meeting.

Nevertheless, contacts between the presidencies of the two sides continued. This provided the opportunity for Arab and European representatives to hold a tripartite meeting in Tunis on 12 and 13 November 1984. During the meeting, the two sides managed to take stock of all aspects of the dialogue, and agreed to hold a further tripartite Euro-Arab meeting in 1985 with a view to preparing for the next General Committee meeting.[121]

After the Tunis meeting, efforts to bridge the gap between them and prepare the ground for the next meeting of the General Committee continued. Two meetings took place between 6 and 8 February 1985, in Tunis and Rome respectively, between representatives from the EEC and the Arab League. During these meetings, the two sides failed to reach agreement on the direction of the dialogue. The Arab side repeated its demand for more emphasis on the political aspects of the dialogue, while the European Community preferred to concentrated on the economic dimension of the talks. The meetings as usual ended with both sides reaffirming their wishes to continue the dialogue with the aim of increasing their co-operation in all fields covered by it.[122]

To break the deadlock, an initiative was taken by the Arab side in the autumn of 1985. The secretary-general of the League of Arab states, Mr Klibi, addressed a letter to the president of the Council of the European Community. In this letter, Mr Klibi suggested that a Euro-Arab ministerial meeting (following the Troika arrangement) could take place to discuss political matters, such as the situation in the Middle East and the Mediterranean region.[123] This approach was examined by the Community at the meeting of their foreign affairs ministers in the Hague on 25 February 1986. During the meeting, the ministers agreed on the following:

(a) a tripartite Euro-Arab Commission could meet to examine political matters of interest to both communities and a statement could be issued following the meeting;
(b) discussions would be restricted to general subjects of interest to the European and Arab sides and would not deal with specific political questions.[124]

On 31 March, the European Commission notified the secretariat-general of the Arab League of the decision adopted in the Hague on 23 February by the European Council of Ministers. The Arab response was negative. The Arabs did not agree to the European conditions. Adnan Omran, Assistant Secretary-General for International Affairs for the Arab League, explained to the Netherlands ambassador the Arab position. He stressed that the Arab League had notified the European Council that there would be no separation between specific political issues (which the Community wanted to avoid in order not to give any political commitment on issues such as the Palestine question and the recognition of the PLO) and those of a more general interest: 'There was a necessity to follow specific discussion of issues as previously defined at Arab summits and meetings of the Arab League Council.' He also confirmed that the Arab side believed positively that in order to ensure the success of the dialogue it was imperative to discuss all aspects of interest, either general dialogue or specific political questions, so that both areas could be covered at the same time.[125]

Before this impasse could be overcome, tension in the area (especially in the Mediterranean) rose and started to sour Euro-Arab relations. The tension was caused by the American raids on Libya in April 1986, and the subsequent EEC adoption of measures against Libya.

THE AMERICAN RAID ON LIBYA, 15 APRIL 1986

After a long period of increasing tension between Libya and the United States, during which the United States government repeatedly accused Libya of supporting international terrorism, on 15 April 1986 American aircraft launched bombing raids on targets in Tripoli and Benghazi. The raids caused a large number of civilian casualties and resulted in considerable international condemnation.

Clash over the Mediterranean

Initially, tension between the two countries had started to mount when the United States Sixth Fleet staged manoeuvres to the north of the Gulf of Sirte from 23 to 30 January, and from 11 to 14 February. On 20 March, American officials declared that some of their ships would cross south of latitude 32 into territorial waters claimed by Libya. On 24 March, three American ships sailed into the disputed waters. Libya's reaction was swift; Libyan shore batteries near the town of Sirte fired surface-to-air missiles. In response, American aircraft attacked a Libyan missile ship and a corvette, while an American cruiser attacked a second missile ship. American air forces also launched two separate raids on the radar installations of the Libyan batteries at Sirte.

The following day (25 March), a second Libyan corvette came under air attack. Libyan casualties were estimated to be between 56 and 97 people. After the initial clashes on 24 March, the American presidential spokesman, Larry Speakes, stressed that the Libyan action 'points out once again, for all to see, the aggressive nature of Col. Kadhafi's regime'. He described the American manoeuvres as 'a peaceful navigational exercise in international waters' and rejected the idea that they had been planned to provoke a Libyan response.

On 28 March, the Secretary of State, George Shultz, threatened that the American forces would launch further action against Libya if required. This threat was again confirmed on 31 March by a State Department Official who stressed that 'the next act of terrorism will bring the hammer down'. On 25 March, Col. Kadhafi warned the United States, stressing that 'this is not a time for speaking... it is a time for war'. He blamed the United States for expanding the conflict and threatened to 'carry it all over the world'.[126]

European and Arab reactions to the USA–Libya confrontation

The American-Libyan confrontation over the Mediterranean on 24 March drew broad reactions from Europeans as well as Arab countries. Among the individual European countries, the United Kingdom endorsed the United States action, while other European countries expressed various degrees of concern. The French, Spanish and West German governments urged restraint, acknowledging at the same time the American right to self defence when attacked in international waters. The Italian prime minister, Bettino Craxi, stressed that the American action against Libya was not a proper way to solve a conflict over territorial waters. He expressed great concern over the armed confrontation in the area and stated that Italy 'does not want a war on its doorstep'. The Greek government stressed that 'provocations and conflict are a danger to peace'.

The Arab reaction was strong. Most of the Arab governments criticized the United States and stressed their support for Libya. Among those countries expressing strong support were Morocco, Algeria and Saudi Arabia. It was reported that King Fahd ibn Abdul Aziz telephoned Col. Kadhafi on 27 March and offered to place all of Saudia Arabia's 'resources at the disposal of the Libyan people'. Similarly, the PLO expressed sympathy and support for Libya. President Mubarak of Egypt stressed Egypt's concern and urged restraint on both sides. The foreign ministers of the League of Arab States held a meeting in Tunis on

27 March, during which they condemned the American action and affirmed their solidarity with Libya.[127]

On 29 March, the Council of the League of Arab States held a meeting at which the question of the American action against Libya was discussed. The Council made the following points:

(a) it strongly condemned the American aggression and confirmed its previous stance with regard to the American threat against Libya;

(b) it stressed its absolute solidarity with Libya and urged all Arab states to lend their support and assistance to Libya;

(c) it called upon the United States to stop its aggression and withdraw its fleets from the area;

(d) it recommended that action must be taken to clarify the situation at the international community level;

(e) it called upon the United Nations Security Council to convene.[128]

Between 26 and 31 March, the UN Security Council discussed the situation in the area, but adjourned without adopting any resolution. Finally, strong criticism came from the Soviet Union when a Soviet spokesman characterized the American exercises as 'deliberate actions taken in order to destabilize the situation in the region'. He added that these actions had 'poisoned the atmosphere' of the relations between the two superpowers. On 27 March, the Soviet leader, Mikhail Gorbachev, repeated his condemnation of the American action and offered to withdraw the Soviet fleet from the Mediterranean if the United States would follow suit.[129]

Escalation of American–Libyan tension

Over the ensuing days of early April, tension between the United States and Libya began to mount. American officials accused Libya of being involved in a number of terrorist acts against American interests in Europe. On 2 April, a bomb exploded on an aircraft of the American airline TWA during a flight from Rome to Athens. The bomb killed four people. Responsibility was claimed by a group called 'the Arab Revolutionary Cells', which declared that the attack was carried out in retaliation for the American aggression against Libya. Libya, denied any involvement in the attack and deplored it as 'an act of terrorism'.

On 5 April, another bomb went off in a discotheque frequented by American servicemen in West Berlin. The casualties were one American soldier and a Turkish woman dead, and an estimated 200 injured, including 60 American citizens. Responsibility for the incident was claimed by three groups. Two were West German: the 'Red Army Faction' and the 'Holger Meins Commando'; the third group was called the 'Anti-American Arab Liberation Front'. Despite Libya's denial of any involvement in these incidents, American officials blamed Libya for having masterminded the attacks. On 5 April, they stated that there was 'strong circumstantial evidence' of Libyan responsibility. On 7 April, the American ambassador to West Germany, Richard Burt, stated that there were 'clear indications' of Libyan involvement in terrorist attacks. On 9 April, the NATO Supreme Commander Europe, Gen. Bernard Rogers, stressed that 'indisputable evidence' existed of Libyan involvement in the bombings. The American campaign against Libya reached its peak when President Reagan, in a televised news conference on 9 April, characterized Col. Kadhafi as a 'mad dog'. He threatened: 'If and when we can specifically identify someone responsible for one of these acts, we will respond'.[130]

Libya's response to the accusations and threats was quick. On 9 April, Col. Kadhafi in a news conference denied all charges against Libya and threatened to launch attacks against American interests throughout the world if its forces attacked Libya. During the five days following President Reagan's threat, American officials repeatedly indicated that a United States attack on Libya was on the way.

Meanwhile, the United States government was pressing Europe to take tough action against Libya. Consequently, and in response to American pressure, on 5 April the French government expelled four Arabs, two of them Libyan diplomats, alleging that they were involved in a plot to attack American interests in France. On 6 April, the West German government declared that it had appointed a special panel to investigate the possibility of foreign governments being involved in terrorist attacks. On 9 April, the West German government ordered two Libyan diplomats to leave the country for their 'impermissible activities'. On 12 April, the Three-Power Allied Command in West Berlin consented to give local police 'exceptional and provisional' powers to stop suspected terrorists entering West Berlin from the eastern part of the city. On 12 April the Spanish government recalled its ambassador to Libya. Joint and coordinated European action against Libya came at a meeting of foreign ministers of the European Community countries, which took place in the Hague on 14 April 1986.[131]

The EEC foreign ministers' meeting, April 1986

The foreign ministers of the Community member states held a meeting in the Hague on 14 April 1986. During it, the ministers adopted a joint statement which highlighted the Community's grave concern over the dangerous situation in the Mediterranean. The ministers vigourously condemned international terrorism and singled out Libya as responsible for the terrorist attacks that had recently taken place in Europe. They refused to accept the threats made by Libyan leaders against the Community countries, which they said would encourage recourse to acts of violence and directly threaten Europe. Hence they stated that any action of this sort would be met with a proper response on the part of the Community. Moreover, the twelve members of the Community agreed on specific sanctions to be applied against Libya. These were as follows:

(a) restrictions on the freedom of movement of diplomatic and consular personnel;
(b) reduction of the staff of diplomatic and consular missions;
(c) stricter visa requirements and procedures.[132]

In addition, they decided to stop all arms sales to Libya and warned that any country lending support to terrorism would not have normal relations with the Community. The ministers also ordered the 'experts concerned' to identify proper measures to be adopted by the Community. These included security measures, the application of international conventions on diplomatic and consular privileges and the safety of civil aviation. The ministers consented to enhance their co-operation with other states in the field of intelligence, to improve security measures and broadly to eliminate terrorist activities. They asked the Arab states to 'analyse jointly and urgently the issue of international terrorism'. Finally the ministers, in order to prevent any military escalation in the area, urged 'restraint' on all sides.[133]

The American air raid—European and Arab reactions

On 15 April, American aircraft launched air strikes on Tripoli, the capital of Libya, and on Benghazi, the second city in the country. They attacked three targets in Tripoli: El-Azizya barracks, Sidi Bilal port and military installations at Tripoli airport; in Benghazi the target was the Benina air force base. The casualties among civilian people were estimated at about 100 dead in Tripoli and around 30 in Benghazi. Residential buildings were damaged, including the French embassy.

After the raid was completed, an American Defence Department spokesman described it as 'a near flawless operation conducted under extremely difficult circumstances'. Similarly, President Reagan, shortly after the raid on 15 April, said: 'Today we have done what we had to do. If necessary, we shall do it again.' He added: 'For us to ignore by inaction the slaughter of American civilians and American soldiers . . . is simply not in the American tradition.' He claimed that the attack on Libya was 'self-defence' and was in conformity with Article 51 of the United Nations Charter. This pre-emptive action, he said, would not only hinder Col. Kadhafi's ability to export terror, it would furnish him with reasons to reconsider his criminal attitude. He went on to stress that the government of the United States had tried different peaceful means but none of them had succeeded in preventing Kadhafi from continuing his mindless policy of intimidation and his unbending pursuit of terror. The following day, President Reagan characterized the attack as 'a single engagement in a long battle against terrorism'.[134]

Libya's response to the attack was strong. Within hours of the American strikes on Tripoli and Benghazi, the Libyan radio broadcast calls to the 'Syrian army, the Algerian air forces and free men in Morocco, Egypt, Tunisia and all the Arab countries' to attack American targets 'wherever they might be, and crush all the interests of America's European allies.' 'The hour of attack and revenge has rung,' the radio announced. The Libyan government urged the Arab countries to 'join in the war, destroy American interests, and impose a political and economic boycott' against the United States.[135] The Libyan delegate to the United Nations, Rajab Azzarouk, appealed to the Security Council to condemn the American strikes as state terrorism. He described them as a 'barbaric and savage', and an 'unprovoked' attack on civilian targets.[136] On 16 April, Col. Kadhafi made a public statement in which he deplored the American raid on Libya, stressing that Libya would not commit similar attacks since Libyans 'do not bomb children like the US does'.[137]

Reactions in Western Europe

The British government aside, the initial reactions of most Western European governments were those of dismay and even anger at the American military attack against Libya. They were particularly upset over the lack of consultation (although Britain was said to have been informed about the action), and over the fact that the American action took place only hours after the European Community's foreign ministers had denounced Libya by name, imposed sanctions against the country and then called for a political solution to the crisis. 'The position adopted by Europe was ignored' said the Italian Socialist premier Bettino Craxi. He described the raid as 'a decision that does not take due account of the value of the European–American partnership'.[138] He also said: 'Far from weakening terrorism, this military action risks provoking explosive reactions of fanaticism and criminal and suicide acts.'[139] The Dutch foreign minister, Han Van den Brok, who was also President of the European Council, described the American raid as a 'slap in the face for Europe'. He stressed that the Netherlands 'deeply deplored' the American attack on Libya so soon after the Community had appealed for a political solution to the crisis.[140]

The Belgian foreign minister, Leo Tindemans, said that the American attacks caught the European Community by surprise. He went on to stress that the Europeans 'do not think the Sixth Fleet is the best way of fighting terrorism'. Chancellor Kohl of West Germany stated: 'We advised against the use of force. Force is not a promising way of dealing with things'. The French prime minister, Jacques Chirac, expressed his regret that 'the intolerable and inadmissible escalation of terrorism has led to an action of reprisals that itself revives the chain of violence'. The Greek government deplored the raid and demanded an emergency meeting of the foreign ministers of the Community to examine the 'abnormal and dangerous situation'. Karolos Papoulias, the Greek foreign minister, stressed that despite the fact that some European allies had been informed by the United States of the impending attack, these allies did not convey the information to their partners. He described this as 'an unpleasant surprise' and 'a violation of the moral rules of political co-operation'.[141]

The Spanish foreign ministry spokesman in Madrid voiced his 'alarm and concern' at the American action against Libya. EEC diplomats also stressed that British endorsement of the American action and suspicions that the British foreign secretary, Sir Geoffery Howe, who was aware of the impending attack, formed a fatal blow to the European hopes of enhancing co-operation on foreign affairs. Britain was the only country in the Community that supported outright the American attack against Libya. The British government had allowed the FIIIs stationed on British airfields to be employed in the attack. On 15 April, the prime minister, Margaret Thatcher, stated that it was 'inconceivable' for her to reject the American demand. She added that the United States had deployed more than 300,000 men in the defence of Europe. Hence it was in Britain's interest to assist the United States when it came under attack.[142]

The joint EEC reaction

Despite the fact that the initial reactions of most of the European governments were critical of the American action, the Community leaders did link their criticism of the United States with condemnation of Libya. Furthermore, the Community member states decided, in their joint reaction, to support the American position. Hence the first Community joint reaction was favourable to the United States stance. At a foreign ministers' meeting which took place in Luxembourg on 17 April, the Community ministers avoided taking an anti-American stance. Instead they re-emphasized their previous position which was adopted during the Council meeting on 14 April in the Hague, which had favoured the imposition of sanctions against Libya.[143]

The Community went further in its meeting in Luxembourg on 21 April. The ministers then agreed on a number of measures against Libya, some of which involved the implementation of the decisions adopted on 14 April, while the rest were new. The new measures were the following:

(a) staff of member states' missions in Libya to be reduced to the level strictly necessary to conduct relations;

(b) Libya's non-diplomatic missions in member states to be considered with a view to the possible imposition of restrictions similar to those agreed on 14 April;

(c) Libyans expelled from one of the 12 member states under suspicion of terrorism to be refused entry to any other member states;

(d) abuse of diplomatic privileges and immunities to be kept under review.[144]

In conformity with the Community decisions of 14, 17 and 21 April, the sanctions envisaged against Libya were put into effect. On 18 April, four Libyans were expelled from France. On 21 April, a former Libyan diplomat in Rome was arrested by Italian police in connection with a plot to assassinate the Egyptian, Saudi and American ambassadors. On 22 April, the United Kingdom ordered 21 Libyans to leave the country because of their 'revolutionary activities' in support of the Kadhafi regime. On 23 April, the West German government expelled 22 Libyan People's Bureau staff on the ground that the government had found clear evidence of Libya's responsibility for the Berlin bombing. The number of West German diplomats in Libya was reduced. On 24 April, the Danish government reduced the number of Libyan diplomats in Copenhagen from eleven to six. The following day, Spain expelled ten Libyans, two of whom were diplomats. On 26 April, the Italian government expelled ten Libyan diplomats and imposed severe restrictions on the movements of the rest; two days earlier Belgium, Luxembourg and the Netherlands ordered the reduction of People's Bureau staff by half. In response to these measures, on 30 April, Libya ordered over one hundred foreign workers, including 53 Italian, 36 Spanish and 19 British citizens, to leave the country.[145]

The Arab reaction

Apart from Iraq, which made no comment on the attack, most of the Arab countries reacted strongly against the American raid on Libya and expressed their grave concern over the dangerous situation in the area. In Amman, Jordan's Information Minister, Muhammad Al-Khatib, stressed that the attack 'may lead to more dangerous results'.[146] The Egyptian government issued this statement: 'Egypt has received with extreme worry and resentment news of the US bombing of Libyan targets and the subsequent casualties in lives of innocent Libyan people in violation of the United Nations Charter.' In Saudi Arabia, the government issued a statement saying that it 'expresses deep regret and condemns this attack and method, which contradicts acceptable international behaviour'. The statement went on: 'We are alongside Libya and any Arab state which is subject to attack.'[147]

The secretary-general of the League of Arab States, Mr Klibi, stated: 'It is regrettable that a nation which for more than two centuries was the champion of freedom and democracy sees its force used in the service of those who can only compromise, perhaps irreversibly, US relations with Arab peoples.' The Kuwaiti government characterized the action as 'an act of terrorism and flagrant aggression'.[148] The Algerian government denounced the attack and expressed solidarity with Libya.

Syrian support for Libya was the most outspoken. The statement issued by the Syrian government stated that it 'now stands by Libya with all its strength and calls on Arab governments to perceive the dangers of this act and confront it'. The PLO chairman Mr Arafat, who was in Sanaa at the time, issued a joint statement with President Ali Abdullah Saleh, stating that 'the American attack is nothing but aggression on the entire Arab nation and should be condemned'. The statement also called for an 'urgent' Arab summit meeting.[149]

Against this background, it was obvious that Euro-Arab relations would be affected and through that the Euro-Arab dialogue. Indeed that was what happened. When the American action took place, the secretary-general of the League of Arab States, Mr Klibi, was in Brussels. He was discussing with Leo Tindemans, the Belgian foreign minister, and the European Commissioner for Mediterranean policy, Claude Cheyesson, broad issues of future peace and security in the Mediterranean. Immediately after the attack, the secretary-general cut short his visit and returned to Tunis in protest against the American attack. It was reported that he was very critical of the Community, stressing that Europe was not forceful enough with the United States. He added that Europe 'should have made its voice heard for a return to reason'.[150] As the relations between the two sides had reached a zero-sum-game, it was impossible for the General Committee to hold any meeting. Hence the dialogue remained in deadlock.

THE DUTCH FOREIGN MINISTER AND THE ATTEMPT TO
REVITALIZE THE DIALOGUE

When tension escalated in the Mediterranean, the Europeans
felt that their interests were at stake, and that to ease the tension
it was necessary to revive the dialogue as quickly as possible.
Consequently, the Dutch foreign minister, Mr Van den Broek
(who was also President of the European Council), visited Tunis
on 25 and 26 May. During the visit, he held talks with the
secretary-general of the Arab League, Mr Klibi, and the Tunisian
minister for foreign affairs. The talks focused mainly on the
possibility of revitalizing the dialogue.[151] During the talks, the
Dutch foreign minister stressed mainly two points:

(a) the necessity to revitalize the dialogue and pursue it in all its
    aspects;
(b) the willingness of the Twelve to continue discussions with
    the Arab side in order to enable the General Committee to
    overcome its impasse.

The desire to revitalise the dialogue, from the European point of
view, was confirmed again in a letter addressed to the secretary-
general of the Arab League, Mr Klibi, in September 1986. The
so-called 'Hindawi affair', however, soon dashed hopes
again.[152]

THE HINDAWI AFFAIR

Nezar Hindawi, a Palestinian of Jordanian nationality, was
arrested under the Prevention of Terrorism Act in London on 18
April. He was found guilty on 24 October of attempting to blow
up an Israeli airliner in mid-air on 17 April. During the trial,
which started on 6 October, he gave evidence that implicated
Syria in the act. He was reported to have said that he had
planned the operation under the supervision of the Syrian intelligence service, had travelled to London under a false name
on a Syrian diplomatic passport, and had been given the encouragement of the Syrian embassy staff, including the ambassador,
Loutof Al-Haydar. Following the trial on 24 October, the United
Kingdom severed diplomatic relations with Syria. In justifying
the decision, the Foreign and Commonwealth Secretary, Sir
Geoffrey Howe, stated that there was 'conclusive evidence' of

Syrian involvement in the operation. Some of this had appeared during the trial, while further proof had been gathered through intelligence operations.[153] On 30 October, the British government announced that it would not approve the renewal of Syria's financial protocol with the EEC for the years 1987–91.[154]

The Syrian government denied all charges and stated that the British action was part of a major conspiracy against Syria by Israel and the United States. In response to the United Kingdom's decision, the Syrian government shut down the offices of the British Council and closed Syrian air space and territorial waters to British craft. British citizens resident in Syria were, however, allowed to stay in the country. On 29 October, it was announced that the Lebanese embassy would handle Syrian interests in Britain.

Support for the British decision came from the United States, which endorsed the action and withdrew its ambassador from the Syrian capital Damascus in protest against Syrian involvement. Within the European Community, the foreign ministers, at their meeting on 27 October, adopted a statement stressing their 'common sense of outrage' at the alleged Syrian responsibility for the bombing attempt.[155] The European foreign ministers went even further at their meeting in London on 10 November. They approved the following measures to be applied against Syria:

(a) the banning of arms sales to Syria;
(b) the suspension of high-level visits to or from Syria;
(c) the review of the activities of Syrian diplomatic and consular missions accredited in the Community countries and applying proper measures;
(d) the tightening of security precautions on the movement of Syrian airliners.[156]

Syria's stance against these accusations was endorsed by most of the Arab countries.[157]

EEC SUPPORT FOR AN INTERNATIONAL PEACE CONFERENCE AND THE PROSPECTS FOR THE REVIVAL OF THE DIALOGUE

On 23 February 1987, the foreign ministers of the European Community held a political co-operation meeting, during which they adopted a statement on the situation in the Middle East. In this statement, the ministers supported the idea of convening an international conference under the auspices of the United Nations to solve the Palestinian problem. They stated that the conference must be attended by all the parties directly concerned, and by any party 'able to make a direct and positive contribution to the restoration and maintenance of peace and to the region's economic and social development'. The foreign ministers expressed their belief that such a conference would provide a proper framework for the necessary negotiations between the parties directly involved in the conflict. Moreover, they stressed the principles on which solutions must be based. In this respect, they emphasized the Venice Declaration of 1980, which called for the PLO to be associated with any peace negotiations. The Community ministers also offered to play a role with respect to such a conference.[158]

The concept of an international conference on the Arab–Israeli conflict was widely welcomed by most of the major interested parties, including the Israeli foreign minister, Shimon Peres (Prime Minister Itzhak Shamir was opposed to the idea). However, despite consent on the principle of holding a conference, significant differences remained among the interested parties on the question of its function.[159]

The Community's support for an international peace conference under the auspices of the United Nations was reiterated at a foreign ministers' meeting in Bonn on 8 February 1988. During this meeting, the ministers adopted a statement in which they expressed their belief that the only solution to the conflict in the Middle East was through a comprehensive, just and lasting political settlement, as suggested by the Community in their Venice Declaration and their subsequent statements. They reaffirmed their strong support for an international peace conference under the auspices of the United Nations, as the proper framework for negotiations between the parties concerned.[160]

The Bonn Euro-Arab meeting, June 1988

The Community declarations supporting an international peace conference created a positive atmosphere in Euro-Arab relations. Hence it gave new impetus to the Euro-Arab dialogue and once again brought representatives from the Arab League and the EEC together around the table.[161]

On 24 June 1988, a Euro-Arab meeting took place in Bonn. The meeting was held according to the 'Troika arrangement' (past, present and future presidencies of the Community and the Arab League). The European delegation was composed of the German foreign minister, Hans-Dietrich Genscher, in his capacity as President of the European Council of Ministers, State Secretary Benny Kimberg, representing the previous presidency (Denmark), and Foreign Minister Karolos Papoulias representing the next presidency (Greece). The European Commission was also represented by Commissioner Claude Cheysson. The Arab delegation consisted of Foreign Minister Farouk Shara'a (Syria) in his capacity as President of the Council of Ministers of the Arab League, State Minister Mohamed Ali Hamoud (Somalia) representing the incoming Arab League presidency, Foreign Minister Hussein Suleyman Abu Salih (Sudan) representing the previous presidency, and Arab League Secretary-General Chedli Klibi.[162]

During the meeting, the representatives took stock of the different aspects of the dialogue and stated that they were ready to give 'a new impetus to the work of the various bodies of the Euro-Arab dialogue'. They also expressed their 'strong interest in a swift reactivation of all institutions and activities set up in the framework of the Euro-Arab dialogue'. However, despite the fact that 'thorough discussion' took place on the important issues related to the Euro-Arab relations, there was no statement on the content of the discussion. Also, there was no date fixed for a sixth meeting of the General Committee of the dialogue. At the end of the meeting, both sides stressed the will to create a positive atmosphere for the continuation of the dialogue.[163]

NOTES

1. *Development of the Community from June 1980 to June 1981*, Directorate General for Research and Documentation, European Parliament, Luxembourg, 1981, p. 2.
2. John C. Campbell, 'The United States and the Middle East', in Colin Legum (ed.), *Crisis and Conflict in the Middle East. The changing Strategy: From Iran to Afghanistan*, Holmes and Meier publishers, New York and London, 1981, pp. 77–9.
3. M.D. Wormser, *The Middle East*, p. 3.

4. Dankwart A. Rustow, *Oil and Turmoil America Faces OPEC and the Middle East*, W.W. Norton and Company, New York, London, 1982, p. 181.

5. R. K. Ramazani, *The United States and Iran: The Patterns of Influence*, Praeger Special Studies, New York, 1982, p. 138.

6. Dankwart A. Rustow, *Oil and Turmoil*, pp. 182–3.

7. *Ibid*, pp. 183–4.

8. John C. Campbell, 'The United States and the Middle East', in Colin Legum (ed.), *Crisis and Conflict in the Middle East*, p. 68.

9. C. Paul Bradley, *Recent United States Policy in the Persian Gulf (1971–1982)*, Tompson and Rutter, USA, 1982, pp. 89–90.

10. *Ibid*, p. 90.

11. Robert J. Lieber, 'The European Community and the Middle East', in Colin Legum (ed.), *Crisis and Conflict in the Middle East*, p. 92.

12. *Ibid.*

13. Barry Rubin, *Paved with Good Intentions: The American Experience and Iran*, Penguin Books, Great Britain, 1981, p. 379.

14. Brig. Kenneth Hunt, 'Overview: The Military and Political Battleground', in Colin Legum (ed.), *Crisis and Conflict in the Middle East*, pp. 5–6.

15. Geoffrey Kemp and Michael Vlahos, 'Military and Strategic Issues in the Middle East–Persian Gulf Region in 1978', *Middle East Contemporary Survey*, p. 68.

16. John C. Campbell, 'The United States and the Middle East', in Colin Legum, *Crisis and Conflict in the Middle East*, p. 69.

17. Geoffrey Kamp and Michael Vlahos, 'Military and Strategic Issues in the Middle East–Persian Gulf Region in 1978', *Middle East Contemporary Survey*, pp. 68–9.

18. C. Paul Bradley, *Recent United States Policy in the Persian Gulf*, p. 86.

19. Michael Vlahos and Geoffrey Kemp, 'The Changing Strategic Tapestry in the Middle East', in Colin Legum (ed.), *Crisis and Conflict in the Middle East*, p. 25.

20. James R. Kurth, 'American Leadership: The Western Alliance and the Old Regime in the Persian Gulf', in Steven L. Spiegel, *The Middle East and the Western Alliance*, p. 120.

21. C. Paul Bradley, *Recent United States Policy in the Persian Gulf*, p. 92.

22. Leila Meo, *U.S.Strategy in the Gulf:Intervention Against Liberation*, Association of Arab–American University Graduates, USA, 1981, pp. 82–3.

23. *Keesing's Contemporary Archives*, 9 May, 1980, pp. 30, 236–7.

24. *Ibid*, pp. 30, 229–30, 234.

25. Brig. Kenneth Hunt, 'The Military and Political Battleground', in Colin Legum (ed.), *Crisis and Conflict in the Middle East*, pp. 7–8.

26. *Bulletin of the European Communities*, No. 6, 1979, p. 93. See also, *Middle East International*, 22 June, 1979, pp. 14–15.

27. *Bulletin of the European Communities*, No. 9, 1979, pp. 67–9.

28. *Bulletin of the European Communities*, No. 11, 1979, pp. 80–2.

29. See *Twenty Seventh Review of the Council's Work (1 January–31 December, 1979)*, Office for Official Publications of the European Communities, Luxembourg, 1980, p. 140.

30. *Fourteenth General Report of the Activities of the European Communities in 1980*, Office for Official Publications of the European Communities, Luxembourg, 1981, p. 280.
31. Saleh A. Al-Mani and Salah Al-Shaikhly, *The Euro-Arab Dialogue*, p. 114. See also, *Bulletin of the European Communities*, No. 9, 1979, pp. 107–14.
32. Robert J. Lieber, 'The European Community and the Middle East', in Colin Legum (ed.), *Crisis and Conflict in the Middle East. The Changing of Strategy: From Iran to Afghanistan*, p. 95.
33. *Middle East International*, 3 August 1979.
34. Robert J. Lieber, 'The European Community and the Middle East', in Colin Legum (ed.), *Crisis and Conflict in the Middle East*, p. 94.
35. *Le Monde*, 12 March 1980.
36. *Middle East International*, 3 August 1979.
37. Ilan Greilsammer and Joseph Weiler, 'European Political Co-operation and the Palestinian–Israeli Conflict: An Israeli Perspective', p. 142.
38. Robert J. Lieber, 'The European Community and the Middle East', in Colin Legum (ed.), *Crisis and Conflict in the Middle East*, pp. 94–5.
39. Janice Gross Stein, 'Alice in Wonderland: The North Atlantic Alliance and the Arab–Israeli Dispute', in Steven L. Spiegel (ed.), *The Middle East and the Western Alliance*, p. 77.
40. *Middle East International*, 20 July 1979.
41. *New York Times*, 5 June 1980.
42. See *The Daily Telegraph*, 5 June 1980.
43. *New York Times*, 31 May 1980.
44. *Middle East International*, 20 July 1979.
45. *Ibid*.
46. *Ibid*.
47. Ilan Greilsammer and Joseph Weiler, 'European Political Co-operation and the Palestinian–Israeli Conflict: An Israeli Perspective', p. 141.
48. *Ibid*, p. 142.
49. *New York Times*, 1 June 1980.
50. *New York Times*, 31 May 1980.
51. *New York Times*, 1 May 1980.
52. *New York Times*, 31 May 1980.
53. *Europe*, Agence Internationale d'Information Pour La Presse, Brussels, 9/10 June, 1980.
54. *New York Times*, 9 June 1980.
55. Nassif Hitti, 'The United States, The European Community and the Arab–Israeli Conflict', in Bichara Khader (ed.), *Co-operation Euro-Arabe*, p. 288.
56. William B. Quandt, 'The Western Alliance in the Middle East: Problems for US Foreign Policy', in Steven L. Spiegel (ed.), *The Middle East and the Western Alliance*, p. 15.
57. Ilan Greilsammer and Josph Weiler, 'European Political Co-operation and the Arab–Israeli Conflict: An Israeli Perspective', p. 142.
58. *Ibid*, p. 143.
59. *The Times*, 13 June 1980.

60. *New York Times*, 12 June 1980.
61. *Europe*, Agence Internationale d'Information Pour La Presse, Brussels, 9/10 June, 1980.
62. *Europe*, Agence Internationale d'Information Pour La Presse, Brussels, 13 June 1980.
63. *Ibid.*
64. *Ibid.*
65. *Ibid.*
66. *New York Times*, 12 June 1980.
67. *Bulletin of the European Communities*, No. 6, 1980, p. 10.
68. *New York Times*, 14 June 1980.
69. *Ibid.*
70. See the Memorandum in *New York Times*, 17 September 1975.
71. *New York Times*, 14 June 1980.
72. *Ibid.*
73. *Los Angeles Times*, 14 June 1980.
74. *New York Times*, 16 June 1980.
75. *Ibid.*
76. *Ibid.*
77. *Ibid.*
78. *Ibid.*
79. *Ibid.*
80. Ilan Greilsammer and Joseph Weiler, 'European political Co-operation and the Arab–Israeli Conflict: An Israeli Perspective', p. 145.
81. *Ibid.*
82. *Ibid*, p. 146.
83. *Ibid.*
84. Robert J. Lieber, 'The European Community and the Middle', in Colin Legum (ed.), *Crisis and Conflict in the Middle East. The Changing Strategy: From Iran to Afghanistan*, p. 95.
85. *New York Times*, 15 June 1980.
86. *Europe*, Agence Internationale d'Information Pour La Presse, Brussels, 16–17 June 1980.
87. Ilan Greilsammer and Joseph Weiler, 'European Political Co-operation and the Arab–Israeli Conflict: An Israeli Perspective', p. 146.
88. *Los Angeles Time*, 14 June 1980.
89. *Ibid.*
90. *New York Times*, 31 May 1980.
91. Saleh A. Al-Mani, and Salah Al-Shaikly, *The Euro-Arab Dialogue*, p. 67.
92. Gulshan Dhanani, 'The Euro-Arab Dialogue: A Critique',in K. B. Lall, Wolfgang Ernst and H. S. Chopra (eds.), *The EEC in the Global System*, p. 185.
93. *Fourteenth General Report on the Activities of the European Community in 1980*, p. 280.
94. *Bulletin of the European Communities*, No. 11, 1980, p. 13.
95. *Fourteenth General Report on the Activities of the European Communities in 1980*, p. 280.

96. *Euro-Arab Dialogue, Final Communiqué*, Luxembourg, 12–13 November 1980.
97. *Ibid.*
98. *Twenty Eight Review of the Council's Work (1 January–31 December 1980)*, pp. 152–3.
99. *Euro-Arab Dialogue, Final Communiqué*.
100. *Bulletin of the European Communities*, No. 11, 1980, p. 14.
101. *Twenty Ninth Review of the Council's Work (1 January–31 December 1981)*, p. 166.
102. Bichara Khader, 'Europe and the Arab–Israeli Conflict 1973–1983: An Arab Perspective', in D. Allen and A. Pijpers (eds.), *European Foreign Policy-Making and the Arab–Israeli Conflict*, p. 69.
103. *Twenty-Ninth Review of the Council's Work, (1 January–31 December 1981)*, pp. 166–7.
104. Colette Cova, *The Arab Policy of the EEC*, p. 131.
105. Yehuda Lukacs, *Documents on the Israeli–Palestinian Conflict, 1967–1983*, pp. 236–7.
106. Bichara Khader, 'Europe and the Arab–Israeli Conflict, 1973–1983: An Arab Perspective', p. 174.
107. Colette Cova, *The Arab Policy of the EEC*, p. 133.
108. *Europe*, Agence Internationale d'Information Pour La Presse, Brussels, 25–26 August 1980.
109. Bichara Khader, 'Europe and the Arab–Israeli Conflict, 1973–1983: An Arab Perspective', p. 173.
110. Quoted in *Ibid*, p. 174.
111. *Ibid.*
112. Nassif Hitti, 'The United States, The European Community and the Arab–Israeli Conflict', in Bichara Khader (ed.), *Co-operation Euro-Arabe*, p. 289.
113. *The Times*, 7 January 1981.
114. *Thirtieth Review of the Council's Work (1 January–31 December 1982)*, p. 159.
115. *Note de background sur le dialogue Euro-Arabe*, Brussels, 14 November 1986.
116. *Bulletin of the European Communities*, No. 12, 1983, p. 72.
117. *Thirty First Review of the Council's Work (1 January–31 December 1983)*, p. 151.
118. *Bulletin of the European Communities*, No. 4, 1983, pp. 53–4.
119. Derek Hopwood, *Euro-Arab Dialogue: The Relations Between the Two Cultures*, Croom Helm, Great Britain, 1983, p. 303.
120. *Ibid*, p. 304.
121. *Thirty Second Review of the Council's Work (1 January–31 December 1984)*, pp. 173–4.
122. *Thirty Third Review of the Council's Work (1 January–31 December 1985)*, pp. 153–4.
123. *Note de background sur le dialogue Euro-Arabe*.
124. 'The Euro-Arab Dialogue: Discussion Needed on All Aspects', *Press Release*, League of Arab States, London Office, 15 April 1986.

125. *Ibid.*
126. *Keesing's Contemporary Archives,* June 1986, pp. 34,454–5.
127. *Ibid,* p. 34,455.
128. 'League Council on the U.S. Aggression Against Libya', *Press Release,* League of Arab States, *Op.Cit.*
129. *Keesing's Contemporary Archives,* p. 34,455.
130. *Ibid,* pp. 34,455–6.
131. *Ibid,* p. 34,456.
132. *Bulletin of the European Communities,* No. 4, 1986, p. 108.
133. *Ibid.*
134. *Keesing's Contemporary Archives,* p. 34,457.
135. *Middle East International,* 18 April 1986.
136. *The New York Times,* 16 April 1986.
137. *Keesing's Contemporary Archives,* p. 34,457.
138. *The New York Times,* 16 April 1986.
139. *Keesing Contemporary Archives,* p. 34,458.
140. *The Times,* 16 April 1986.
141. *The New York Times,* 16 April 1986.
142. *Middle East International,* 18 April 1986.
143. *Telex Mediterranean,* 22 April 1986.
144. *Bulletin of the European Communities,* p. 109.
145. *Keesing Contemporary Archives,* p. 34,459.
146. *The Times,* 16 April 1986.
147. *The New York Times,* 16 April 1986.
148. *Keesing's Contemporary Archives,* p. 34,459.
149. *The New York Times,* 16 April 1986.
150. *Telex Mediterranean,* 22 April 1986.
151. *Middle East International,* 30 May 1986.
152. *Note de background sur le dialogue Euro-Arabe.*
153. *Keesing's Contemporary Archives,* November 1986, pp. 34,771–2.
154. *Keesing's Contemporary Archives,* January 1987, pp. 34,883–4.
155. *Keesing's Contemporary Archives,* p. 34,772.
156. *Bulletin of the European Communities,* No. 11, 1986, p. 98.
157. *Keesing's Contemporary Archives,* p. 34, 772.
158. *Bulletin of the European Communities,* No. 2, 1987, pp. 90–1.
159. *Keesing's Contemporary Archives,* September 1987, p. 35,411.
160. *Bulletin of the European Communities,* No. 2, 1988, p. 78.
161. *Telex Mediterranean,* 17 June 1988.
162. *Euro-Arab Dialogue, Ministerial Troika Meeting,* Press Statement, Bonn, 24 June 1988.
163. *Telex Mediterranean,* July, 1988.

VII

CONCLUSION

What emerges from this study of Euro-Arab relations is that the motivations of both parties, the nature of the ensuing dialogue, the formulation of the agenda and the success or failure of proposed objectives have all been moulded by a complex and often contradictory combination of economic and political factors.

In terms of the political dimension, it was apparent that some of the principal dynamics behind the whole process have been extraneous to the Euro-Arab context considered in itself. The Palestinian question and its manifold repercussions have been of decisive significance. The role of the United States has also been important, not simply in terms of its concrete action (e.g. the bombing of Libya) but also in its 'structural' power, that is, the influence it exerts—often invisibly—simply as a function of its preponderance in the structure of international relations. Thus, in the early stages of decision-making, the consideration—explicit or implicit—of likely American responses played an important role both for the European and the Arab sides. For the Europeans, this general strategic significance of the United States was of course intensified through its involvement in Nato.

Nevertheless, the Arab–Israeli conflict must be considered the key extraneous political dynamic, having had both positive and negative effects on Euro-Arab relations. For instance, while the repercussions of the 1973 War proved to be the major catalyst for upgrading and expanding Euro-Arab relations, it was a factor arising from this same underlying conflict, namely, the respective attitudes towards Camp David, that led to the crisis in relations in 1980.

The part played by this conflict, therefore, is certainly not clear-cut or unambiguous, but the following tentative explanatory hypothesis can be offered: if the threat—strategic, political or economic—to the European Community posed by the consequences of the Arab–Israeli conflict is regarded as greater than the risk of unsettling its relations with the United States and Israel, then the impact on Euro-Arab relations will be positive; but if this threat recedes, then the impact of the Arab–Israeli conflict is likely to be negative, the central assumption here being the persistence of Arab grievances in the face of an uncompromising Israeli state, supported by the United States.

As an example of the positive impact, one can cite not only the 1973 War, the oil embargo and the subsequent quadrupling of oil prices as the principal strategic causes of the European approach to the Arab side, but also the fact that this strategic imperative was regarded as sufficiently compelling to ensure the resolution of the problem of Palestinian representation in the dialogue, arrived at in February 1975.

In the period 1979–80 both the negative and positive effects of the Arab–Israeli dispute could be observed: the repercussions of the Camp David accords resulted in a setback for the Euro-Arab dialogue, because the Arab side insisted on a more dynamic political dimension to the dialogue, to assist in the establishment of a genuinely comprehensive settlement of the Palestinian problem. The perceived 'threat', however, to the vital interests of the European Community was insufficient to overcome the consideration of the costs of adopting such an approach, hence a stalemate ensued. However, despite there being no significant action on the part of the Arabs, the strategic context changed dramatically as a result of the Iranian revolution, the Soviet intervention in Afghanistan and the increasing polarization of the Arab world.

These factors, when considered in relation to the potential and actual radicalization of popular Arab opinion, and in the context of the growing force and appeal of Islamic fundamentalism, were sufficient to raise the prospects of serious destabilization in the region, with the consequent high risks of loss of political influence and commercial benefit. In the Venice Declaration of 1980, therefore, the Europeans accepted the need to address political issues and to launch a new approach to the Arab side.

However, compared with the concrete threat of oil embargoes and price hikes in the sellers' market of the mid-1970, the more limited and abstract threat of the early 1980s—or the inability of the Arab side to create any comparable bargaining position—resulted in a further stalemate in 1983, with the failure to agree on a communiqué on the Palestinian issue at the Athens meeting.

Again in 1986, both the positive and negative effects of the conflict on Euro-Arab relations were in evidence. First, the American bombing of Libya, prompted by Libya's alleged support to terrorist—mainly Palestinian—groups, sparked widespread fears in Europe of a radicalized and anti-Western public. The Europeans therefore sought to resuscitate the dialogue, only to suffer a further setback in April following the Hindawi affair—the attempt by a Syrian national to destroy an El Al airliner.

To date, the collective approach of the EEC to the Arab states—despite certain differences between the European states—has been characterized by a gradually increasing desire to accommodate the moderate Arab position on the Palestinian problem, supporting the withdrawal of Israeli forces from the West Bank and Gaza, and allowing a measure of autonomy to the Palestinians, with the PLO being accepted as the legitimate representative of the Palestinian people. This position derives in part from the aforementioned quest of the Europeans for greater political influence in the region, and in part from their desire to maintain, consolidate and increase the economic benefits accruing from trade, investment and financial relations with the Arab world. The moral argument in favour of such a position has also had an effect, with its attendant benefits in terms of international public opinion.

After the 1973 crisis, the mutual benefit derived from the economic/technical dimension of Euro-Arab relations was much appreciated on both sides, and if political factors had not been so significant, this palpable benefit would doubtless have engendered a much less problematic set of relations. It would be a simplification, however, to conclude that the Europeans preferred a more technical form of relations while the Arabs were trying to politicize the dialogue; for this overlooks the question of motivation on the Arab side, and neglects the difference between the real and the apparent agenda. The Arab side, firstly, cannot be considered a homogeneous group; they differed among themselves more than did the Europeans.

Secondly, even if talks did periodically break down over Arab insistence on the question of Palestine, one must recognize the degree to which the conservative Arab states, in particular, were compelled to adopt such positions despite their own real interests. For it can be argued that these states would have preferred a less politicized context for the dialogue and a greater stress on the economic/technical aspects, from which they derived such tangible benefits and without which their attempts at economic diversification would be set back. However, due to the fear of being seen as 'selling out' on the Palestinian cause, and due to the exigencies arising from their already precarious legitimacy structure, these states were constrained to maintain a high political profile in their relations with the Western world.

It is clear then, that however much both sides may wish for expanding and mutually beneficial trade and economic relations, the extent to which these can be boosted by the political process is critically influenced by the imperative created by the Arab–Israeli conflict. Given also the current weakness of the Arab bargaining position, due to the existence of a buyers' market in oil, and the decreasing likelihood that the Arab states can become sufficiently united or courageous to threaten another oil embargo, the main factor that would compel the Europeans to make any major moves in reviving the dialogue and moving closer to the Arab position *vis-à-vis* Palestine, will be the fear of destabilization of the Arab regimes. This consideration applies in particular to the conservative states—brought about by the continued and ever-increasing tensions over the Palestinian issue.

Combined with the threat that Islamic fundamentalism could further radicalize an Arab world already disillusioned with Western ideologies, this seems to guarantee an ongoing security concern of major proportions for the Europeans. This can be expected to translate into pressure to maintain the dialogue, produce concrete results and thus assist the Arab states in shoring up their legitimacy: permitting them to show, as it were, the utility of Western diplomacy, despite the failure of Western ideology.

In conclusion, then, while it has been observed that the content of Euro-Arab relations in terms of economic and technical agreements has greatly benefitted both sides, the political context of these relations has been critically bound up with the central political issue of the Middle East, the Arab–Israeli conflict. The observed fluctuations in Euro-Arab relations can be regarded as a function of the chronic instability brought about by this dispute. Up to the present time, the impact of the Euro-Arab dialogue upon this central dispute has been minimal, but as the instability built into the *status quo* becomes more acute, then one can expect more significant European moves, flowing naturally not simply from the desire to maintain and expand the Community relations with a more stable set of Arab regimes, but also from the underlying quest by the EEC to upgrade its political role in world affairs.

Appendix 1

CODE OF PROCEDURES

The final communiqué of the second meeting of the General Commission of the Euro-Arab Dialogue, held in Tunis from 10 to 12 February 1977, provided for an ad hoc Group to be set up to work out the necessary procedures for using the Arab and European financial contributions to finance preliminary or feasibility studies and other activities sponsored by the Euro-Arab Dialogue, 'with the exception of the financing of the realization of projects'.

The General Commission of the Euro-Arab Dialogue arranged that this Group's proposals would be considered at its next meeting.

This document covers the proposals which the ad hoc Group submits to the General Commission:

1. Applications for the consideration of a particular project are to be submitted to the responsible working Committee.
2. The findings of the working Committees will be referred to the Finance Group to make its comments and recommendations on the financial aspects, the cost and the amount of the project, and a copy will be sent directly to the General Commission.
3. The Finance Group will refer its findings to the General Commission.
4. The General Commission approves or rejects or refers back to the responsible working Committee the proposed projects with the appropriate directives.
5. The Co-Chairmen of the General Commission* will jointly inform the beneficiary of the decision of the General Commission.
6. As regards feasibility studies, the consultant will be chosen, through a restricted invitation to tender, issued to a list of prospective contractors, chosen from two lists prepared by

---

* It is understood that on the European side this letter will be signed by the representative of the Commission of the European Communities.

both sides of the Dialogue and approved by the responsible working Committee.

7. The contract with the successful tenderer drawn up by the responsible working Committee will be examined on its financial terms by the Finance Group before signature by the beneficiary.

8. Concerning contracts for:
   — technical assistance
   — organisation of seminars, symposia and other similar operations, the procedures for execution set out above are to apply mutatis mutandis, with the exception of tendering for technical assistants. The selection of these will be made in consultation with the beneficiary from the candidates put forward by the Arab and European sides.

9. The beneficiary will receive the required documents for finished parts of the contract periodically. It, in turn, will refer it to the two mandated representatives (1 Arab and 1 European) of the responsible working Committee for certification.

10. A mandated representative of the beneficiary, on the basis of the certificate, received from the two representatives of the responsible working Committee, makes out orders to pay, in accordance with the specifications of the contract.Two orders[1] to pay would be made out in the currencies specified in the contract, one, representing the part of the sum to be paid by the Arab side, would be addressed to the Arab payer[2] and the other, representing the part of the sum to be paid by the European side would be addressed to the Commission of the European Communities. The orders to pay would be accompanied by all required documents proving the proper execution of the contract or its parts to be paid.

On reception of the orders to pay, payment would be made by the two payers without delay directly to the contractor. Each of the payers would inform the other of the payment it had made.

Source: The General Committee of the Euro-Arab Dialogue, *Final Communiqué*, Brussels, 1977.

[1] The Arab side accepts the two accounts principle temporarily on the understanding that the European side will refer the Arab request for a common account to the responsible authorities of the European Communities for decision.
[2] To be specified.

Appendix 2

LIST OF ACTIONS

STUDY OR OTHER ACTIVITY	Estimated cost ($)	Estimated Contributions ($)	
		Arab	European
Symposium of the relation between the two civilisations, Hamburg	250.000	125.000	125.000
B *Basic Infrastructure*			
1. *Study on the training requirements of the Arab countries in the field of sea transport*	200.000	160.000	40.000
2. *Harmonization of statistics in Arab ports*	60.000	48.000	12.000
3. *Study for the development of the new port of BASRA, Iraq*	500.000	400.000	100.000
4. *Study for the development of the new port of TARTOUS, Syria*	500.000	400.000	100.000
5. *Symposium on 'New Towns'*	20.000	10.000	10.000
C. *Agriculture and rural development*			
1. *Juba Valley: Study for the Bardera irrigation Scheme, Somalia*	1.200.000	960.000	240.000
2. *Sudan Meat Project*	50.000	40.000	10.000
3. *Seed Potato Project, Iraq*	1.800.000	1.440.000	360.000

Source: The General Committee of the Euro-Arab Dialogue, *Final Communiqué*, Brussels, 1977.

Appendix 3

EURO-ARAB DIALOGUE

PROJECT SUMMARY

TITLE OF PROJECT

Euro-Arab Symposium on the relations between the two civilisations and their role in the contemporary world (Hamburg)

BENEFICIARY COUNTRY/ORGANISATION

Federal Republic of Germany
'Deutsches Orient Institut', Hamburg

PROJECT DESCRIPTION

Project aims to prove that the Dialogue is a civilisation endeavour between two civilisations which, being deeply indebted one to the other, greatly contributed to human heritage and to give a better and more adjourned image of the modern Arab world among the European people nations.

The symposium will include for one week a series of scientific 'seances' with up to 150 participants and should be accompanied by some cultural manifestations.

ESTIMATE OF PROJECT COSTS

250,000 dollars
Estimated European contribution: $125,000
Estimated Arab contribution: $125,000

RESPONSIBLE WORKING COMMITTEE

Working Committee on cultural, social and labour questions, assisted by a specialized Group and by a Task Group.

EURO-ARAB DIALOGUE

PROJECT SUMMARY

TITLE OF PROJECT

Study on the training requirements of the Arab countries in the field of sea transport.

BENEFICIARY COUNTRY/ORGANISATION

All Arab Countries

PROJECT DESCRIPTION

The study covers:

(1) Identification of all Arab countries' requirements in training; technically and in management

(2) Carrying out a program of training:
    (a) personnel training in Europe
    (b) Experts' visits for local training

ESTIMATE OF PROJECT COSTS

(1) $50,000
(2) $150,000
      ‾‾‾‾‾‾‾
    $200,000 Total

Estimated European contribution: $40,000
Estimated Arab contribution: $160,000

RESPONSIBLE WORKING COMMITTEE

Basis Infrastructure Group.

EURO-ARAB DIALOGUE

PROJECT SUMMARY

TITLE OF PROJECT

Harmonization of statistics in Arab ports

BENEFICIARY COUNTRY/ORGANISATION

All Arab Countries

PROJECT DESCRIPTION

The study includes:

(1) Relevant data collection

(2) Coordination and standardization of systems to be proposed for information and statistical records.

ESTIMATE OF PROJECT COSTS

$60,000
Estimated European contribution: $12,000
Estimated Arab contribution: $48,000

RESPONSIBLE WORKING COMMITTEE

Basis Infrastructure Working Group.

EURO-ARAB DIALOGUE

PROJECT SUMMARY

TITLE OF PROJECT

Development of the port of 'BASRA' (North East of the Gulf)

BENEFICIARY COUNTRY/ORGANISATION

Iraq

PROJECT DESCRIPTION

The feasibility study includes:

— Fully detailed description of the present conditions
— Identification and outlining of difficulties, points of unsuitability, bottlenecks, etc
— Proposals for immediate improvement: remedies, solutions, requirements in training and equipment
— Proposals for the future infrastructure based on expectations of economic development in the country and in the region.

ESTIMATE OF PROJECT COSTS

$500,000
Estimated European contribution: $100,000
Estimated Arab contribution: $400,000

RESPONSIBLE WORKING COMMITTEE

Basic Infrastructure Working Group.

EURO-ARAB DIALOGUE

PROJECT SUMMARY

TITLE OF PROJECT

Development of the port 'TARTOUS' (Eastern Mediterranean)

BENEFICIARY COUNTRY/ORGANISATION

Syria

PROJECT DESCRIPTION

The feasibility study includes:

— Fully detailed description of the present conditions
— Identification and outlining of difficulties, point of unsuitability, bottlenecks, etc
— Proposals for immediate improvements: remedies, solutions, requirements in training and equipment
— Proposals for the future infrastructure based on expectations
of economic development in the country and in the region.

ESTIMATE OF PROJECT COSTS

$500,000
Estimated European contribution: $100,000
Estimated Arab contribution: $400,000

RESPONSIBLE WORKING COMMITTEE

Basic Infrastructure Working Group.

EURO-ARAB DIALOGUE

PROJECT SUMMARY

TITLE OF PROJECT

New Towns Symposium

BENEFICIARY COUNTRY/ORGANISATION

All countries

PROJECT DESCRIPTION

Exchange of informations about the new towns existing or in project in Europe and in the Arab world.

ESTIMATE OF PROJECT COSTS

$20,000
Estimated European contribution: $10,000
Estimated Arab contribution: $10,000

RESPONSIBLE WORKING COMMITTEE

Basic Infrastructures.

EURO-ARAB DIALOGUE

PROJECT SUMMARY

TITLE OF PROJECT

Study for the Bardere Irrigation Scheme, Somalia

BENEFICIARY COUNTRY/ORGANISATION

Somalia

PROJECT DESCRIPTION

The study aims to determine the feasibility of irrigated agriculture in an area of 47.000 ha lying downstream from the proposed Bardere Dam. The study will include three main components:

— Resource surveys
— Crop research programme
— Development planning and feasibility studies.

ESTIMATE OF PROJECT COSTS

Total project costs are estimated at US$1,200,000
Estimated European contribution: $240,000
Estimated Arab contribution:　　　$960,000

RESPONSIBLE WORKING COMMITTEE

— Working Committee for Agriculture and Rural Development.

EURO-ARAB DIALOGUE

PROJECT SUMMARY

TITLE OF PROJECT

Sudan Meat Project

BENEFICIARY COUNTRY/ORGANISATION

Sudan

PROJECT DESCRIPTION

Feasibility study for the establishment of an interim project consisting of a feedlot located near Khartum. The feedlot will have a capacity of 12,000 head of cattle per year. Duration three months.

ESTIMATE OF PROJECT COSTS

The study is estimated to cost US$50,000
Estimated European contribution: $10,000
Estimated Arab contribution: $40,000

RESPONSIBLE WORKING COMMITTEE

Working Committee for Agriculture and Rural Development.

EURO-ARAB DIALOGUE

PROJECT SUMMARY

TITLE OF PROJECT

Seed Potato Project, Iraq

BENEFICIARY COUNTRY/ORGANISATION

Iraq and the Arab region

PROJECT DESCRIPTION

The establishment of a potato seed multiplication programme, initially of two years duration. The programme will comprise a centre and outlying trials located principally in the Shahrazur plain. The programme will test potato varieties for multiplication and distribution in the Arab region.

ESTIMATE OF PROJECT COSTS

Total project costs are estimated at	US$1,800,000
of which capital equipment amounts to	US$205,000
technical assistance	US$320,000
supplies	US$830,000
operating costs	US$445,000
Estimated European contribution:	$360,000
Estimated Arab contribution:	$1,440,000

RESPONSIBLE WORKING COMMITTEE

Working Committee for Agriculture and Rural Development.

Source: The General Committee of the Euro-Arab Dialogue, *Final Communiqué*, Brussels, 1977.

STUDY OR OTHER ACTIVITIES (Annex 3)	Estimated total costs	Contributions in US$	
		Arab	European
Industrialization 1. Setting up of Euro-Arab documentation and information centres for standardization	450,000	360,000	90,000
2. Study on petrochemical industries	165,000	132,000	33,000
3. Study on oil-refining industries	165,000	132,000	33,000
4. Study on policy and programmes for education and training in the fields of standardization, metrology and quality control.	135,000	108,000	27,000
Culturo and social questions 5. Publication of the proceedings of the Venice Seminar on 'Means and forms of co-operation for the dissemination in Europe of knowledge of the Arabic language and literary civilisation'	20,000	10,000	10,000
6. Draft Catalogue of Cultural and Scientific Institutions	6,000	3,000	3,000
7. Technical assistance for the establishment of an Arab vocational and instructor training-centre	880,000	704,000	176,000
Scientific and Technological Co-operation 8. Study for the establishment of an 'Arab Institute for Water Desalination and Resources'	600,000	480,000	120,000
9. Feasibility study for the creation of an Arab Polytechnic Instituto	1,000,000	800,000	200,000
10. Survey of scientific infrastructure on marine science in the Arab countries	160,000	128,000	32,000
Additional amount for the Hamburg symposium on the relationship between the two civilizations	115,000	57,500	57,500
	3,696,000	2,914,500	781,500

Source: The General Committee of the Euro-Arab Dialogue, *Final Communiqué*, Damascus, 1978.

Appendix 4

JOINT DECLARATION ON THE PRINCIPLES
GOVERNING THE LIVING AND WORKING
CONDITIONS OF MIGRANT WORKERS IN
THE TWO REGIONS

December 1978

The Arab and European Delegations of the Euro-Arab Dialogue,

Conscious of the magnitude of the problems facing foreign workers and their families who are nationals of the States participating in the Dialogue and are resident in the territory of these States,

Hereby adopt this declaration,

With a view to reaffirming the principles by which their policies in this field are guided.

A migrant worker and the members of his family shall, in the country where they legally reside and work, enjoy equality of treatment as to living and working conditions, wages, economic rights, rights of association and the exercise of the basic public freedoms.

This equality of treatment shall operate within the limitations imposed by considerations, of public policy, public security and public health and according to the provisions in force in the States participating in the Dialogue. Subject to these conditions, equality of treatment shall compromise the principles specified in the following paragraphs:

1. Equality of treatment as to working conditions, wages and economic rights shall imply the following principles in particular:

— as regards employment-related social security benefits, granting to migrant workers and members of their families living with them of treatment free from any discrimination based on nationality as compared with nationals of the States in which they are employed;

— the extension of these benefits to members of families who remain in the country of origin in so far as provided for in bilateral agreements;

— entitlement to the same employment-related social advantages as those enjoyed by a national worker;

— under the rules governing the labour market:
  = assistance from employment exchanges in finding jobs;
  = access to vocational guidance;
  = access to apprenticeship schemes, to baic and advanced vocational training, to re-adaptation and to retaining and eligibility for redeployment measures;
  = access to activities organized for the unemployed.

Information on the various schemes open to the migrant workers hall be made available to him;

— freedom to choose a job in a given country following a period of paid employment laid down by the provisions in force in that country which could be about five years;

— protection equal to that enjoyed by a national worker as regards industrial hygiene and safety.

2. Language courses and basic vocational training shall be organized in accordance with the possibilities so that a migrant worker taking a vocational training course can do so with the same chance of success as a national worker.

3. A migrant worker shall enjoy treatment no less favourable than a national worker as regards taxes and contributions relating to his occupation.

4. Equality of treatment in the exercise of rights of association shall imply:
   — the freedom to join trade union organisations;
   — the right to vote and the right to stand for and be appointed to office both in trade union organizations and in bodies governing industrial relations within an undertaking between workers and employers.

5. It must be possible for a migrant worker to be joined by his spouse and any dependent children who are minors.

6. A migrant worker may leave the territory of the country of employment without losing his rights, in particular as regards his residence permit, provided that his absence does not exceed his statutory or contractual annual holiday entitlement, plus necessary travelling time, which should not exceed one month.

   The granting of special facilities to a migrant worker to enable him annual holidays in his country of origin may be encouraged.

   His family shall be allowed to enter and reside temporarily in the country of employment.

7. A migrant worker shall enjoy all the rights and benefits granted to a national worker as regards accommodation, including the right to home ownership.

8. Equality of treatment as regards living conditions shall in particular imply:
   — for the children of a migrant worker
      = access to general and vocational education;
      = promotion of a reception system, including intensive courses in the language or languages of the host country;
   — access to welfare and medical services.

9. A migrant worker and the members of his family shall have the right to exercise the freedoms of speech, association and assembly.

   A migrant worker and the members of his family shall have the same rights as nationals to assert their rights before the competent bodies, particularly by going to law.

10. A migrant worker and the members of his family shall enjoy the same legal protection of their person and possessions, as do nationals.

11. A migrant worker and the members of his family shall also be granted the same legal aid arrangements as nationals. They may be granted special facilities to enable them to assert their rights on an equal footing with nationals.

12. To help and encourage the efforts of migrant workers and members of their families to protect their national identity

and their attachment to the cultural values of their country of origin:

— a migrant worker and the members of his family may receive regular information in their own language about both their country of origin and the host country;
— the children of migrant workers shall have access, as far as possible, to the teaching of their mother tongue and culture; the general conditions applicable to such teaching, including those relating to co-ordination with standard teaching, shall be laid down by the host country in co-operation with the country of origin.

13. The social integration of migrant workers and of the members of their families in a host country shall be facilitated by:
    — making the general public in the host country more aware of the problems of migrant workers and members of their families;
    — promoting cultural activities for migrant workers and nationals with a view to better mutual understanding.

14. The voluntary return of migrant workers and members of their families to their country of origin may be facilitated in particular under co-operation agreements or programmes.

*   *   *

The Arab and European delegations of the Euro-Arab Dialogue, in adopting the present declaration on the principles governing the living and working conditions of migrant workers, who are nationals of the States participating in the Dialogue,

— reaffirm the principle of the need for close co-operation between States of immigration and emigration concerned with the problems of migrant workers and recall the bilateral and multilateral agreements in which such a co-operation is already being implemented,

— believe it is important to seek, within a bilateral and multilateral framework, appropriate solutions in the future to the problems which the States concerned consider still remain to be solved.

Source: The General Committee of the Euro-Arab Dialogue, *Final Communiqué*, Damascus, 1978.

BIBLIOGRAPHY

A PRIMARY RESOURCES

I. *OFFICIAL DOCUMENTS*

EEC OFFICIAL DOCUMENTS
Eighth General Report on the Activities of the Community (1 April 1964–31 March 1965), Publishing Services of the European Communities, Brussels, 1965.
Eighth General Report on the Activities of the European Communities in 1974, Office for Official Publications of the European Communities, Luxembourg, 1975.
Eighteenth General Report on the Activities of the European Communities in 1984, Office for Official Publications of the European Communities, Luxembourg, 1985.
The Euro-Arab Dialogue, Joint Memorandum, Cairo, 1975.
The Euro-Arab Dialogue, Joint Working Paper, Rome, 1975.
The Euro-Arab Dialogue, Joint Working Paper, Abu Dhabi, 1975.
The Euro-Arab Dialogue, Joint Working Paper, Luxembourg, 1976.
The Euro-Arab Dialogue, General Committee Meeting, Final Communiqué, Luxembourg, 1976.
The Euro-Arab Dialogue, General Committee Meeting, Final Communiqué, Tunis, 1977.
The Euro-Arab Dialogue, General Committee Meeting, Final Communiqué, Brussels, 1977.
The Euro-Arab Dialogue, General Committee Meeting, Final Communiqué, Damascus, 1978.
Euro-Arab Dialogue, Final Communiqué, Luxembourg, 1980.
Euro-Arab Dialogue: Ministerial Troika Meeting, Bonn, 1988.
European Parliament, Information, Parliament in Session, Luxembourg: European Parliament, 1973.
European Parliament, Information, Parliament in Session, Luxembourg: European Parliament, 1977.

Eleventh General Report on the Activities of the European Communities in 1977, Office for Official Publications of the European Communities, Luxembourg, 1978.

Fourteenth General Report on the Activities of the European Communities in 1980, Office for Official Publications of the European Communities, Luxembourg, 1981.

Memorandum on a Community Policy on Development Co-operation, Commission of the European Communities, Brussels, 1972.

Meeting Between the European Community and the Gulf Co-operation Council, Final Text, Luxembourg, 1985.

Nineteenth General Report on the Activities of the European Communities in 1985, Office for Official Publications of the European Communities, Luxembourg, 1986.

Report to the Council on the Exploratory Talks with the Mediterranean Countries and the Applicant Countries, Commission Proposal Concerning the Implementation of a Mediterranean Policy for the Enlarged Community, Commission of the European Communities, Com (84) 107 Final, Brussels, 1984.

Sixteenth General Report on the Activities of the European Communities in 1982, Office for Official Publications of the European Communities, Luxembourg, 1983.

Seventeenth General Report on the Activities of the European Communities in 1983, Office for Official Publications of the European Communities, Luxembourg, 1984.

Twentieth Review of the Council's Work (1 January–31 December 1972), Office for Official Publications of the European Communities, Luxembourg, 1972.

Twenty Fifth Review of the Council's Work (1 January–31 December 1977), Office for Official Publications of the European Communities, Luxembourg, 1978.

Twenty Sixth Review of the Council's Work (1 January–31 December 1978), Office for Official Publications of the European Communities, Luxembourg, 1979.

Twenty Seventh Review of the Council's Work (1 January–31 December 1979), Office for Official Publications of the European Communities, Luxembourg, 1980.

Twenty Eighth Review of the Council's Work (1 January–31 December 1980), Office for Official Publications of the European Communities, Luxembourg, 1981.

Twenty Ninth Review of the Council's Work (1 January–31 December 1981), Office for Official Publications of the European Communities, Luxembourg, 1982.

Thirtieth Review of the Council's Work (1 January–31 December 1982), Office for Official Publications of the European Communities, Luxembourg, 1983.

Thirty First Review of the Council's Work (1 January–31 December 1983), Office for Official Publications of the European Communities, Luxembourg, 1984.

Thirty Second Review of the Council's Work (1 January–31 December 1984), Office for Official Publications of the European Communities, Luxembourg, 1985.

Thirty Third Review of the Council's Work (1 January–31 December 1985), Office for Official Publications of the European Communities, Luxembourg, 1986.

Thirty Fourth Review of the Council's Work (1 January–31 December 1986), Office for Official Publications of the European Communities, Luxembourg, 1987.

Tenth General Report on the Activities of the European Communities in 1976, Office for Official Publications of the European Communities, Luxembourg, 1977.

Twelfth General Report on the Activities of the European Communities in 1978, Office for Official Publications of the European Communities, Luxembourg, 1979.

Twenty First General Report on the Activities of the European Communities in 1986, Office for Official Publications of the European Communities, Luxembourg, 1987.

Twenty Second General Report on the Activities of the European Communities in 1987, Office for Official Publications of the European Communities, Luxembourg, 1988.

OAPEC OFFICIAL DOCUMENTS
Fifth Annual Report, Secretary-General, Kuwait, 1978.

ARAB LEAGUE OFFICIAL DOCUMENTS
Press Release, League of Arab States, London Office, 1986.

II. *EEC PUBLICATIONS*

Ysse, D. *The Effects of Enlargement on Other Mediterranean Countries,* Europe News Agency, Brussels, 1984.

Co-operation Agreements Between the EEC and the Maghreb Countries, Commission of the European Communities, Directorate-General for Information (D.G.), Brussels, 1982.

The Court of Justice of the European Communities, Office for Official Publications of the European Communities, Luxembourg, 1986.

Cova, C. *The Arab Policy of the EEC*, Bureau d'Information Européen, S.P.R., Brussels, 1983.

Dauderstadt, M. *et al. The Outlook for Community Policy on Co-operation with the Developing Countries in the Light of Changing North–South Relations and the Future Development of the Community*, Commission of the European Communities, D.G. for Information, Brussels, 1982.

Development of the Community From June 1980 to June 1981, D.G. for Research and Documentation, European Parliament, Luxembourg, 1981.

EEC–Morocco Co-operation Agreement, Commission of the European Communities, Spokesman's Group and D.G. for Information, Brussels, 1980.

Europe–South Dialogue, Commission of the European Communities , D.G. for Information, Brussels, 1984.

Europe–Third World Rural Development, Commission of the European Communities, D.G. for Information, Brussels, 1979.

The European Community and the Arab World, Commission of the European Communities, D.G. for Information, Brussels, 1982.

European Unification, the Origins and the Growth of the European Community, Office for the Official Publications of the European Communities, Luxembourg, 1986.

Europe at a Glance: A Brief Guide to the European Community and Britain's Share in its Activities, Commission of the European Communities (London Office), 1982.

The European Community External Trade (1958–1974), Office for Official Publications of the European Communities, Luxembourg, 1976.

The European Community and the Developing Countries, Office for Official Publications of the European Communities, Luxembourg, 1975.

The EEC's Trade Relations with the Developing Countries, Commission of the European Communities, D.G. for Information, Brussels, 1985.

The European Parliament and the World at Large, Office for Official Publications of the European Communities, Luxembourg, 1981.

EEC–Syria Co-operation Agreement, Commission of the European Communities, Spokesman's Group and D.G. for Information, Brussels, 1978.

EEC–Egypt Co-operation Agreement, Commission of the European Communities, Spokesman's Group and D.G. for Information, Brussels, 1978.

EEC–Jordan Co-operation Agreement, Commission of the European Communities, Spokesman's Group and D.G. for Information, Brussels, 1978.

EEC–Lebanon Co-operation Agreement, Commission of the European Communities, D.G. for Information, Brussels, 1980.

The Europe–United States–Japan Trade Controversy, Office for Official Publications of the European Communities, Luxembourg, 1983.

The Enlargement of the European Community, Commission of the European Communities, D.G. for Information, Brussels, 1983.

The European Community and the Gulf Co-operation Council, Commission of the European Communities, D.G. for Information, Brussels, 1985.

Fact Sheets on the European Parliament and the Activities of the European Community, European Parliament, D.G. for Research, Office for Official Publications of the European Communities, Luxembourg, 1987.

The Institutions of the European Community, Office for Official Publications of the European Communities, Luxembourg, annual publication (1982–1986).

The Mediterranean Policy: Thirty Years of Community Law, Office for Official Publications of the European Communities, Luxembourg, 1983.

Meyer, E. *Euro-Arab Relations*, Commission of the European Communities, (London Office), 1980.

Note de background sur le dialogue Euro-Arabe, Commission of the European Communities, Brussels, 1986.

Problems of Enlargement: Taking Stock and Proposals, Commission of the European Communities, D.G. for Information, Brussels, 1983.

Subhan, M. *The EEC's Trade Relations with the Developing Countries*, Commission of the European Communities, D.G. for Information, Brussels, 1985.

The Second Enlargement of the European Communities, Office for Official Publications of the European Communities, Luxembourg, 1979.

Taylor, R. *Implications for the Southern Mediterranean Countries of the Second Enlargement of the European Communities*,

Commission of the European Communities, D.G. for Information, Brussels, 1980.

Zeul, Wieczorek. *Trade Relations between the EEC and the Gulf States*, European Parliament, Luxembourg, 1981 (First and Second Editions).

B SECONDARY RESOURCES

1 *BOOKS AND CHAPTERS IN EDITED VOLUMES*

Al-Dajani, A.S. *Munazamat al-tahrir al-filastiniya wal-hiwar al-arabi al-urubbi (The PLO and the Euro-Arab Dialogue)*, Research Centre, Palestine Liberation Organization, Beirut, 1979.

Al-Dajani, A.S. *The Euro-Arab Dialogue*, Research Centre, Palestine Liberation Organization, Beirut, 1981.

Al-Mani, S.A. and Al-Shaikly, S. *The Euro-Arab Dialogue*, Frances Pinter, London, 1983.

Al-Rumaihi, M. 'Factors of Social and Economic Development in the Gulf in the Eighties', in Gantzel, K.J. and Mejcher, H. (eds.), *Oil, the Middle East, North Africa and the Industrial States*, Paderborn: Schoningh, 1984, pp. 207–21.

Biroli, C.P. 'Foreign Policy Formation within the European Community with Special Regard to the Developing Countries', in Hurewitz, L. (ed.) *Contemporary Perspectives on European Integration*, Aldwych Press, London, 1980, pp. 225–54.

Bradley, C.P. *Recent United States Policy in the Persian Gulf (1971–1982)*, Tompson and Rutter, USA, 1982.

Coffey, P. *The External Economic Relations of the EEC*, The Macmillan Press, London, 1976.

Cordesman, A.H. *The Gulf and the Search for Strategic Stability*, Westview Press, Boulder, Colorado, and Mansell Publishing Limited, London, 1984.

Campbell, J.C. 'The United States and the Middle East', in Legum, C. (ed.) *Crisis and Conflict in the Middle East. The Changing Strategy: From Iran to Afghanistan*, Holmes and Meier Publishers, New York and London, 1981, pp. 67–80.

Carre, O. 'The Future for the Gulf/Europe/America Relationship: A European View', in Pridham, B.R. (ed.) *The Arab Gulf and the West*, Croom Helm, London, 1985, pp. 234–243.

Dhanani, G. 'The Euro-Arab Dialogue: A Critique', in Lall, K.B. et al. *The EEC in the Global System*, Allied Publisher Private Limited, New Delhi, 1984, pp. 171–190.

Dishon, D. 'The Middle East in Perspective', in Legum, C. (ed.), *Crisis and Conflict in the Middle East. The Changing of Strategy: From Iran to Afghanistan*, Holmes and Meier, Inc., New York and London, 1981. pp. 15–23.

Friedlander, M.A. *Sadat and Begin*, Westview Press, Boulder, Colorado, 1983.

Fahmy, I. *Negotiating for Peace in the Middle East*, Croom Helm, London, 1983.

Fesharaki, F. and Tsaak, D.T. *OPEC, the Gulf, and the World Petroleum Market: A Study in Government Policy and Downstream Operations*, Croom Helm, London, 1983.

Gadel Hak, H.A.H. *The Mediterranean Policy of the European Economic Community, with Special Reference to Egypt* (published doctoral thesis) Institute of Arab Research and Studies, League of Arab States, Cairo, 1978.

Greilsammer, I. and Wiler, J. 'European Political Co-operation and the Palestinian–Israeli Conflict: An Israeli Perspective', in Allen, D. and Pijpers, A. (eds.), *European Foreign Policy-Making and the Arab–Israeli Conflict*, Martinus Nijhoff Publishers, The Hague, 1984, pp. 121–60.

Golan, G. *Yom Kippur and After*, Cambridge University Press, London, 1977.

Garratt, J. 'Euro-American Energy Diplomacy in the Middle East 1970–1980: The Pervasive Crisis', in Spiegel, S.L. (ed.), *The Middle East and the Western Alliance*, George Allen and Unwin, London, 1982, pp. 82–103.

Hager, W. 'The Community and the Mediterranean', in Kohnstamm, M. and Hager, W. (eds.) *A Nation Writ Large? Foreign Policy Problems before the European Community*, Macmillan, London, 1973, pp. 195–221.

Hager, W. 'Western Europe: The Politics of Muddling Through', in Hurewitz, J.C. (ed.) *Oil, the Arab–Israel Dispute, and the Industrial World: Horizons of Crisis*, Westview Press, Boulder, Colorado, 1976, pp. 34–51.

Hatem, S. A. *The Possibilities of Economic Co-operation and Integration between the European Community and the Arab League*, (published doctoral thesis) München, Florentz, 1981.

Henderson, W.O. *The Genesis of the Common Market*, Frank Cass, London, 1962.

Henig, S. *External Relations of the European Community: Association and Trade Agreements*, Chatham House, London, 1971.

Henig, S. 'Mediterranean Policy in the Context of the External Relations of the European Community: 1958–1973', in Shlaim, A. and Yannopoulos, G.N. *The EEC and the Mediterranean Countries*, Cambridge University Press, 1976, pp. 305–25.

Hitti, N. 'The United States, The European Community and the Arab–Israeli Conflict', in Khader, B. (ed.), *Co-operation Euro-Arabe*, Vol. 1, Louvain-La-Neuve: Université Catholique de Louvain, 1982, pp. 277–91.

Hunt, B.K. 'Overview: The Military and Political Battleground', in Legum, C. (ed.), *Crisis and Conflict in the Middle East. The Changing Strategy: From Iran to Afghanistan*, Holmes and Meier Publishers, New York and London, 1981, pp. 5–12.

Hopwood, D. *Euro-Arab Dialogue: The Relations between the Two Cultures*, Croom Helm, London, 1983.

Ifestos, P. *European Political Co-operation: Towards A Framework of Supranational Diplomacy?*, Gower Publishing, England, 1987.

Imperiali, C. and Agate, P. 'France' in Allen, D. and Pijpers, A. (eds.), *European Foreign Policy-Making and the Arab–Israeli Conflict*, Martinus Nijhoff Publishers, the Hague, 1984, pp. 1–17.

Jaidah, A.M. *An Appraisal of OPEC Oil Policies*, Longman, London, 1983.

Khader, B. 'Europe and the Arab–Israeli Conflict 1973–1983: An Arab Perspective', in Allen, D. and Pijpers, A. (eds.), *European Foreign Policy-Making and the Arab–Israeli Conflict*, Martinus Nijhoff Publishers, The Hague, 1984, pp. 161–86.

Kolodziej, E.A. *French International Policy Under De Gaulle and Pompidou*, Cornell University Press, Ithaca, New York, London, 1974.

Kubursi, A.A. *Oil, Industrialization and Development in the Arab Gulf States*, Croom Helm, London, 1984.

Kurth, J.R. 'American Leadership: The Western Alliance and the Old Regime in the Persian Gulf', in Spiegel, S.L. (ed.), *The Middle East and the Western Alliance*, George Allen and Unwin, London, 1982, pp. 117–28.

Lieber, R.J. 'Expanded Europe and the Atlantic Relationship', in Alting Von Geusau, F.A.M. (ed.), *The External Relations of the European Community*, Saxon House, England, 1974, pp. 33–67.

Lieber, R.J. *Oil and the Middle East War: Europe in the Energy Crisis*, Center for International Affairs, Harvard University, 1976.

Lenczowski, G. *Middle East Oil in A Revolutionary Age*, Washington D.C., 1976.

Lewis Jr, J.W. *The Strategic Balance in the Mediterranean*, American Enterprise Institute for Public Policy Research, Washington DC, 1976.

Lukacs, Y. *Documents on the Israeli–Palestinian Conflict: 1967–1983*, Cambridge University Press, London, 1984.

Lieber, R.J. 'The European Community and the Middle East', in Legum, C. (ed.), *Crisis and Conflict in the Middle East. The Changing Strategy: From Iran to Afghanistan*, Holmes and Meier Publishers, New York and London, 1981, pp. 92–8.

'La Communauté Européenne et Le Monde Arabe', in Khader, B. (ed.), *Co-opération Euro-Arabe*, Vol. 1, Louvain-La-Neuve: Université Catholique de Louvain, 1982.

Macdonald, R.W. *The League of Arab States, A Study in the Dynamics of Regional Organisation*, Princeton University Press, Princeton, 1965.

Mishalani, P. *et al.* 'The Pyramid of Privilege', in Stevens, C. (ed.), *EEC and the Third World: A Survey (1)*, Hodder and Stoughton in Association with the Overseas Development Institute of Development Studies, London, 1981, pp. 60–82.

Maull, H. *Europe and the World Energy*, Butterworths, London, 1980.

Maull, H. 'The Strategy of Avoidance: Europe's Middle East Policies After the October War', in Hurewitz, J.C. (ed.), *Oil, the Arab–Israel Dispute, and the Industrial World: Horizons of Crisis*, Westview Press, Boulder, Colorado, 1976, pp. 110–37.

Moisi, D. 'Europe and the Middle East', in Spiegel, S.L. (ed.), *The Middle East and the Western Alliance*, George Allen and Unwin, London, 1982, pp. 18–32.

Meo, L. *US Strategy in the Gulf: Intervention Against Liberation*, Association of Arab–American University Graduates, USA, 1981.

Pickles, D. *The Government and Politics of France*, Methuen & Co. Ltd., London, 1973.

Pomfret, R. *Mediterranean Policy of the European Community: A Study of Discrimination in Trade*, Macmillan (Trade Policy Research Study Centre), London, 1986.

Quandt, W B. 'The Western Alliance in the Middle East: Problems For US Foreign Policy', in Spiegel, S.L. (ed.) *The Middle East and Western Alliance*, George Allen and Unwin, London, 1982, pp. 9–17.

Ramazani, R.K. *The Gulf Co-operation Council: Record and Analysis*, the University Press of Virginia, USA, 1988.

Regelsberger, E. and Wessels, W. 'European Concepts for the Mediterranean Region', in Luciani, G. (ed.), *The Mediterranean Region*, Croom Helm, London, 1984, pp. 239–66.

Ramazani, R.K. *The United States and Iran: The Patterns of Influence*, Praeger Special Studies, New York, 1982.

Rubin, B. *Paved with Good Intention: The American Experience and Iran*, Penguin Books, Great Britain, 1981.

Rustow, D.A. *Oil and Turmoil: America Faces OPEC and the Middle East*, W.W. Norton & Company, New York and London, 1982.

Siotis, J. 'The European Economic Community and its Emerging Mediterranean Policy', in Alting Von Geusau, F.A.M. (ed.), *The External Relations of the European Community*, Saxon House, England, 1974, pp. 69–83.

Shlaim, A. and Yannopoulos, G.N. *The EEC and the Mediterranean Countries*, Cambridge University Press, 1976.

Shwadran, B. *Middle East Oil Crisis Since 1973*, Westview Press, Boulder, Colorado, and London, 1986.

Stein, J.G. 'The Politics of Alliance Policy: Europe, Canada, Japan, and the United States Face the Arab–Israel Conflict', in Stein, J.G. and Dewitt, D.B. (eds.), *The Middle East at the Crossroads*, Mosaic Press, Canada, 1983, pp. 145–175.

Saied, A.M. *Al-hiwar al-arabi al-urubi*, (The Euro-Arab Dialogue), Centre for Political and Strategic Studies, Cairo, 1977.

Steinbach, U. 'The European Community and the United States in the Arab World', in Shaked, H. and Rabinovich, I. *The Middle East and the United States*, New Brunswick, US and London, 1980, pp. 121–39.

Sicherman, H. *Broker Or Advocate? The US Role in the Arab–Israeli Dispute 1973–1978*, Foreign Policy Research Institute, Philadelphia, Pennsylvania, 1978.

Hadid, M.K. *The United States and the Palestinians*, Croom Helm, London, 1981.

Shurydi, M. 'The Baghdad Summit Conference: A Critical Evaluation', in Zeady, F. (ed.), *Camp David: A New Balfour Declaration*, Association of Arab–American University Graduates, Detroit, Michigan, 1979, pp. 24–9.

Stein, J.G. 'Alice in Wonderland: The North Atlantic Alliance and the Arab–Israeli Dispute', in Spiegel, S.L. (ed.), *The Middle East and the Western Alliance*, George Allen and Unwin, London 1982, pp. 49–81.

Taylor, P. *When Europe Speaks with One Voice: The External Relations of the European Community*, Aldwych Press, London, 1979.

Taylor, R. 'Implications of EEC Enlargement for Arab Exports', in *Euro-Arab Co-operation*, Colloquium held in Brussels 20–22 April 1983, Arab–British Chamber of Commerce Publication, London, 1983, pp. 89–95.

Tovias, A. *Tariff Preferences in Mediterranean Diplomacy*, Trade Policy Research Centre, London, 1977.

Townsend, J. 'The Extent and the Limits of Economic Interdependence', in Pridham, B.R. (ed.), *The Arab Gulf and the West*, Croom Helm, London, 1985, pp. 51–67.

Vaughan, R. *Twentieth-Century Europe: Paths to Unity*, Croom Helm, London, 1979.

Vlahos, M. and Kemp, G. 'The Changing Strategic Tapestry in the Middle East', in Legum, C. (ed.), *Crisis and Conflict in the Middle East. The Changing Strategy: From Iran to Afghanistan*, Holmes and Meier Publishers, New York and London, 1981, pp. 24–35.

Weil, G.L. *A Foreign Policy for Europe? The External Relations of the European Community*, College of Europe, Bruges, Belgium, 1970.

Wilson, R. *Euro-Arab Trade: Prospects to the 1990s*, EIU Publications, London, 1988.

Wormser, M.D. *The Middle East*, Washington DC, 1981.

2 JOURNAL ARTICLES

Allen, D. 'The Euro-Arab Dialogue', *Journal of Common Market Studies*, Vol. 16, 1977–1978, pp. 323–42.

Al-Dajani, A.S. 'The PLO and the Euro-Arab Dialogue', *Journal of Palestine Studies*, Vol. IX, No. 3, Spring 1980, pp. 81–98.

Alnasrawi, A. 'Arab Oil and the Industrial Economies: The Paradox of Oil Dependency', *Arab Studies Quarterly*, Vol. 1, No. 1, Winter 1979, pp. 1–27.

The Arab–British Chamber of Commerce, 'Saudi Arabian Petrochemicals Exports: The EEC Protectionist Measures and Sabic's Prospects', *The Arab Gulf Journal*, Vol. 5, No. 1, 1985, pp. 9–20.

Artner, S.J. 'The Middle East: A Chance for Europe?', *International Affairs*, Vol. 56, No.3, Summer 1980, pp. 420–42.

Colord, D. 'La Politique Méditerranéene et Proche-Orientale de G. Pompidou', *Politique Etrangère*, Vol. 43, No.3, 1978, pp. 283–306

Goldsborough, J.O. 'France, The European Crisis and the Alliance', *Foreign Affairs*, Vol. 52, No.3, 1974, pp. 538–55.

Ghareeb, E. 'The US Arms Supply to Israel During the War', *Journal of Palestine Studies*, Vol. III, No. 2, Winter 1974, pp. 114–21.

Gammer, M. 'The Negotiating Process: Attitudes of Interested Parties', *Middle East Contemporary Survey*, Vol. 11, 1977–1978, pp. 156–84.

Itayim, F. 'Arab Oil: The Political Dimension', *Journal of Palestine Studies*, Vol. III, No. 2, Winter 1974, pp. 84–97.

Kemp, G. and Vlahos, M. 'Military and Strategic Issues in the Middle East–Persian Gulf Region in 1978', *Middle East Contemporary Survey*, Vol. 11, 1977–1978, pp. 62–9.

Rogana, A. 'The Maghreb Economic Co-operation in Retrospect', *The Maghreb Review*, Vol. 3, No. 7–8, May–August 1978, pp. 12–15.

Rubin, B. 'US Policy, January–October 1973', *Journal of Palestine Studies*, Vol. III, No. 2, Winter 1974, pp. 98–113.

Shlaim, A. 'The Maghreb Countries and the EEC', *The Maghreb Review*, Vol. X, No. 2, August–September 1976, pp. 10–13.

Sus, I. 'Western Europe and the October War', *Journal of Palestine Studies*, Vol. III, No. 2, Winter 1974, pp. 65–83.

Steinbach, U. 'Western European and EEC Policies toward Mediterranean and Middle East Countries', *Middle East Contemporary Survey*, Vol. II, 1977–1978, pp. 40–48.

'Statement Issued by the Ninth Arab Summit Conference', *Journal of Palestine Studies*, Vol. VIII, No. 2, Winter 1979, pp. 202–4.

Sicherman, H. 'Politics of Dependence: Western Europe and the Arab–Israeli Conflict', *Orbis*, Vol. 23, 4, Winter 1980, pp. 845–57.

Stournaras, Y.A. 'Is the Industrialisation of the Arab Gulf a Rational Policy?', *The Arab Gulf Journal*, Vol. 5, No. 1, April 1985, pp. 21–7.

Taylor, A.R. 'The Euro-Arab Dialogue: Quest for An International Partnership?', *Middle East Journal*, Vol. 32, No. 4, 1978, pp. 429–43.

Ullman, R.H. 'After Rabat: Middle East Risks and American Role', *Foreign Affairs*, Vol. 53, No. 2, January 1975, pp. 284–96.

3 PERIODICALS

Bulletin of the European Communities
Daily Star
Daily Telegraph
The Financial Times
Europe
The Guardian
International Herald Tribune
Jerusalem Post
Keesing's Contemporary Archives
Los Angeles Times
Le Monde
Middle East International
The New York Times
Telex Mediterranean
The Times
Telex Africa
Trade and Industry
The Washington Post

INDEX

The index is arranged using letter-by-letter alphabetisation. Prepositions etc are ignored in determining the order of subheadings.

The following abbreviations have been used:
AL   Arab League
EEC   European Economic Community
GCC   Gulf Co-operation Council
GSP   Generalised system of preferences
PLO   Palestine Liberation Organization